Wealth, Welfare
and the Global Free Market

Corporate Social Responsibility Series

Series Editors:
Professor Güler Aras, Yildiz Technical University, Istanbul, Turkey
Professor David Crowther, De Montfort University, Leicester, UK

Presenting applied research from an academic perspective on all aspects of corporate social responsibility, this interdisciplinary series edited by Güler Aras and David Crowther includes titles of interest to all those with an interest in ethics and governance; corporate behaviour and citizenship; regulation; protest; globalization; responsible marketing; social reporting and sustainability.

Forthcoming titles in this series

Global Perspectives on Corporate Governance and CSR
Edited by Güler Aras and David Crowther
ISBN: 978 0 566 08830 8

Making Ecopreneurs
Developing Sustainable Entrepreneurship
Edited by Michael Schaper
ISBN: 978 0 566 08875 9

Social and Environmental Reporting
Ethical Disclosure and Socio-economic Factors
Riham R. Rizk
ISBN: 978 0 566 08997 8

Ageing Populations and Changing Labour Markets
Social and Economic Impacts of the Demographic Time Bomb
Edited by Stella Vettori
ISBN: 978 0 566 08910 7

A Handbook of Corporate Governance and Social Responsibility
Edited by Güler Aras and David Crowther
ISBN: 9780566088179

Towards Ecological Taxation
The Efficacy of Emissions-Related Motor Taxation Regimes
David Russell
ISBN: 978 0 566 08979 4

Wealth, Welfare and the Global Free Market

A Social Audit of Capitalist Economics

IBRAHIM OZER ERTUNA
Okan University, Istanbul, Turkey

GOWER

Gower Applied Business Research
Our programme provides leaders, practitioners, scholars and researchers with thought provoking, cutting edge books that combine conceptual insights, interdisciplinary rigour and practical relevance in key areas of business and management.

Published by
Gower Publishing Limited
Wey Court East
Union Road
Farnham
Surrey, GU9 7PT
England

Ashgate Publishing Company
Suite 420
101 Cherry Street
Burlington,
VT 05401-4405
USA

www.gowerpublishing.com

British Library Cataloguing in Publication Data
Ertuna, Ibrahim Ozer.
    Wealth, welfare and the global free market : a social audit
    of capitalist economics. -- (Corporate social
    responsibility series)
    1. Capitalism. 2. Capitalism--Social aspects.
    I. Title II. Series
    306.3'42-dc22

    ISBN: 978-0-566-08905-3 (hbk)
    ISBN: 978-0-566-08906-0 (ebk)

Library of Congress Cataloging-in-Publication Data
Ertuna, Ibrahim Ozer.
    Wealth, welfare, and the global free market : a social audit of capitalist
economics / by Ibrahim Ozer Ertuna.
        p. cm. -- (Corporate social responsibility)
    Includes index.
    ISBN 978-0-566-08905-3 (hardcover) -- ISBN 978-0-566-08906-0
(ebook) 1. Economics. 2. Capitalism. 3. Wealth. 4. Welfare economics. 5.
Free enterprise. 6. Globalization. I. Title.
    HB71.E78 2009
    330.12'2--dc22

                                                            2009011511

Mixed Sources
Product group from well-managed forests and other controlled sources
www.fsc.org Cert no. SA-COC-1565
© 1996 Forest Stewardship Council

Printed and bound in Great Britain by
MPG Books Ltd, Bodmin, Cornwall.

Contents

Introduction   1

Chapter 1   Economics and Economic Systems Today   9
Systems and People   9
What is Economics?   12
Economic Systems   13
Market Economies   16
Capitalism   20
Socialism   26
Change and Transformation in Economic Systems   28
The Rivalry between Capitalism and Socialism   29
Change in the Competitive Environment
    – The *New Economic Design*   31
Conclusion   32

Chapter 2   Capitalism's Definition of Human Beings   35
Economic Systems and People   35
Definition of Human Beings in Capitalism   38
Definition of People in Production   42
Definition of People as Consumers   46
The Results of these Assumptions   49
The Dilemma: Producing and Consuming People   51
Other Belief Systems' Perception of People   52
Summary   53

Chapter 3   Competition: The Driving Force of Economics   55
Capitalism and Competition   56
Differences in Practices   58
Other Types of Behavior   59
Competition in Anatolian Culture   61
Economic Behavior in the Vedas   64
Propositions of Islam   64
Conclusion   66

Chapter 4   **The Market Guidance of the Economy**   **69**

The Competitive Market Economy   69

Markets and Prices   75

The Globalization of Markets   81

Parities Among the Prices   82

Prices Determined Outside the Markets   84

Summary   85

Chapter 5   **The First Concession of Market Economies**   **87**

Wage Determination in Labor Markets:

    The Collective Bargaining System   88

Problems of the Collective Bargaining System   90

The Balance of Power in Other Markets   92

Conclusion   95

Chapter 6   **Misguidance of the Markets and Crises**   **97**

Problems in Exchange Rate Determination   98

Interest Rates and Price of Risk   104

Market Gains   108

Conclusion   111

Chapter 7   **Costs and Benefits that are not Reflected in Markets**   **113**

Social Costs not Reflected in Markets   114

Human Beings as a Cost Factor   119

Social Benefits   123

Conclusion   125

Chapter 8   **Demand and Production: The Theory and the Reality**   **127**

Demand Theory in Economic Science   128

Assumptions of Demand Theory   130

Utility and Needs   132

Production Theory in Economic Science   135

Production Function   139

Recent Developments in Production

    and Production Factors   141

Production and Income Sharing   144

Summary   147

Chapter 9 **What is the Objective: Profit or Income?** **149**
The Definition of Profit 150
The Definition of Value Added 152
The Conflict between Profit and Value-added
 Maximization 153
Labor's Replacement by Robots 154
Re-engineering 156
Privatization Practices 158
Globalization Trends 161
Conclusion 162

Chapter 10 **Foreign Trade** **165**
The Foreign Trade Model 167
The Law of Comparative Advantages 168
Price Impositions in Foreign Trade 169
Foreign Trade in Real Life 170
The Lack of Mobility of Production Factors 170
Misunderstanding Prices 171
Imbalance in Bargaining Power 172
Existence of Non-tradable Products 173
Conclusion 174

Chapter 11 **The *New Economic Design*** **177**
Competitive Conditions 177
The General Agreement on Tariffs and Trade (GATT) 179
The Missing Pillar of the *New Economic Design*: MAI 185
Globalization and Trade Blocs 188
The Objectives of the *New Economic Design* 189
The First Phase of the *New Economic Design* 190
The Second Phase of the *New Economic Design* 193
Conclusion 198

Chapter 12 **An Interrogation of Capitalism** **199**
Capitalism Turning into a Religion 200
The Joy of Victory 201
The Point Now Reached 202
Resistance to Globalization 203

Opposition Against the Global Companies   205
An Interrogation of Capitalism   208
The Post Autistic Economics Movement   209
The Santa Fe Institute   211
Capitalist Companies' Search for Solutions   212
The Insistence on Capitalism for Survival   214
Inconsistent Principles and the Conflicting System   217
Epilogue   222

Index   *225*

I wrote this book because
I met people of many different countries
I learned their aspirations and
I loved them.
I dedicate this book to all nice people with hearts full of aspirations to serve
humankind.

O enlightened men! Through My power all the creatures
Take breath, eat, see and hear;
Even if they do not know, they dwell in my love;
I am in them, they are in me.

(Rig Veda 10.125.4, p. 70)

Introduction

Rise O man! To fall is not your nature
You alone are blessed with
A piercing intellect to avoid pitfalls.

(*Atharva Veda 8.1.6 s:246*)[1]

In our day, as science gains importance and becomes a leading force, economics, which is one of the fields of science, is fast losing its scientific nature. Today, capitalism, converting itself to a faith system, has become a contemporary religion. In this new religion, money has become the God, and stock exchanges are temples of worship. Capitalism, with its dogmas, rules of conduct and its prophets, has developed into a complete religion. As in the case of previous religions, the God of this religion is also a jealous god.[2] It considers respecting a rival god to be the greatest sin of all. Everything must be for the sake of money, for *profit*. Destroying the environment, blocking the implementation of environmental control measures, endangering human health, and increasing hunger are all approved for the sake of profit. This religion has developed since the eighteenth century. Starting with Adam Smith, it has had a number of prophets, and vast ranks of clergymen. This religion attained its most significant growth in the twentieth century, when the realities were very different from the assumptions of its founding fathers; as economies were being dominated by monopolies, and as the international companies were solidifying their hegemony. In fact, the inconsistency between reality and the assumptions capitalism rested upon helped the system to diverge from its scientific foundations and to evolve as a religion.

Capitalism gained momentum after the so-called Washington Consensus among the World Bank, the International Monetary Fund (IMF) and the US Treasury in the 1980s, and the fall of the Union of Soviet Socialist Republics (USSR) in 1990. After the fall of economic system of the USSR, the victory of capitalism was proclaimed. This declaration was one of the most successful

---

1   The Vedas are the holy books, said to be revealed 4,000 years ago, which can be considered to be the basis of Hinduism. *Atharva Veda* is one of the four Veda books, the others being *Rig*, *Yajur* and *Sama*.

2   Deuteronomy, Chapters 5, 9.

propaganda coups of all time. In reality, there was no winner; the fact was that an alternative system had failed. An economic system which did not respect individual choices but relied on the guidance of central administrative planning had failed. The fall of this system does not mean that the remaining capitalist system meets the aspirations of humanity; furthermore, it does not indicate that the capitalist system is itself immune from a possible fall from grace one day. However, capitalism has exploited this opportunity very successfully. It has converted itself into such a religion that even questioning it is a great sin. The name of the new religion became *Globalization*: an economic design meant to worship profits. The world has fast journeyed into a new form: an unsustainable form that is bound to have a short life if it does not change itself in a way that respects and meets the aspirations of mankind.

Today the opponents of what I call the *new economic design*[3] are challenging the system. These opponents of globalization have gained enough strength to block some World Trade Organization meetings; alternative meetings are being organized under the banner of "A Better World is Possible." Greenpeace members are able to raise their voice with greater confidence. The ranks of advocates of the Post Autistic Economics movement, which started in France, are growing.[4] The Santa Fe Institute, which embraces many Nobel Prize winners among its members, is striving to create, in the words of its founder George Cowan, "*the Science of the twenty-first-century*," believing that the way science is perceived today will not be able to solve the problems, including the economic problems, of the twenty-first century.[5] More importantly, many organizations that are working for the advance of humanity and prioritizing the elimination of poverty rather than making rich richer, have entered a constant search for alternatives to capitalism. Additionally, in line with its nature, science has started questioning the developing system. Scientists who are considered *Critical Theoreticians* have started to be effective in all areas of science, especially

---

3   The way it is used in this book, the *new economic design* refers to the economic system promoted to secure the economic privileges of the developed countries. The design is an integral part of the "new world order" spelled out in 1990 by US President George H.W. Bush, and often bears the title "globalization." In our opinion, globalization is a dynamic system that will evolve. The *new economic design* is just a transition state of globalization.

4   In June 2000, a group of disaffected French economics students claimed that the way economics was being taught in universities had made it into an autistic science. The argument evolved into the Post Autistic Economics movement, supported by many academics and a quarterly journal. See: <www.paecon.net>.

5   According to the Santa Fe Institute, a world worth living "should be a society that is adaptable, robust, and resilient to lesser disasters, that can learn from mistakes, that isn't static, but that allows for growth in the quality of human life instead of just the quantity of it." See M. Mitchell Waldrop, *Complexity, The Emerging Science at the Edge of Order and Chaos*, New York: Touchstone Books, 1993, p. 351.

in the social sciences. Many critical economists, deviating from the classical economics of the nineteenth century, have been striving to create a society of integrated people, living in peace with each other, preserving human cultures and values.

The world does not have many choices. Either capitalism will change, or the world will face an end. Capitalism is consuming the world. The ozone layer is thinning, the greenhouse effect is warming the world, with the result that the glaciers are melting, and the rainforests are vanishing. Each year, the world is losing to other uses an area of forest land equal to the size of Portugal.[6] The probability that capitalism's life will be short is increasing. Capitalism is a system conflicting with the aspirations[7] of humanity as cultivated for thousands of years: it is a system that promotes competition rather than mutual support and cooperation. Capitalism justifies any means in order to make profits or to gain money, and takes sides with the strong instead of those who are right. On the other hand, the great majority of the world's people respect the values upheld by humanity over thousands of years and urges us to glorify them. Humanity aspires to use the opportunities created by technological advances to serve and uplift all the people. For all these reasons, capitalism as it is practiced today needs to change fundamentally; otherwise it must come to an end, as the Soviet system did in the 1990s.

Currently, the beneficiaries of capitalist faith claim that capitalism is based on scientific foundations. They also introduce seemingly scientific modifications in its design so that it will continue to serve their interests. The claim and the modifications are not scientific themselves. Science itself is a continuous search of knowledge, attempting to expand the borders of our knowledge. Since economic systems are developed to serve people, science should be in a continuous search of better economic systems that can serve humanity. Capitalism is one of the possible economic systems designed to meet the economic needs of people. It can be tested by scientific methods to see if its results are consistent with the assumptions made, or to see if it meets the objectives set for the system. Using scientific methods, one can show that the results of the capitalist system are consistent with its assumptions. But this would not necessarily mean that the assumptions are correct and the results are appropriate; that is, appropriate in terms of serving humanity. The

---

6 "The World's Forests, Balancing Economic Demands and Conservation," *Finance and Development*, December 2003, p. 40.

7 The Turkish word for this is *özlem*, which means more than aspirations. It includes aspirations, dreams, longings, yearnings, nostalgia and ardent desire.

scientific approach also requires being in search of assumptions that are more appropriate, and a design that produces better results on this latter criterion.

In this book, our approach will be a scientific one. With this study, we will question the assumptions and the results of the capitalist system. By doing so, we will try to explain if capitalism can serve humanity to reach the aspirations of mankind. Throughout the study, we will abide by scientific objectivity and methodology.

Here we may need to explain what we mean by scientific methodology. Science reaches its conclusions by applying scientific methodology, which may be defined as the use of conventional logic, mathematics and statistics based on objective observations and measurements. When the scientific method is used, the same assumptions and methods must lead to the same conclusions; that is, scientific methods should not result in conflicting conclusions. But, by using scientific methodology, it would not be possible to prove whether a system is *better* or *worse* than another. Systems may be considered to be *better* or *worse* depending on their assumptions, the methodologies used, or the objectives set for them. But systems cannot be classified as *good* or *bad* purely on scientific grounds. Being *good* or *bad* depends largely on value structures. These value structures are the aspirations of humanity. Science, faith and aesthetics, together and in complex ways, help us to determine what is correct, what is right, and what is beautiful. If we simplify and generalize, we may say that science tries to expand the borders of the current state of knowledge, scientific methods help us to differentiate between correct and incorrect; faith systems differentiate between good and bad, and aesthetics differentiate between beautiful and ugly. We may succinctly say: science increases what we know, faith systems lead us toward good, and art helps us to appreciate and create beauty. Science, faith and aesthetics, all together, help humanity to excel.

Scientific methodology requires objectivity. But the principle of objectivity should not be misunderstood. There are many scientists who believe that science must take sides with the advancement of humanity and must defend the principle of *science for mankind*.[8] I also adopt this perspective and believe that it is important not diverge from it. All systems, economic, political and cultural, must focus on serving the people. That is, the goal must be the welfare of human beings; systems are only the means to achieve this goal. Unfortunately, not human beings but money, profits and wealth are the objectives (the goals) of capitalism. Capitalism is not a system designed to serve the happiness and

---

8   Çiğdem Kağıtçıbaşı, "Science is for mankind," *Koç Üniversity Bulletin*, 2002.

well-being of people, but to increase (or maximize) the wealth of the rich. As the world's income increased by 2.5 percent a year between 1990 and 1998, the number of people who face poverty and earn less than $2 a day has increased by 100 million people.[9]

As excessive consumption destroys the natural environment and depletes the wealth of our planet, concurrently hunger expands its domain. A United Nations Food and Agricultural Organization (UNFAO) report states that *hunger rates*, which declined in the 1970s and 1980s, reentered its increasing trend after 1990. Every year, 14 million children die of hunger in the world. Hunger is no longer a tragedy faced only by poor countries. Rich countries also face the same problem: 6.1 million adults and 3.3 million children suffer hunger in the US.[10] This is a natural result of capitalism, and a shame on humanity.

It can be easily claimed that alternative systems which seek to make people happy are no more than ideologies or dreams and would fail to attain their objectives. It can even be argued that those systems don't suit human nature. But it is very important to preserve the ideal of spreading happiness, and putting all the means created by science and technology to the service of this ideal. Ideologies to serve humanity have not been successful in the past; but capitalism was successful in reaching its own objectives. Since capitalism is designed to serve the interests of fortunate people, capitalism increases the well-being of the rich. Eliminating hunger is not an objective of capitalism, so hunger is not eliminated. But it is very unfortunate that, due to the observed success of capitalism, science itself has also accepted the objective of serving capitalism.

It is a humanitarian crime to have millions of people face hunger while others waste enormous amounts of resources and enjoy superfluous consumption. This crime should not be committed behind the mask of science. Science and scientists must serve humanity. In his book *Gülistan*, Sadi has said it poetically: "*A scholar who does not abstain from sin is a blind man, holding the torchlight. He reveals the correct path but does not see it himself.*"[11] In our day, it is questionable whether some of these scholars are even revealing the correct path.

---

9   Joseph E. Stiglitz, *Globalization and Its Discontents*, New York: W.W. Norton, 2002, p. 27.
10   A Report of The International Forum on Globalization, *Alternatives to Economic Globalization, A Better World is Possible*, San Francisco, CA: Barrett-Koehler Publishers, 2002, p. 7.
11   Sadi is one of the famous Iranian poets whose works are respected as guidelines by many. *Gülistan* means "rose garden".

The personal profile of capitalism, which has become a faith, and the personal profile of the other faith systems that have tried to glorify human beings over the centuries are very different from each other. Human beings defined by capitalism are:

- self-centered,

- competitive with others, and

- seeking solely in their own self-interest.

On the other hand, other belief systems such as Hinduism, Buddhism, Taoism, Judaism, Christianity and Islam, which have received widespread acceptance from the overwhelming majority of the world's population even today, downgrade and sometimes even condemn self-centeredness, competitiveness and advocating only personal interest. The human characteristics that these belief systems have been trying to cultivate over the centuries are:

- altruism,

- cooperation with others, and

- seeking right and justice.

Capitalism as it is practiced today creates a paradox in the inner self of human beings. On the one hand, the values created by capitalism expand its domination as a new system; on the other hand, a different set of values glorified by mankind over the centuries warms the hearts of human beings.

In this book, our aim is not to develop an alternative to the *capitalist free market economy*. I believe that such an alternative will emerge as a result of an intense interaction among people made possible by the advances in communication technology. In this book, we want to promote awareness, prevent misunderstandings and help everyone to determine their own *values* and *rights*. We want to analyze the contradictions within capitalism and explain the conflicting aspects of capitalist system with the aspirations of humanity as developed over thousands of years. We believe that such awareness will help us to find our direction within the current system, and at the same time it will help us contribute to the development of a new system. My personal conviction is that, with the means and opportunities created by today's communication technology, the *alternative economic design* established will be in line with the aspirations that humankind has nurtured and preserved with care for thousands of years. These aspirations have been captured inside belief systems which have been developed in both the East and the West.[12] These aspirations are the fruits of the cultures of human societies. In my opinion, the problems faced by humankind and the increasing awareness of these problems in all communities will facilitate the process of replacing the capitalist system with a system that is developed to realize the aspirations of humankind. Capitalism is designed to serve just a small minority; the replacing system will try to serve all.

In this respect, I also believe that the Anatolian culture has an important duty in the development of a new economic system. The new system that will emerge needs to be based not on the "clash of civilizations,"[13] but on the enrichment of cultures by cross-fertilization. Anatolia has become the fertilization ground for various cultures through the centuries. This interaction has produced a very significant synthesis. The roots of Anatolian cultures are Hattie, Hurry, Hittite, Roman, Greek, Persian, Arabic, Ottoman, Turkish, and European. Recently, as the new developments in communication technology integrate different lands and eliminate distances, Anatolian culture is also being influenced by American and Far Eastern cultures. Anatolian culture has emerged as a fruit of this cultural fertilization, which will continue in the decades to come. With this cultural accumulation and potential, Anatolian culture will be able to make significant contributions to the development of a new economic system in the world.

The main intention of the book is presenting a view of economics outside the conventional mainstream. In the twenty-first century, our problems, our capacity to solve our problems and our aspirations have all been amplified. Identifying our problems, creating our solutions and reaching our aspirations all require new innovative viewpoints. Economists, constrained by the classical concepts, models and arguments, may face difficulties in bringing new viewpoints and solutions to this rapidly changing world. I believe the new innovative solutions will come from those who are not conditioned by the current system. They will have to take a fresh look at the problems and search for new solutions to these problems in order to meet their aspirations. This book aims to assist the reader in this endeavor. For that reason, this book

---

12 It is very unfortunate that Eastern and Western cultures have been strongly prejudiced against each other. I have a feeling that Western culture wants to dominate: Eastern culture accepts coexistence. I believe we need cross-fertilization between cultures.

13 See Samuel P. Huntington, *The Clash of Civilizations and the Remaking of World Order*, New York: Simon and Schuster, 1998.

is not one that generates solutions, it is one that poses questions. Solutions will be created by the broader public participation enabled by the means of the new century. Today, economic developments are not moving in the right direction. It is the responsibility of all of us to put them on the right track.

Economics and Economic Systems Today

For the love of money is a root of all kinds of evil.

(New Testament, 1 Timothy 6:10)

Lest strangers feast on your wealth
And your toil enriches another man's house.

(Old Testament, Proverbs 5:10)

Gold is a wonderful thing! Whoever possesses it is master of everything he desires. With gold one can even get souls into heaven.

(Christopher Columbus)[1]

Systems and People

Humankind has been developing various systems to live better and to be happy. All these systems are developed by people, applied by the participation of people, and exist to serve people.[2]

That this is a fact as clear as can be is not open to any doubt or question, but has been many times forgotten. It is often forgotten that systems are just tools to reach objectives, and they often become the objective themselves. In such cases, people become simply the means to serve the systems. People are sacrificed to make the systems endure. This is true for government, religion

---

1 Robert L. Heilbroner, *The Worldly Philosophers, The Lives, Times and Ideas of the Great Economic Thinkers*, New York: Simon and Schuster, New York, 1966, p. 21.

2 One of the best ways of expressing this idea comes from Abraham Lincoln, who was president of the US during the Civil War. Abraham Lincoln, in his Gettysburg Address, defined the nature of the political system that people yearn for: "Government of the people, for the people, by the people shall not perish from the earth."

and the economy. The question inevitably arises of whether the people exist for the sake of government rather than government existing for the sake of people. Throughout the centuries, the most fierce and cruel wars have been fought for the sake of religion. Economic systems lose their bearings, become the ends instead of the means, and spread misery instead of happiness among the people.

Systems are composed of institutions, means and rules. Factories are institutions of production. Markets, fairs, shops and shopping malls are institutions of distribution. Labor, capital, knowledge and technology are means of production. Money is a means of exchange. Rules define the operations of these institutions, relations among the institutions and relations between the institutions and the people. The way the institutions use their means and their rules show variations in different systems. But one fact should not differ: systems must be designed to serve people. This means that the ultimate goal must be that of serving people. Unfortunately, as we have mentioned above, from time to time this fact is forgotten. Serving institutions, serving the rules and preserving the means for doing so become the goal themselves. Let us take an example: in the capitalist system, the *profit motive* is a means to guide the owners of enterprises to reach their objectives. According to the economic theory, it is believed that the system will serve people better if participants are motivated to earn a profit. In actual practice, the profit may became an end, instead of a means. The environment may be polluted and destroyed, people may be deprived of health services and education, or even be left to poverty. In fact, it may not stop there: money, which is a means of exchange, may lose its function and go beyond being an objective; it may become an object of worship and be regarded as a God.

Systems – that is, institutions, means and the rules governing them – are constantly changing and developing. The reason for this constant change may be the dynamic nature of people and their needs and aspirations. Perhaps the actual reason is the inability of the current systems to attain their changing objectives. These changing objectives may reflect the aspirations (longings) of a group of people or the people as a whole. The interesting thing is that the people's aspirations as a whole do not change much, and have not changed much over thousands of years. But, with all the developments in knowledge and technology, our capacity to serve the aspirations of people has been increasing. With this increasing knowledge and technology, the current system needs to change to serve people's aspirations and to solve their problems. On this point, I want to share a meaningful and inspiring anecdote with you:

A young new faculty member arrives at a university. As he develops his way of teaching, he keeps an eye on the approaches of the other (and particularly the older) professors. He notices that an old professor has developed a habit of asking the same final exam questions at the end of each semester. To satisfy his curiosity, he decides to talk to the professor. "Dear Sir," he says, "I see that you are asking the same final exam questions to your students every semester. As you know, the students keep an archive of the exams. Doesn't it create any problems? The old professor responds with all contentment: "No," he says, "it creates no problem at all. Every semester I change the answers."

As far as we know, people have been asking the same questions since the beginning of life on earth. What needs to be produced? Who should produce it? How can they produce it? How shall it be shared? What do people deserve? What are good and bad? There are thousands of questions like these. The questions have remained the same but the answers have changed, and will continue to change. What is important is that we should not tire in searching for answers; we should not confuse the means with the ends, and we should not make people the slaves and victims of the systems we create. This is the scientific approach. Following this approach, we should not be satisfied with what we know and what we have; we need to be constantly in search of new knowledge and new solutions.

In this section, we will study the systems developed in the field of economics. Economic systems are the systems developed for people's production and consumption activities. The "economy" relates to production and sharing the fruits of production. As a branch of science, economics studies the economic systems developed by people and searches for ways to improve them. Economic systems, like other systems, have their own institutions, means and rules. Economics studies these institutions, means and rules, and tries to understand how these institutions, means and rules serve the people. Questions relating to production and sharing are not easy ones to answer. Throughout history, economics has searched for answers to the questions "How shall we produce?" and "How shall we share?" The answers provide for a wide range of solutions. Currently, at one end stands the principle "Every one contributes to production according to his means, and consumes according to his needs." Various collective systems exist to meet this principle, such as the *kolkhoz* and the *kibbutz*. At the other end, the principle is that "Every one contributes to production according to his competency which is rewarded with a commensurate income, and consumes according to his income." The capitalist system follows this second principle. Here we will try to study some of these economic systems.

What is Economics?

Economics is a field that specifies the institutions, the means and the rules for participating in the production of goods and services and sharing the outputs of that production. From a different point of view, we can define economics as the allocation of scarce resources to the areas of production and consumption in order to increase the satisfaction of the people. This point of view emphasizes the fact that the resources we can allocate to production and consumption are limited, and the objective of the allocation system is the satisfaction of the people. Whatever the definition, the answers sought in economic studies do not change: questions such as "How are the goods and services produced?", "Who owns or should own the factors of production?", "What should be the method of sharing the goods and services produces?", and so on. Only very recently have people realized that these questions lack an important dimension: sustainability, and that the economic systems, tools and rules we have developed so far are depleting the resources of our planet.

People need to consume and to own things, and they need to express themselves. People produce some of the things they need and get some from other people. They need a place to shelter, food to satisfy hunger, clothing to protect them from the elements, and they have a desire to express themselves to others. These needs have always existed. In the beginning, people sheltered in caves, hunted animals, wore the skins of the animals they hunted, and drew pictures on the walls of their caves. But these needs are just a few of the basic needs of humans. Similar to these needs, there are all manner of other ones, some defined as basic, some as essential and some as non-essential. It is assumed that all these are needed in order to get satisfaction from life. But the relation between needs and life-satisfaction may not be a positive one. Some may get satisfaction from meeting their needs by their own efforts, some by getting help from others, and some by suppressing their needs.

People may or may not have a given set of needs. They develop their structures of needs by interacting with the environment and the developments in the environment, comprising the physical, cultural, religious domains. In the environment, there are many agents persuading and convincing people about what they need and providing prescriptions for their satisfaction. The process of persuasion may result in consumption patterns harmful to society and the natural environment. The objective of such persuasion may be serving the interests of a few who benefit from the outcome, but may not be serving society in general. The needs can become so elevated that consumption may only soothe the pangs of the hunger created by the persuasion. The level of consumption may result in waste and may harm the environment. What we need may be the creation of an educated awareness of the effects of our need structure, and how we satisfy our needs, on ourselves, society, the environment and the planet we live in. By creating such an educated awareness, people may have a better chance to formulate their structure of needs and their satisfaction in a rational manner.

Today, the economic systems we have designed persuade people that they have an endless number of needs which can only be satisfied by consumption. Economic success is measured by the amount of consumption an economic system provides to its members.[3] But in fact, economic success may not depend on the amount of consumption provided. The relation between the level of consumption and the level of satisfaction may be much more complicated than that. If people's happiness is the objective, it may even be possible to increase happiness while reducing consumption. It may be possible to increase happiness with a lower level of consumption by eliminating waste.[4] Many religions and belief systems, with millions and millions of followers, try to teach their adherents to be happy with less rather than more.

People either produce the things they need or purchase them from others. Today, it is not possible for individuals to produce all that they need. For that reason, people need to produce some things themselves, produce jointly with others, and buy other things from other producers.[5] We can say that people have developed economic systems to obtain, to produce, and to share the things they need. The systems people develop are composed of institutions, means and rules.

Economic Systems

Most of the things people acquire from others are not even within the domain of the study of economics. There are many alternative ways of acquiring things from others. One way is acquiring the things produced or owned by others by force, for example, by using military power. Although these methods

---

3   The capitalist system of our day may be called "the economics of waste."

4   In Islam "waste" is considered "haram" (illicit). " … do not act extravagantly; He does not love the extravagant" the Koran, Surah 6:141, Surah 7:31.

5   There are things that increase the level of satisfaction or happiness, which cannot be purchased from others, but must be produced by people themselves. The most important ones are developing one's taste for nature, art and culture, and establishing love of mankind in one's heart.

of acquisition are not within the domain of economic studies, it is very well known that the real motives behind most wars are economic motives. Though the process is one of using force through military means, the act itself is an economic act: in exercising military power, the purpose is to obtain the goods essential to consumption or production, and acquiring wealth.[6] These kinds of acquisitions may not be considered morally appropriate. They may be inconsistent with the values of people and communities. For that reason, these procedures are carried out behind masks to hide the *shame*. For example, as everyone knows very well, in the First Gulf War in 1990 the real intention was not to bring freedom to Kuwait, and in the Iraq War in 2003 it was not to save the world from terrorist activities.

Another method used is exploitation, that is, taking more than one's *fair share* from what is produced with others. There are many methods of exploitation: using slave labor, paying labor subsistence wages in colonies, and imposing import and export duties in foreign trade, have been some of the ways used throughout the centuries. Exploitation is so attractive, and differentiating it from competitive advantage so difficult, that it cannot be eliminated easily. That is why it has been used so widely by some societies throughout history. In the initial stages, exploitation systems were established by force. In time, in parallel with global social and economic developments, exploitation systems became more subtle. Developed countries found methods to exploit many developing countries, under the guise of helping them. It is even possible to exploit some countries by praising their leaders for collaborating in the exploitation of their own people. The well-accepted principle of our day in international relations is that countries do not seek justice; they only look after their own interest. Being right or just is not important at all, nor is there a need for fairness in economic relations among countries.[7] Since 1994, a *new economic design* called "globalization" has been in the process of development. This *new economic design* is developing on the principles of *interest* and not *fairness*. The current system that is spreading through the world does not have the objective of serving people, whoever they are and whatever country they come from.

---

6   In his book *Confessions of an Economic Hit Man*, John Perkins explains the process used to acquire the control of the resources of developing countries: first, financial measures are used; if not successful, then intelligence services stage plots; and if intelligence services fail, military power is used. See John Perkins, *Confessions of an Economic Hit Man*, San Francisco, CA: Barret-Koehler Publishers, 2004.

7   It is important to note here that supporters of the "Alternatives to Economic Globalization" movement are asking for fair trade and fair prices, rather than free trade and market prices.

Exploitation of the people of developing countries is not well regarded by great majority of people all around the world in different cultures. Most belief systems, whether religious or secular, have tried to convince people that it is their duty to establish equitable economic systems on earth. It is very difficult to claim that the free market economy accomplishes the fair and equitable allocation of resources and the products of these resources. Therefore people have been searching for alternative economic systems that may be considered more equitable. *Kibbutzim*[8] *and moshavs* in Israel, socialism and *kolkhozes* in the former USSR, Mondragón Cooperatives in the Basque region in Spain,[9] may be considered to be examples of the fruits of such quests. The basic objective of these systems is that everyone participates in production according to their means, and shares the produce according to their needs. The systems mentioned above have strong scientific foundations. But these systems have not received wide acceptance in our day. Economic systems providing equitable sharing are still considered to be *ideal* systems that people aspire to, but are in reality just a dream.

It is very difficult to define equitable sharing. What may seem to be equitable sharing to some people may seem to be very unequal to others. Some people may claim that it is very unjust for those who have not contributed to the production to take a share from the output. Being just or unjust is a normative evaluation. The economic science we have today does not base its findings on normative choices; it claims to be objective. The economic science of today does not consider moral issues to be in its domain of interest; it has left the normative issues to the moral and belief structures of communities.

Societies have also developed concepts, means and rules to meet the needs of the poor and people in poverty. Helping the poor, donations, aid, alms, *fitre*,[10] *zekat*[11] are widely used concepts and means to help those in poverty. Institutions

---

8   A *kibbutz* (Hebrew: "gathering, clustering"; plural *kibbutzim*) is a collective community in Israel that was traditionally based on agriculture. The *kibbutz* is a form of communal living that combines socialism and Zionism. *Kibbutzim* began as utopian communities, but have gradually embraced a more capitalistic approach. Today, farming has been partly supplanted by other economic branches, including industrial plants and high-tech enterprises. *Kibbutzim* members comprise 5 percent of the Israeli population,

9   The *Mondragón* Cooperative Corporation (Spanish: *Mondragón Corporación Cooperativa* – MCC) is a group of manufacturing and retail companies based in the Basque Country and extended over the rest of Spain and abroad. It is one of the world's largest worker cooperatives and one important example of workers' self-management. See <http://en.wikipedia.org/wiki/Mondrag%C3%B3n_Cooperative_Corporation>.

10 *Fitre* are the donations Muslims are obliged to make to those in need during the month of fasting (Ramadan).

11 As one of the five prerequisites of Islam, Muslims must donate one-fortieth of their wealth to the needy as *zekat*.

such as charitable foundations, *imarethane* (soup kitchens), and *misafirhane* (hostels) are commonly found in many countries to help those in need. In the current understanding of economics, these institutions, concepts, means and rules that are designed to help the poor are in the domain of moral systems.[12]

Today, the widely accepted system for people to obtain the things they need is the exchange of goods in the market environment. These economies are called "market economies."[13] These kinds of economic systems are considered virtuous in our time.

Market Economies

Markets are the economic structures where supply and demand meet. In markets, the suppliers of products and services, capital, labor and various rights meet with those who demand them. Both suppliers and demanders act out of their own interest and free will. No authority forces them to act in any predetermined way. That is, in product markets, no one forces the sellers to sell their product or requires someone to purchase them. The free will of the sellers and buyers in free markets determines the free prices that clear the market. The free prices determined in the markets, in turn, guide the economy. That is, economic agents make their economic decisions under these prices, determined freely in the market. This is called the "invisible hand" that guides free market economies. But this guidance may or may not be in the interests of society. It is currently believed that to serve the interest of society, these free markets would have to be competitive; both buyers and sellers must compete in their own interest. On the other hand, even such competitive free markets may not be able to serve the interests of society as a whole.

Markets may develop to be competitive, oligopolistic, or monopolistic. Today's economists believe that if transactions in the markets take place under the rules of perfect competition, there would be no room for exploitation in the

---

12 It may be appropriate to say few words about foundations (*vakifs* in Turkish) here. Foundations are institutions established to serve a mission. The sources of revenue of foundations may be donations as well as commercial or productive operations. The objective of these Foundations is not making a profit, but realizing their mission. Foundations may use their revenues to realize their social or economic missions. In the twenty-first century, such foundations may serve to realize the aspirations of people of the world.

13 According to some economists, market economies have evolved over the centuries through a revolutionary process in which the land, labor and capital became commercial products. Previously, economics was guided either by tradition or central authorities: Heilbroner, *The Worldly Philosophers*, pp. 1–27.

markets. Under such a conviction, great effort is spent to liberalize the markets and to increase their competitiveness. In 1994, institutions like the World Trade Organization established "competition boards" in many countries, as well as regulations like the General Agreement on Trade and Tariffs (GATT), and antitrust laws and competition laws in many countries, all in an attempt to increase the competitiveness of markets. In competitive free market economies, the individuals, economic institutions, and nations compete in order to serve the general interest. It is believed that this form of competition to serve the interests of buyers and sellers will serve society as a whole, and thus all the individuals in that society as well. But this is only a belief. Economic science has developed models and rules to support this belief, and has succeeded in doing so under various assumptions. The conclusions reached using these models and rules are only correct under the assumptions made. These assumptions may conflict with the humanitarian values and aspirations of many whose dream is to uplift the well-being of every individual in the society. In the chapters that follow, we will evaluate the basic assumptions of economic theory when appropriate.

In these markets, the buyers are only those who have money to purchase. Only their free will and choices are reflected the prices in the markets, and the economy is guided with these prices. In market economies, the choices of those without purchasing power are not considered at all. The "invisible hand" guides these economies not according to the choices of everyone, but according to the choices of those who have money. And, in this guidance, each individual's choices are weighted by the amount of money they have.

From the point of view of the production of goods and services, the market approach may not be able to guide the economy within the framework of the choices of the people. There are basically two reasons for this. The first is the existence of costs and benefits that are not reflected in the market. The second is the existence of monopolies that control the markets or market mechanism. Let us take a short look at these conditions.

Let us start with our first claim: free market economies are guided by the prices determined in the markets. The prices are determined so as to balance the forces of supply and demand.[14] Demand itself depends on the benefit ("utility" in economic parlance) that the purchaser derives from the goods and services he or she buys; and the supply depends on the costs of the goods and services to the producer. If all the costs and benefits are reflected in the markets, the prices determined in the markets may guide the economy properly. But there

---

14 Using economic terminology, prices clear the market.

are great varieties of costs and benefits that are not or cannot reflect the markets. For example, the costs of polluting the physical and social environment in the production of certain products or services are not costs to the economic agents producing them. Those costs accrue to society as a whole. For that reason, these costs are not taken into account in the markets. As the result, these goods and services are produced and consumed in greater quantities. The consequence is excess production and consumption and an increased burden on the social and physical environment. Reduction of the world's rainforests, the melting of the polar glaciers, and the thinning of the ozone layer are the consequences of the inability to reflect some of these costs in the markets. The opposite is also true. The social benefits of some products may not appear to the companies as benefits (revenues). For that reason, the production of some goods and services may be less than what they might be. Health care, education, cultural services are very important products benefiting society as a whole, as well as those who purchase them. When these social benefits are not reflected in the markets, reductions in health care, education, and cultural services have great negative impacts on society's welfare. Similarly, if people without sufficient means are deprived of health care, education and cultural services, society suffers significantly.

The second reason for constraining production to serve the interests of society as a whole is the existence of national and international monopolies and the control these monopolies exercise on the markets. As economic science has proven clearly, monopoly power provides chances to the monopolist to exploit the buyers. Classical economic theory does not approve of monopolies. In fact, it recommends developing means and regulations to eliminate it. But, as we will see in the following chapters, in order to defend the market mechanism, economic science develops new models and concepts of competition to prove that different types of competition among agents with monopoly power may serve the interests of the people and society.[15] At one time, authorities used to study mergers and acquisitions cases in order to prevent the formation of powerful monopolies. Under the new definitions of competition, it is possible to claim that the strong competitors created by mergers and acquisitions may serve the public interest. There are new assertions that not just the quantity, but the quality of competition also matters.

---

15 J.A. Schumpeter and Joan Robinson developed the "monopolistic competition" concept, which is more in tune with real-life conditions. The "creative destruction" concept of Schumpeter is a very important one, which defends the assertion that even in a monopolist environment, competition is the driving force of economic development. In Schumpeter's vision of capitalism, innovative entry by entrepreneurs was the force that sustained long-term economic growth, even as it destroyed the value of established companies that enjoyed some degree of monopoly power. See <http://en.wikipedia.org/wiki/Creative_destruction>.

Economic science claims that in competitive free market economies everyone receives their share of output according to their contribution, and gets their share of consumption according to their income. This seems to be a *good* solution provided by the system. But, in order to make a proper assessment two points require closer attention. This assertion may be correct under the full employment of resources, including full employment of workers.[16] But in the real world, the unemployment of resources, especially those of laborers is a very significant problem that many countries are facing. Also, those who do not have the required talents needed in the production system may not be able to find employment and earn an income.

Economic theory assumes the goods and services in the market to be homogenous. In the case of labor, it is assumed that all laborers have the same talents. For that reason, there are many who believe that systems which allow labor to contribute to production according to their means (talents) and to take their share from the output according to their needs are more equitable systems. But being equitable or not, being fair or not, are not the concern of the market economies that are defended today. The economic results reached by implementing the capitalist market economic system may be undesirable from social points of view. But, these are not the concerns of these market economies. Concepts such as being equitable, just, or fair are left to the domains of belief and religious systems throughout history. Almost all religions, past and present, urge fair and equitable distribution and recommend alms and donations to redress the poverty caused by the application of inequitable systems.

Competitive free market economies do not have to be capitalistic economies. There are systems that require competitive free markets, but are not capitalist systems. One of these systems is the *labor-managed market economy*.[17] In capitalist economies, the capitalist owner supplies the capital and has all the rights to run the company in his own interest to earn a profit. The capitalist owner hires labor from the markets. On the other hand, in labor-managed market economies, labor as a group owns the company and runs it for their collective purposes. Their purpose is earning income to share. They hire capital from the well-functioning capital markets, paying the market interest. Laborers participate in company decisions according to their *quality* and *intensity* of their

---

16 Full employment is a well-defined term in economics. It indicates a state of equilibrium in which supply and demand clear the market. It is a state where there is no one who is willing to buy but cannot, and there is no one who is willing to sell but cannot find a buyer at the current price.

17 Jaroslav Vanek, *The General Theory of Labor Managed Market Economies*, Ithaca, NY: Cornell University Press, 1970.

involvement. The *Mondragón* cooperatives in the Basque region in Spain are one of the best examples of the application of such a labor-managed market economic system.

Although the means the people use to acquire goods and services from others that are explained above – by force, by exploitation, and by market access – follow an evolutionary order and time sequence, all those systems are still observed in our day in one way or another. The important point is that the relevant puzzles of how to produce and how to share have not been solved, and their complete solution is not expected. People and societies are in constant search of solutions to the dilemmas of how to produce and how to share. In fact, it is what they should be doing.

Now we want to concentrate on the economic systems that were popular and widely applied in the twentieth century, that is, the capitalist and socialist systems. Today, the favored economic system, which is spreading all over the world with an assertion that it has no rival or alternative, is the capitalist system.

Capitalism

Broadly speaking, capitalism is an economic system in which some people own the capital or "means of production", and the ownership of capital grants them the right to run the company in their own interest, that is, that of the capitalist owner. In capitalist market economies, companies acquire the labor they employ from the labor market, the funds they need from the capital markets, and the raw materials they use in the production from the product markets; they sell the products they produce in the product markets. Companies are managed in the interest of the capitalist owners, in most of cases to maximize their profit.

Capitalism believes in *private initiative* and entrepreneurship. Entrepreneurs, acting in their own interests, try to maximize their gains by competing with others. These entrepreneurs provide the dynamism of the capitalist system. Their desire to maximize their individual profits results in serving society by providing economic growth. In the competitive environment, each entrepreneur must develop a comparative advantage over the others. Through these comparative advantages, they are able to serve their customers better. All this ensures that capitalism fuels overall economic development and serves the well-being of society. This is the well-accepted and common belief of our times.

Free enterprise and the profit motive play a very significant role in the success of the capitalist economic system.[18] In any capitalist system, free enterprise should not be restricted at all. Private individuals, and they alone, should engage in economic activities in order to maximize their benefits. Governments should not undertake economic activities and become competitors to private individual interests, but should leave all their economic operations to individuals. Governments may invest in infrastructure that is not attractive enough to attract private investment, and take measures to help the private sector to flourish.[19] It is a common belief in capitalist thinking that governments' participation in economic activity reduces the span of control of the private sector and their chance to maximize their profits, thereby causing a disservice to society. This is also a common belief of our times.

The profit motive of capitalism, that is, having profit maximization as the main objective, creates its own dilemma in the capitalist system. The type of competition needed for the success of the entrepreneur in the capitalist system is not the same type of competition needed for the success of the capitalist economic system itself. The entrepreneur tries to create monopoly power in order to increase his or her profits. From the entrepreneurs' point of view, competition means overcoming rivals.[20] Overcoming rivals may require destroying the competitive market and establishing a monopoly. The means of overcoming rivals is important as well. To eliminate rivals, companies may divert their energies to practices that are considered "unfair competition." On some occasions, entrepreneurs, through what is called collusion, may act together to exploit the customers. All these types of behavior violate the rules of competition. This is why these behaviors are outlawed to create a healthy competitive environment. In countries that seek to implement healthy competition, there are institutions, laws and rules to prevent establishment of monopolies and trusts, and the exploitation of customers.

The capitalist system is expected to serve the interests of people as a whole only under the type of competition that is defined as "perfect competition" in capitalist economic theory. The conclusion of this economic theory, which

---

18 Free enterprise is a term similar to entrepreneurship, but a broader one. Entrepreneurship is a talent, a gift of God, while free enterprise is a right to engage in economic activities without any restrictions.

19 Previously the common belief was that the private sector is not interested in infrastructure investments due to their magnitude. Today, the supranational companies are very much interested in investments such as transportation, telecommunication and energy investments because these types of investments provide monopolistic power.

20 In the Japanese economic system, competition and solidarity may go hand in hand in so-called *keiretsu* organizations and behavior.

can be summarized as "each individual's seeking his own interest will end up in serving the society as a whole," only holds true if economic activities are carried out under the kind of "perfect competition" that is specified in economic theory. The system does not serve the interests of all if that type of perfect competition does not exist. In fact, even the theory itself acknowledges that it may result in exploitation. Economic theory defines fully competitive markets as markets where buyers and sellers are so marginal that they cannot influence the market, where there are no barriers to enter or exit the market, where all products traded in the market are homogeneous, where everyone has full and perfect information about all relevant facts about the markets and products, and where transportation costs are zero. Under these conditions, as entrepreneurs compete to increase their profits, they will best serve consumers and there will be no exploitation. But, economic theory proves that under such an environment profits will also be zero. Everyone will get their equitable share of income, as determined by the markets. This means in that in the capitalist system, entrepreneurs are motivated by the idea of profits they will not be able to secure. This is what the economic theory claims.

As explained above, in the capitalist system, entrepreneurs will try to maximize their profits by moving away from perfect competition, while on the other hand, government will try to create and improve the conditions for competition. Because of this dilemma, the capitalist system needs a government that is not itself active in economic activities, but rather oversees and protects the implementation of the rules of capitalism. Even such governmental regulations are not well accepted in our day: deregulation in the markets has been the recent trend.

In spite of the recent deregulation trend, governments have been trying to regulate misbehavior in the markets, taking measures to eliminate monopolies and cartels, unfair competition, and similar practices to protect consumers. That is, governments have been trying to protect their people from the misbehaviors of capitalism. Governments also provide incentives to entrepreneurs to carry out activities that are expected to serve the economic objectives of the people as a whole. The role of government in the economy is a subject that is not resolved in capitalist economies yet.

In the capitalist system, companies are managed to serve the interests of the owners of capital, that is, the stockholders. Stockholders have sole rights on the profits of the company. Labor is one of the factors of production, employed by the company by paying wages. Wages are among the costs of production that must be deducted from the revenues to realize profit. In the process of production, stockholders seek to maximize their profit, and the laborers seek to get more wages. That is, the interests of the stockholders and the laborers are in conflict. In case of such a conflict between the owners of capital and the laborers, laborers are assumed to be weaker than capital, especially when the rate of unemployment is high. In such a case, the capitalist owner, that is the employer, can exploit the laborers. This has been a very important phenomenon, especially during and after the Industrial Revolution. It was found that free labor markets are unable to provide a solution to eliminate the exploitation of labor.

In order to protect labor from exploitation, a system outside the free labor markets had to be established. The system created was the *collective bargaining* system. In this system, labor, represented by labor unions, and the employers, represented by employer unions, strike a bargain on the wages and the working conditions of the laborers. To assure the balance of power of the employers and the laborers, deadly weapons are provided to the two groups who are assumed to have conflicting interests. The two weapons provided are labor's right to strike, and employers' right to lockout. The important thing is that the capitalist system is constructed on the assumption that the interests of capital and labor are not complementary but in conflict. This is seen to be a very significant deficiency of capitalism.[21] Fortunately, capitalism shows some important differences in its application in different countries. There are many cases where capital and labor are considered complementary and they collaborate in the production process. In Japan, sub-systems such as "lifetime employment", "quality circles", "total quality" and the like help to draw attention to the complementarities of capital and labor in the production process. Unfortunately, with increased popularity of capitalism, such "lifetime employment" implementations are disappearing in Japan.

In recent years, capitalism has been going through a transformation. Terminologies such as "capitalist" and "labor class" are changing fast, and new concepts, such as "stakeholder" and "intellectual capital" are emerging.[22] In the US, mutual funds, insurance companies and pension funds own more than half of the capital of corporations. The benefits of these funds are shared to some degree by the employees of those companies. These

---

21 Jaroslav Vanek calls this deficiency "negative sign syndrome" and considers it to the main single problem of the twenty-first century: Jaroslav Vanek, *General Theory of Social Systems* <http://ecommons.library.cornell.edu/handle/1813/642>.

22 Today, "intellectual laborers" such as designers, fashion and image developers don't see themselves as members of the "working class."

companies and the institutional investors are not managed by capitalists, but by professional managers.[23]

In modern corporations, management and ownership are well separated. But in the capitalist system, it is believed that the interests of managers and owners may conflict. This assumed conflict is the result of the understanding that in capitalism, no one, including managers and owners, has any common interest; they each seek their own interest. This conflict is called the "agency theory" in management literature. The agency theory claims that the agents (managers) have better and more information about the company; agents may use this asymmetric information to their benefit, at the cost of the principals (owners). The agency theory is built on the expectation of unethical behavior by the agents. On the other hand, stock exchanges have introduced new dimensions to the relationships between owners and managers. Stockholders of highly traded companies do not buy their stocks just to gain dividends from the earnings of the companies and to vote for new management once a year. They buy their stocks primarily for their capital appreciation value. If they like the way the company is run and find the company successful, they will hold their stocks; otherwise they sell them. Some people claim that this is a new way of supervising the managers of a company.

In short, the recent trends in the world indicate that today's capitalism has already deviated from the capitalism of the classic teachings. But one thing has not changed: the typical individual living in the capitalist economic system is assumed to be seeking only their own interest (they may even be considered selfish), and he or she competes with others, trying to eliminate competitors and gain a bigger piece of the pie when it comes to sharing the benefits. We will study in a later section capitalism's definition of human beings.

DIFFERENT FORMS OF CAPITALISM

Today, capitalism, which has gained widespread acceptance, is applied in different forms in different countries. We may say that it is implemented in its purest form in the US, where it has been quite successful in its application. The US has been trying to redesign the economic systems of primarily developing countries in order to increase its control of the world economy. It would not be a mistake to argue that *globalization* was a concept developed by the US. The World Bank, the IMF (International Monetary Fund) and the WTO (World Trade Organization) are the institutions that have assumed the role of

---

23   Peter F. Drucker, *Post-Capitalist Society*, New York: Harper Business, 1993.

developing a *new economic design* for the world.[24] The way that capitalism has been implemented in the US since the nineteenth century is also called "wild capitalism." On the other hand, the way that capitalism has been implemented in European, especially northern Scandinavian, countries, is a form of capitalism which incorporates social justice. In these countries, although in production and trade capitalist principles are adhered to and free markets are respected, attempts have been made to develop efficient social spending systems that will guarantee the basic necessities of their people.

After the 1997 East Asian economic crises, the circles close to the World Bank claimed that the form of capitalism implemented in East Asian countries was responsible for the crises. These circles created a new term for the type of capitalism implemented in those countries: "crony capitalism," that is, capitalism where interpersonal relations guide economic activities.[25]

The argument is that crony capitalism is a kind of capitalism where friends and relatives receive favorable treatment in commercial transactions. Economic systems take their forms and shapes under the prevalent culture of societies. Systems appropriate to some cultures may not be appropriate in others. In Eastern cultures, interpersonal relations are important, for social and economic reasons. Eastern cultures praise collaborative or cooperative rather then competitive relations, and rely on trust rather than doubt. Therefore, economic behavior in different cultures can be misunderstood if their cultural foundations are not properly taken under consideration. The concept of "crony capitalism" may be the result of such a misunderstanding. Nobel Prize-winning economist Joseph Stiglitz has a different view of the way capitalism is implemented in Asian countries. According to Stiglitz, there are alternatives to the way capitalism is exercised in America:

> ... the Asian Development Bank argues for "competitive pluralism," whereby developing countries will be provided with alternative view of development strategies, including the "Asian model"– in which governments while relying on markets, have taken an active role in creating, shaping, and guiding markets, including promoting new technologies, and in which firms take considerable responsibility for the social welfare of their employees – which the Asian Development

---

24 The International Forum on Globalization, *Alternatives for Economic Globalization, A Better World is Possible*, San Francisco, CA: Berrett-Koehler Publishers, 2002, p. 37.

25 In this type of capitalism, favors extended under interpersonal relations also observed in governmental levels. Socialists claim that crony capitalism is a natural outcome of the capitalist system <http://en.wikipedia.org/wiki/Crony_capitalism>.

Bank sees as distinctly different from the American model pushed by Washington-based institutions.[26]

In fact, the Japanese type of capitalism is spreading in Asia. The main driving force behind this process is the increasing number of subsidiaries and suppliers of Japanese companies operating in China. The economic system of Japan is a system that can neither be called capitalist nor a socialist system. It is a different system, informed by Japanese culture. According to Locke:

> *Simply put, Japan has done almost everything wrong by Neoliberal standards and yet is indisputably the second-richest nation in the world ... Japan's economy is highly regulated, centrally-planned by the state, and often contemptuous of free markets. But it has thrived.*[27]

In guiding the economy, the Ministry of Finance and the *keiretsus*[28] play an important role. The financial institutions, under the control of the Ministry of Finance, provide very cheap credit to Japan's industry. Because of that, Japan's economy has a long-term vision and highly competitive position and is able to pay high wages to its employees. For all these reasons, Japan's economy can be called a capitalist economy with socialist financial markets.

Socialism

Both capitalism and socialism are the systems created by the dominant Western thought. In fact the best known form of socialism, the way it was implemented in the Union of Soviet Socialist Republics, can be called state capitalism. According to Jaroslav Vanek:

> *Following [the Second World War] the winning systems were both capitalist systems, one based on private capital ownership, the second based on state capital ownership. That is, both systems were seeking to serve the interests of capital – one that of the private owners, the*

---

26 Joseph Stiglitz, *Globalization and its Discontents*, New York: W.W. Norton and Company, 2002, p. 10.

27 Robert Locke, "Japan, Refutation of Neo-liberalism", *Post-Autistic Economics Review*, 23, January 5, 2004, article 1 <www.paecon.net/PAEReview/issue23/Locke23.htm>.

28 *Keiretsu* are vertical or horizontal holding companies organized around a bank. They provide coordination and cooperation among the companies <http://www.rotman.utoronto.ca/evans/teach363/keiretsu.htm>.

*other the interest of the state – as if the workers were just a resource
to serve capital.*[29]

On the other hand, there have been significant differences in socialism's view
of human beings. Socialist systems are more egalitarian systems with a claim
that people deserve certain economic rights simply because they are human
beings. Socialist systems defend rights such as the right to employment, to meet
basic needs, to receive appropriate education, to receive health care, as these
rights are stated in the Universal Declaration of Human Rights. But in socialist
systems, people do not have the right to own property and to guide production
decisions. In socialist systems, the authorities and experts who claim to know
what individuals need make all the production decisions, such as who will
produce and what will be produced, in the planning offices. In socialist systems,
it is also claimed that people seek not their own interest but the interests of
their society. The socialist system assumes that people are basically good and
the system has the duty to bring this into the sunlight. Everyone participates
in production, and everyone gets their share from the output. Socialist systems
are expected to evolve into communist systems, where everyone contributes
to production according to their means, and take their share from production
according to their needs. This is the ideology of the socialist system.

As is the case for capitalist systems, in socialist systems, theory and practice
may conflict. In practice, socialist systems have elevated society (perhaps in
the form of the government) above the individual. That is, existing socialist
systems started serving only the state, rather than the individual, and thus
became state capitalism.

Socialism gets its theoretical base from the works of Karl Marx, who claimed
that the value of products is determined by the amount of labor used in their
production. Starting from this assertion, it is argued that the profit-seeking
capitalist pays labor less than it deserves, keeping the *surplus value* created by
labor for themselves. Therefore, Marx believed that capitalism exploits labor.
He also believed that the laborers that are exploited (proletarians) would revolt
against those who exploit them (bourgeois) and a classless society, under a
system of communism, would be established. It is interesting to note that the
revolt of the working class that Marx expected to occur in the industrial countries
of the time did not occur there, but rather took place in 1917 in Russia, then an

---

29 Jaroslav Vanek, *The Future, Dynamics And Fundamental Principles Of Growth Of Economic
Democracy*, A four-part paper presented to the IAFEP in Mondragón, July 2006 <http://www.
eteo.mondragon.edu/IAFEP/IAFEP2006/Vanek.pdf>.

agricultural country. It is usually asserted that, after 70 years of implementation, with the downfall of socialism, communism was relegated to the torn pages of history. This is propaganda, which convinced many after the fall of the Berlin Wall. In reality, what had collapsed was not socialism but the way socialism had been implemented in the USSR. The fall of the USSR in 1990–1991 was declared to be the victory of the capitalist system. But this claim was not correct: there was a loser, but no winner, on the scene. Both socialism and capitalism have strengths and weaknesses, and these strengths and weaknesses may differ from different points of view. The fall of the USSR revealed some of the weaknesses of socialist systems. This could help us to improve the economic systems we develop. The capitalist system itself may have similar weaknesses that could be repaired. Or the capitalist system may need to benefit from its strengths. If we do not benefit from the lessons of history in improving our economic systems, the economic systems we have may fail to satisfy the aspirations of the people. And they may also fall.

Change and Transformation in Economic Systems

The world is changing fast, science is advancing fast, people are realizing needs they were unaware of before, and new means are emerging to satisfy these needs. In such an environment, one cannot expect economic systems to remain the same. Economic systems need to change in order to address the new needs and develop new means to meet them. The objective of the change must be to contribute to the happiness of people as a whole.

At present, the world is facing a very basic problem in achieving this objective. A *new economic design*, which is under construction, is shaping itself over the foundations of capitalist economic system. It is clearly observed that the current capitalist system is inflicting great damage on the environment and falls short in meeting the aspirations of humankind. In the way the *new economic design* is developing, it provides benefits from the fruits of technological advances, but at the expense of damaging the ecology of the planet. Those who manage to use this new capitalism to serve their own interests exploit the planet and the people in it. These beneficiaries of the system have converted capitalism into a religion or conviction which cannot be questioned, a feature shared by both capitalism and Marxism.

One of the prominent economists of the twentieth century, who was an advocate of capitalism, Joseph Alois Schumpeter, claimed that Marxism was a religion, with Karl Marx being its prophet. Schumpeter claims:

In one important sense, Marxism is a religion ... To the believer it presents, first, a system of ultimate ends that embody the meaning of life and are absolute standards by which to judge events and actions; and, secondly, a guide to those ends which implies a plan of salvation and the indication of the evil from which mankind is to be saved. We may specify still further: Marxist socialism also belongs to that subgroup which promises paradise on this side of the grave.[30]

As we have stated above, after the 1990s, capitalism also became a religion. For this reason, capitalism may also share the same destiny as Marxism. Schumpeter also claims that capitalism will come to an end and it will transform itself into another economic system (probably a socialist system). But its demise will not be of the kind described by Marx. It will end neither by failure nor by revolution. Schumpeter's theory is that the success of capitalism will lead to a form of corporatism and a fostering of values hostile to capitalism, especially among intellectuals. Capitalism will transform itself into a better system in a democratic way.

The Rivalry between Capitalism and Socialism

During the Cold War, the world had two competing economic systems. The West was promoting the capitalist economy and the East was trying to expand the socialist system. As it is well known, in 1990 the USSR disintegrated. It was a surprising downfall of the stronghold of the socialist bloc. The incredible developments in information technology played a key role in this collapse. People living in the USSR used to believe that they were living in the most prosperous and socially just country in the world: perhaps they were made to believe so. They believed that they should consider themselves the most gifted people in the world. Developments in communication technology brought all parts of the world into their living rooms; they realized that what they believed was not the actual case. It became quite clear that the way the USSR had implemented the socialist system was not serving the aspirations of the people, and it was not using the new benefits of technological advances to meet the people's demands. There was a need to implement new policies. In the late 1980s, Mikhail Gorbachev put into effect some polices and reforms,

---

30 Joseph A. Schumpeter, *Capitalism, Socialism and Democracy*, Routledge, 1994. p. 5. It seems that most religions use the dialectical method. For example, in the Zoroastrian religion, light (representing Ahuramazda) and darkness (representing Ahriman) compete to attract the people to their side. In the Koran, it is also stated that the prophet is sent to take the people to light from the darkness: "He may bring you from utter darkness into light" (Surah 57:9).

which became known as *perestroika* (economic restructuring) and *glasnost* (transparency). The move towards economic liberalization and the ensuing political dissent resulted in the disintegration of the USSR.

It is possible to present a different argument about the cause of the failure of the Soviet socialist system. That is, the system implemented fell short in motivating the people, it was not able to mobilize their creativity in the area of production, and instead of respecting the choices of the people to shape the markets, it relied on the decisions of the bureaucrats responsible for planning. The system did not respect people and their choices in production and consumption. This economic system could not meet the aspirations of people in the twenty-first century. The failure of the Soviet socialist system was not the capitalist system's victory. When we put all the arguments together, we notice that the failure of the Soviet socialist system showed that in the twenty-first century, people desire to live in economic systems where they have a better chance to control their own destinies.

It was very unfortunate that the failure of the Soviet socialist system was declared to be the victory of the capitalist system. The world should have learned the lessons from this failure by analyzing the reasons for the Soviet socialist system's weaknesses and strengths. For example, socialism had shown great success in the areas of education and health care coverage.[31] But socialism, in the way it was implemented in the USSR, was not able to incorporate a *customer-oriented* design in its system that would meet the rising aspirations of the people towards the end of the twentieth century. The lessons taken from Soviet socialist system's failure could have helped to address some of the shortages and benefits of other economic systems that we are trying to improve in the twenty-first century.

The error committed did not help capitalism either. No one expected the fall of the Soviet socialist system. If one had made such a claim before it happened, they would have been ridiculed. But the fact is that it failed. The same may happen in the case of the capitalist system as well. No one could claim that capitalism meets all the aspirations of people. The World Trade Organization was established in 1995 to implement the globalization agenda, which is the current, expanding form of capitalism. Yet the discontent with globalization of

---

31 In one of the trips I made to Russia after 1990, I observed that Russians were actually making this evaluation. For example, I remember the comment one of our guides made: "We used to have money, bur we were not able to find something to buy; now shop windows are full of products but we don't have money to buy them."

those who claim "A better world is possible" are increasing, as they themselves are in number, every day. If the changing aspirations of people, and the new means developed to meet these aspirations are studied thoroughly instead of declaring the victory of capitalism, and if the weaknesses of capitalism were repaired and its strengths capitalized, capitalism itself might benefit.

Change in the Competitive Environment – The *New Economic Design*

Competition is emerging as the main rule in all markets, and among all economic agents in the world. Liberalization in trade and capital markets is unifying all the goods, services and capital markets of the world, and increasing the competition in these markets. It is common to state that the entire world is becoming a single market. But, it seems awkward that, as the world is becoming a single market, regional blocs are also emerging. At least three powerful trade blocs have emerged and are competing with each other: the European Union (EU), the North American Free Trade Agreement (NAFTA) and the Shanghai Cooperation Organization (SCO). These blocs provide for cooperation among their members to improve their competitive positions in the emerging *new economic design*.

The 1995 signing of the General Agreement on Trade and Tariffs (GATT), and the subsequent creation of the World Trade Organization (WTO) by GATT, was the turning-point in world economics that we are calling the *new economic design*. GATT aims at full liberalization of world trade, and sets down the rules of trade and competition on world markets. Trade liberalization of agricultural products, together with the elimination of agricultural subsidies, will have a significant impact on both developing and developed countries. On the other hand, the *new economic design* does not allow for the free mobility of the labor force among countries. Lack of labor mobility is expected to limit the equalization of wages over boundaries. The kind of competitive environment brought by the *new economic design* is very different from the type of competition defined in classical economic theory. GATT strongly protects trade-related intellectual property rights (TRIPS) such as copyrights, trademarks, brand names, design, patents, printed circuits and trade secrets. That means that the system established by GATT gives strong monopoly powers to those who own intellectual property. This monopoly power granted by the system may easily be used for the exploitation of other producers, customers and countries.

Two competition areas are created by the *new economic design* established by GATT. In the first, the countries that do not have intellectual properties such as brand names and designs fiercely compete for the manufacturing of the products of those who have them. These countries are those with abundant labor forces and low wages. Since the GATT system does not allow for the mobility of labor among countries, and since the machinery used in production is almost the same in all countries, the competitive power of these countries depends on how low their respective wages are. On the other hand, those countries that own brand names and designs compete in product markets with the monopoly power granted to them by the protection of their brand names and designs. This monopoly power granted to companies by the TRIPS agreement of GATT provides the companies new opportunities to exploit their producers and customers. The *new economic design* is developed to favor those who have advanced technology and intellectual property. The beneficiaries may be countries or supranational firms. The widening gap between the rich and the poor both within and among countries is a sure sign of the exercise of this power to exploit.

The beneficiaries of the *new economic design* will be those who can develop intellectual property, who can invest in research and development, and most important of all, those who can invest in human capital.

Conclusion

People have developed a vast variety of systems to meet their economic reeds. But, considering the rapid change in our times, the growing needs of the people, and the new means developed by technological advances to satisfy these needs, none of these systems can be expected to meet the future aspirations of humanity. On the contrary, the present economic systems are creating severe problems. Our current economic systems are damaging the earth's ecological balance by polluting and depleting the environment due to our excess consumption, while at the same time resulting in an inequitable sharing of the benefits of our economic endeavors. Today, one of the two major economic systems of the past century, the Soviet socialist economic system, has failed. This failure has been interpreted as the victory of its rival capitalist system. This interpretation has been very unfortunate. Capitalism has strengths and weaknesses. The strengths, weaknesses and limitations, of both Soviet socialism and capitalism, should have been evaluated properly in order to develop economic systems that might serve the aspirations of humanity in this century. Economic systems are developed to serve people. Unfortunately, some economic systems seem to be designed for the people to serve the systems. Today, in the way capitalism is expanding its influence all over the world, it is questionable whether it is serving the aspirations of people. However, it is not possible to question the virtues of capitalism since it has transformed itself into a new kind of religion. This expanding capitalist religion is contrary to the aspirations of humanity as developed throughout its history. We will expound on this thesis in the following chapters.

2

Capitalism's Definition of Human Beings

See, I am creating a mortal of clay of mud molded. When I shaped him and breathed My Spirit in him, fall you down, bowing before him!
(The Koran, Surah 15:28, 29)

Economic Systems and People

What do people seek? What is their main purpose? It is difficult to generalize and find answers to these questions. In spite of this difficulty, we can roughly say that people try to be happy; they seek the way to happiness. People become happy when they reach the objectives they have set for themselves without sacrificing their standards and principles. When we look at these questions from an economic point of view, we can say that most people want to increase their affluence. Economic science accepts affluence to be an economic goal of people. Would an increased level of affluence make people happier? It is usually assumed that there is a relation between affluence (material well-being) and happiness. But this relationship is not as strong as one thinks. We know that people's affluence has increased to a great extent during the last half-century. But, it is difficult to claim that people's happiness has increased by the same proportion. We may even question that claim with our casual observations. Even today, comparing rich and poor countries, it is difficult to defend the proposition that those in rich countries are happier than those in the poor countries.

People have some basic needs. One cannot expect people to be happy unless their basic needs are satisfied. But, after these basic necessities are satisfied, it could easily be claimed that affluence is only one factor, but not the main factor that makes people happy. Besides, the concept of "basic needs" is not a well-defined one. Some consumption items considered to be essential for some people may not be considered necessary for others. If we were to generalize again, we could say that different people with the same level of affluence may be at different levels of happiness, and people with the same level of happiness may be at different levels of affluence. The reason for the lack of any simple relationship between affluence and happiness rests in the belief systems of individuals.

Perhaps, the relationship between success and happiness is stronger than the one between affluence and happiness. Perhaps people derive happiness from their success in meeting small or big challenges. As people reach higher levels of affluence, the span of their challenges may decrease. Perhaps, this may be one of the reasons for the lack of relationship between affluence and happiness.

Since the beginning of human existence, people have been searching for economic systems to increase their affluence, and they have been developing belief structures to increase their happiness. The economic systems and belief systems (one of them being religion) they have developed may support each other on some occasions, or may influence each other on other occasions, while sometimes these two systems may be in conflict. Throughout history, each one of these economic and belief systems have struggled to establish dominance and governance over the others. But there is a well-known reality: it is wrong to assume these economic and belief systems stand independent of each other.

For thousands of years, people have developed and implemented many different types of economic system. People have always needed the products produced by others. Complete self-sufficiency is almost impossible. People have either confiscated the produce of others or developed economic systems to exchange their products with the products of others. The dominating feature of these systems differed along a wide spectrum, ranging from plunder, exploitation, competition, cooperation, mutual support, trade, grants, to finally, aid. On the other hand, all the belief systems, which have a strong base in human nature, almost without exception, have advised people to cooperate, to support each other, to be generous and to be just in all economic activities.

Today, the economic system that is expanding all over the world is the liberal market economy based on private initiative, that is, the capitalist system. This system has achieved its development on economic foundations during the last two centuries, but has recently transformed itself into a belief system with a growing congregation. In spite of the fact that capitalism's assumptions about human beings and human nature are questionable, and its promises to humanity lose their validity as time goes on, ever since the capitalist system has been elevated to a religion, questioning it has been taboo. Since its institutions, means and rules have become divine, it has been perceived as a sin to question some of its principles and values: the virtues of the market mechanism, benefits of privatization and foreign investment, and liberalization, to cite but a few examples.

This new religion – capitalism – promises full employment, equitable income distribution and economic growth under the guidance of the prices established in liberal, competitive markets. Compared to the promises of the other belief systems about life after death, it is not difficult to find adherents to the promises of the capitalist system. But the reality does not match the promises: increasing unemployment, a worsening income distribution, depleted natural resources and increasing misery is apparent everywhere and hurting the consciences of increasing numbers of people and violating even the most basic ethical rules.[1]

The most significant danger we are facing today is the delusion that in capitalism we have found the ideal economic system; this belief has been spreading since the fall of the Soviet socialist bloc in 1990. In reality, compared to the past, with the developments in new technology, our chances of designing a better system have greatly improved. We have the means and duty to develop a *new economic design* that will serve people better in the twenty-first century. For that reason, it is imperative to study and question the assumptions of capitalism, to understand to what extent it is consistent with the nature of human beings and the needs of society, and the inherent contradictions in it. We begin our inquiry with the assumptions of capitalism about the human nature. And then, we will explore the way capitalism defines humanity in productive operations and in consumption.

---

1 Although there is no agreement on what is "right" and what is "wrong," the belief systems define rules to differentiate between right and wrong. These rules are moral and ethical rules. It is possible to claim that ethical and moral rules to be the same. But in this book we differentiate between them. We call religious rules moral ones, and secular rules ethical ones. There may be differences in the moral rules of different religions. For example, in Islam, receiving interest (usury) is wrong but this may not be the case for other religions. Ethical rules are developed by people of all denominations throughout time and adhered to by all. An example may be the consensus stated in the Universal Declaration of Human Rights. However, we should note that moral and ethical rules may conflict.

Definition of Human Beings in Capitalism

It is very important to understand how an economic system perceives human beings. This is obvious because the subject – the means and the ends of economic systems – is human beings. The main factor of production is the human being. It is the human being who creates capital, who makes machinery, who accumulates knowledge and who develops technology. All economic systems are developed by humans, run by humans, in order to serve humans: economics of the people, by the people, and for the people.

According to the assumptions of capitalist economics, human beings are selfish; they compete in fulfilling their self-interest, and any effort they make needs to be compensated. There is no giving or sacrifice without compensation or reward; the core principle is exchange. In their exchanges, individuals try to get as big a share as possible at the expense of their competitors. Capitalist economics defends these claims, arguing that capitalism must be realistic in its assumptions about the nature of human beings. According to the capitalist belief system, even if selfishness is not an admirable attitude, the economic design needs to be realist and accept human beings exactly as they are. Assuming men to be virtuous suits better the dreamers and poets. In the science of economics, there is no room for dreams and dreamers. According to one of the architects of capitalist thinking, Alfred Marshall:

> If competition is contrasted with energetic co-operation in unselfish work for the public good, then even the best forms of competition are relatively evil; while its harsher and meaner forms are hateful. And in the world in which all men were perfectly virtuous, competition would be out of place; but so also would be private property and every form of private right. Men would think only of their duties; and no one would desire to have a larger share of the comforts and luxuries of life than his neighbors ... Such is the Golden Age to which poets and dreamers may look forward. But in the responsible conduct of affairs, it is worse than folly to ignore the imperfections which still cling to human nature.[2]

There is room for cooperation among human beings because they are not individually strong enough; therefore they are bound to cooperate. Recently, there have been attempts to define the relationship between cooperation and

---

2   Alfred Marshall, *Principles of Economics*, New York: Macmillan, 1920, pp. 8–10.

competition and creation a new concept: "co-opetition."[3] But in capitalist economic thought, man by nature is not cooperative but is endowed with a fiercely self-centered nature;

> *It is only because man is a socially cooperative creature that he has succeeded in perpetuating himself at all. But the very fact that he has had to depend on his fellow man has made the problem of survival extraordinarily difficult. Man is not an ant, conveniently equipped with an inborn pattern of social instincts. On the contrary, he is pre-eminently endowed with a fiercely self-centered nature. If his relatively weak physique forces him to seek cooperation, his untamed unconscious drives constantly threaten to disturb his social working partnerships.[4]*

The assertion is that economics is not built on moral values defining good or bad. Economics presents the facts as they are. The moral values are left to the domains of other studies, mainly to the domain of religion. In fact, this is the main reason for the success of economic science: working under its own assumptions, economic science has proven that in the capitalist system everyone's urge to seek their own interest will end up serving the interest of the society as a whole. Perhaps we should say it in a more correct way: defenders of capitalist thought have accepted it as their mission to prove that capitalism will serve society. Our economics education is designed for this duty. Our schools are commissioned to teach this "scientific truth" to their students. In fact, this is not a reality; it is just a theoretical conclusion underpinned by a series of assumptions, most of which conflict with reality. Exactly at this point lies a dilemma of capitalism. With its claims of being realistic, capitalism assumes humans to be selfish and self-centered, but it tries to present a humanitarian solution to people that their selfish conduct will benefit society as a whole. The fact that the solution and the reality do not agree does not bother the advocates of capitalism at all.

Capitalism's definition of humans is more important than one thinks. If people were defined as being altruistic instead of being self-oriented, the solutions reached by economic science would have been very different. For that reason, with a different set of assumptions, economic science can develop very different economic systems using the same scientific methods. The assumptions

3   Adam J. Brandenburger and Barry J. Nalebuff, *Co-opetition*, New York: Doubleday, 1997. "Co-opetition" is defined by the authors to be a revolutionary new mindset that combines cooperation and competition, the game theory strategy that's changing the game of business.
4   Robert L. Heilbroner, *The Worldly Philosophers, The Lives, Times and Ideas of the Great Economic Thinkers*, New York: Simon and Schuster, 1966, p. 6.

the theory starts with are crucially important. The assumptions the economic theory starts with reflect the values and beliefs of groups in societies.

Economics is claimed to be a science rather than being a belief system. This claim is also questionable. Economic science, as is the case with other belief structures, starts with its own assumptions and reaches some conclusions using scientific methods. For that reason, the conclusions reached by scientific methods are accepted as scientific conclusions. The solutions reached by economics become principles and guidelines. These principles and guidelines have a tendency to be converted into belief systems if the underlying assumptions are disregarded. These we will try to explain below. The point we are trying to clarify is, no matter how strongly economics denies that it is a belief system, it starts with the assumptions of belief structures, and it has a tendency to end up with scientifically proven belief structures. If the starting assumptions, axioms[5] in scientific parlance, are not correct, neither will be the conclusions reached by the scientific methods.

Scientific methods are not as comforting and conclusive as one might believe. Scientific methods rely on observations. It is easy to argue that in many areas we do not have sufficient and reliable observations. To get down to the roots, the observations we are able to make are limited by our capacities, perception and our current knowledge. One cannot claim that the universe is constructed only on the dimensions that we can perceive and that, for example, there is no fourth (or fifth!) dimension. The scientific approach requires us to be *suspicious*. Science itself is the attempt to remove the question marks. On the other hand, there are many things we perceive or observe today, which were not known or observable just a century or two ago. Certainly, there are still many things we are not able to observe with the present state of our knowledge, but we will be able to observe in the future. Science cannot claim that we are able to make observations on everything that exists or that there are no dimensions we cannot now observe.[6] Such a claim would be scientific fanaticism.[7]

---

5   Axioms are the basic propositions which are assumed to be true without requiring any proof.
6   A great mathematician and poet Ömer Hayyam (1048–1131 AD) put it nicely: "They are crumbs of the universe these beautiful stars/Appearing and disappearing shedding light on earth they are/On the sky's lap and the bosom of the land/So many things to born and to twinkle there are."
7   The distinction between science and belief (religion) has captured the thoughts of many philosophers. For some, the real distinction is not between science and belief (religion) but between free thought and fanaticism. Free thought and fanaticism can be found in belief systems, but can also be found in science.

We know very well that both the means and end of economics is serving human beings. But we are not able to observe and measure many aspects and variables relating to human beings. What do the people feel about various economic events? Can these feelings be expressed in mathematical formulas? On these kinds of questions we have no scientifically meaningful and comforting observations, measurements, or statistical formulations. But what people feel is very relevant in economics. Let us take a very simplified example. Economics assume that people derive *utility* from their consumption. This utility is something like satisfaction or happiness. Economists have searched for a meaningful measure of utility for a long time. When we eat an apple, how much utility do we get? What will be the amount of increase in utility when we eat the second apple? Economists were not able to find an objective measure of utility. Perhaps there is no such measure. So, they solved the problem by making some assumptions, such as "each additional unit one eats would increase his satisfaction," or "the satisfaction one gets from each additional unit he eats would decrease." These assumptions are the foundations of the economic beliefs of our time. We will discuss these assumptions in the following sections. What we acknowledge here is that the solutions we reach using scientific methods are not indisputable. The science itself requires us to question everything we know at present. Returning back to our example, if we change our assumptions on the *utility* derived from consumption – let us say, after reaching a satiation level, further consumption would result in *negative* utility – our scientific conclusions would be very different from the ones we have now.

People have developed *ethical* and *moral* values and rules in order to establish order in their societies. These values and rules help to define what is right and what is wrong. Capitalism does not take into consideration these ethical and moral values and rules in making its assumptions and reaching its conclusions.[8] Today, there is a growing recognition that ignoring ethical values in economics has caused a significant amount of damage to society. This recognition has opened new areas of research in harmonizing ethical and economic rules.[9] Today *ethics* is an important area of academic studies and it offers a new dimension for solving scientific questions.

---

8   In contrast to the neo-classical view, some economists question the assertion that economics is independent of the value judgments of people. Charles K. Wilber, a retired professor of Notre Dame University claims that since both the economists' (the theoreticians and policy advisors) and economic agents' (sellers, consumers and workers) behaviors are influenced by their ethic and moral values, economic and ethical values cannot be independent: Wilber, "Ethics in Economic Theory", *Post-Autistic Economics Review*, issue no. 20, June 3, 2003 <http://www.paecon.net/PAEReview/issue20/Wilber20.htm>.

9   For example, in the Anatolian region, *akhi* organizations have been successful in unifying economic, trade and ethical rules and have served the people for more than 600 years.

The two major areas of study in economics are production and consumption. Economic science tries to determine rules for the efficient allocation of production factors to the production of goods and services, the allocation of the overall income generated to various contributors, and the allocation of personal income to the consumption of various goods and services and savings. Human beings are the main actors in both production and consumption. Capitalism has clearly but separately defined the producing and the consuming person. Capitalism sees the producing and consuming individuals as separate persons.

Definition of People in Production

According to capitalist theory, firms hire input factors to produce the products they sell. The input factors are called the factors of production and generically they are classified as land, labor and capital. According to the capitalist theory, the capitalist provides the capital and has the right to run the company to serve her or his interest. The firms may borrow from capital markets while paying interest, to earn additional profits for the capitalist entrepreneur. People sell their labor to firms to earn wages. In the capitalist system, labor is a cost item. For a company to be competitive, it would have to reduce its costs as much as possible. For that reason, labor would have to compete with the other factors of production in order to be employed, which means to find a job. Today, people would have to compete with machines and robots in the production process. This competition is getting more and more difficult as technology advances. The capabilities and productivity of both machinery and robots increase in parallel with the developments in technology. In order to compete with them, human workers must develop new capabilities and talents, which is getting more difficult every day. In order to preserve their competitive position in the market, firms will have to hire the factor inputs that produce at a lower cost. Therefore as the technology advances, labor faces the danger of losing its job. This is how the capitalist production system works and this is the role of people in this system.

Considering labor a cost factor in production may be the root of many problems we face in our times. Jaroslav Vanek, a strong advocate of economic democracy, certainly claims that it is. Jaroslav Vanek names this the "negative sign syndrome." In one interview, he claimed that:

> Perhaps the most important aspect of capitalism, its objective function, is to maximize profit. If you look at it more carefully, profit is revenue minus labor costs and other costs. This means then human beings enter

the defining objective function of the system with a negative sign. By contrast, economic democracy has an objective function where people are on the positive side of the equation. The idea is to maximize the welfare of the people participating. This is an enormous difference, and I'm convinced that the tragic difficulties of our culture – ecological devastation, starvation, etc. – can be traced to this negative side.[10]

Capitalism believes that the lower the cost of production, the lower the selling price of goods and services can be. Lower selling prices, on the other hand, mean more consumption for individuals under a given income. More consumption is assumed to increase the welfare of individuals. These assumptions and beliefs do not have a sound basis. Lowering the cost of production may mean paying less to labor or even firing workers. This may mean a loss in income and a corresponding decrease in welfare.

As we have already mentioned above, in the process of production, the laborer would have to compete with machinery and robots in order to keep their job. In order to do that, they would have to increase their efficiency and productivity. The laborer's compensation would depend on the level of their productivity. It is all right to talk about the efficiency of machinery and robots, but when it comes to labor the anxiety caused by the need to be more efficient, and the fear of losing their job may be very damaging to the lives of laborers. But it is not only machinery and robots the laborer must compete with; they must also compete with other laborers. The capitalist system eliminates laborers who cannot cope with increases in productivity. Vanek, in the interview cited above, claims that "Productivity is not measured only in dollars and output but also in happiness and job security. Job security is more important than whether you earn three or four or five hundred dollars a week."

When labor is regarded as a substitutable factor input, and can be displaced if the conditions justify it, workers are laid off in great masses as technology advances. In order to reduce the brutal appearance of these mass unemployment implementations, unemployment payments and retraining options are usually provided to laborers who lose their jobs. In modern terminology, these measures are called "safety nets." But it is important to note that unemployment is not only about losing income, it is also about losing self-respect. The increasing level of unemployment in the world certainly reduces the welfare of societies and triggers much social disorder. But mass unemployment serves the profit-

---

10   Albert Perkins, "Cooperative Economics: An Interview with Jaroslav Vanek", *New Renaissance*, 5:1 (1995) <http://www.ru.org/51cooper.html>.

maximization motive of capitalist economies. Profits and the prices of stocks of companies that lay off thousands of workers increase, but the happiness and the welfare of those societies, even the overall national income, may decrease. For example, if a company increases its profit by $100 by reducing its wage bill by $1,000, its profit will increase but the income generated by the company will decrease by $900.

In summary, we can say that in capitalist theory, human beings are production factors just like machinery and robots. In order to be employed or keep their job, workers need to be as efficient as those robots. There are many questions requiring answers here. Can we treat labor, machinery and robots as the same? Which one is more relevant for people: to be efficient, or to enjoy their jobs, to be happy with what they are doing? The efficiency concept: does it suit human beings or do we have better concepts such as productivity, effectiveness and motivation? Recently, there have been observations indicating that when people like the job they do and are happy doing it, they are more motivated to reach their working or professional objectives.

Now we turn to another assumption of capitalism related to work. In capitalist theory, work is a burden on individuals. When a person works, this burden needs to be compensated with a wage. The alternative to working is assumed to be leisure. In capitalist theory, the individual, being a factor of production, tries to find a balance between the burden (disutility) of this work and the benefits (utility) of the wage, in order to maximize their level of satisfaction. According to the assumptions made, as an individual's participation in production increases, that is, as they work longer, the disutility of the work increases, and the utility created by the wage received decreases. According to capitalist formulation, people decide how much to work by equating the utility received for the last hour's wage and the disutility of the last hour worked.[11] These are the assumptions and conclusions of the capitalist economic theory.

We need to raise a question here: is participation in production really a burden or bliss? There is no clear-cut answer to this question. The answer may depend on the role each individual plays in the production process. In those production processes where the laborer sells time to participate in production using their physical power, work could be seen as a burden. Of course, if people were to break and haul stones, dig ditches, and do heavy manual work, work

---

11 In technical language, people allocate time to work and leisure: work is assumed to be a burden, leisure is bliss. In an optimal allocation of an individual's time, the time spent on work is the time when marginal disutility of work is equal to marginal utility of bliss.

would be a burden. Perhaps these were the working conditions in most jobs until very recently; at least it was the case when the capitalist economic theory was developed. On the other hand, today, people participate in production with a very different spectrum of competencies. Working may be providing them a chance to prove themselves and their skills; people need these opportunities in order to be happy. In such a productive environment, working itself may be bliss, rather than a burden. People may derive happiness from producing, being creative, feeling that they are needed, and attaining a share in the production process. Creating an environment for people to develop themselves, to produce something, to prove themselves, and to share in the output to which they have contributed may help them to be happy. That is, participating in production may be a source of happiness itself. It may not be the burden that capitalist theory assumes.

Today, the concept of work is changing. Until quite recently, people used to sell their time of work to employers. They worked for the employer for certain hours per day or week using their physical and mental power. In the expanding practice, people develop for themselves a *portfolio of competencies* and earn their income by selling these competencies to those who need them. The competencies developed make up the human capital owned by the people. The interesting thing is that people develop most of these competencies as they work for others. In the work they do, they obtain competencies, add new talents to their competencies and increase their human capital. As people sell their competencies, these do not decrease or diminish; in fact, they increase as people become more experienced. These increasing competencies contribute to the effectiveness of the individuals in their new assignments. Work itself becomes an investment in human capital. People could even make payments to realize such an investment. Seen from this point of view, work, which was once a burden, has become transformed into bliss as the working conditions have changed.

The opposite of working is losing one's job. To lose a job is not only to lose a wage or salary. People may lose their self-respect and confidence when they lose their job. In more social forms of capitalist economies, unemployment insurance was developed to cure the damage unemployment inflicts on individuals. This unemployment insurance partially compensates for the loss of income, but falls well short of repairing all the physical and moral damage people suffer when they are unemployed. In spite of the promise of capitalist liberal market economies to provide full employment, existing and growing unemployment is one of the major economic problems of both developing and developed countries. Unemployment increases among well-trained and well-educated individuals are also very common. Unemployment is a very unfortunate waste of resources in an economy, but capitalism does not take into consideration the economic, social and moral costs of unemployment.

During recent years, there has been a growing tendency to recognize the importance of human factors in the process of production. Increasing numbers of firms have started to believe that people are the main source of production. *Total quality* and *quality circle* applications are good examples of these trends. Through these implementations, companies try to improve the working conditions in their production processes. The total quality concept aims at improving the product, production process, working conditions, and, in short, the quality of life of the workplace. Quality circles are voluntary groups of people in workplaces trying to find ways and means of applying total quality concepts. But, today, the purpose of all these activities is maximizing the profit of companies. Improving working conditions is not the goal in itself. It is believed that promoting the productivity and creativity of the people in the workplace will increase the profitability of the companies.

Definition of People as Consumers

The capitalist system has great respect for consumers as long as they have money to spend. Consumers will allocate their income to products and services to maximize their levels of satisfaction. The levels of satisfaction they can reach is constrained by the amount of income they have. In the capitalist system, "the customer is king" – as long as he has money. It is very important to be "customer oriented," that is, to cherish the customers. Perhaps the main reason for the fall of the socialist system the way it was practiced in the USSR was the lack of customer orientation and consideration of the "customer as king." In the USSR, decisions on who will produce and what will be produced were not made according to the choices of the people, but by bureaucrats in the central planning departments. This, of course, put constraints to what could be purchased and how it was purchased. On the other hand, the capitalist system also has limitations. As we have stated above, only those who have money to spend are kings. Only their choices reflect to production, proportionate to their spending. In the capitalist approach, social support systems or philanthropic organizations are developed for those who do not have sufficient means to meet their needs. But these systems and organizations are outside the domain of economic systems.[12]

In Eastern cultures, the customer is considered to be *velinimet.* This concept is similar to the "customer is king" concept, but there is also a significant difference. *Velinimet* means "source of blessings." Blessings may not be only profit or material gains. What is important is the blessing of God. For that reason, the main duty of the companies is serving consumers, which may require honesty, caring and empathy.[13] In certain cases *hayır dua* (thanking God for your service) can be a *nimet* (blessing) also.

Today, economic science assumes that people become happy by consuming. More specifically, people derive utility from consumption. That means economic science believes that satisfaction depends on the amount of consumption. The more an individual consumes, the more satisfaction they gain. In fact, you cannot be happy *unless* you consume. The science of economics makes two assumptions about the relationship between the level of satisfaction and the amount of consumption. According to the first assumption, additional consumption grants a decreasing amount of satisfaction. The second assumption is, no matter how much you consume, you get additional satisfaction from additional consumption (however small).[14]

Let us examine the first assumption. In real-life cases, the satisfaction derived from the additional amount of consumption may not be decreasing. Until a level of concentration is reached, the satisfaction derived from additional units of consumption may increase. Only after that level of concentration has been reached may the marginal utility of consumption decrease. Consumption of products and services of art and culture may be good examples for these cases. As people consume more and more of the products and services of arts and culture, their taste for these may develop and they may get more enjoyment out of additional consumption.

---

12 In Iran, donating to the poor (*sadaka*) has developed to be part of daily life for people. In Tehran, in the walkways of the big boulevards there are *sadaka* boxes, almost as big as the mail boxes of the old days, at nearly every corner. People drop their donations into these boxes as they go to work or do their shopping.

13 I want to share one of my experiences on one of my business trips to Turkey. We went to Kula, near Smyrna to share ideas on a problem. Our meeting was much shorter than we had planned. We wanted to buy some oranges and apples. There were two shops selling fruit. When the shop owner learned that we were from Istanbul, he said, "The apples are good; but the quality of my oranges would not meet your expectations. So I will give you my neighbor's oranges." And he did. His neighbor was standing there. He did not ask him; we did not even meet him.

14 In technical language, the first assumption states that the marginal utility of consumption decreases. The second assumption claims that the marginal utility of consumption is always positive.

The second assumption is much more critical. It claims that no matter how much an individual consumes, consuming more will still increase their level of satisfaction. This is identical to claiming that people will *never* reach a state of full satisfaction, no matter how much they consume. In other words, this means that people will seek to consume more no matter how affluent their present position is. Perhaps the most problematic assumption of the capitalist theory is this endless hunger for consumption. This hunger may be one of the major causes of the damage inflicted on nature: polluting our waters, diminishing our rainforests and thinning our ozone layer. On the other hand, it is not wrong to claim that people could reach the same level of satisfaction at very different levels of consumption. In fact, most belief systems, primarily religions, advise people to be satisfied at lower levels of consumption.

In fact, for many types of consumption, there does exist a level where people become satiated. And the level of consumption where one might be satiated depends on one's personality or identity. People's identity is conditioned and shaped by their social and cultural environment. Many different popular cultures and religions try to establish a human character structure in such a way that people could be happy at lower levels of consumptions. Many cultures and religion require people not to be wasteful, to be satisfied with what they have, to be thrifty and not to overburden nature and nature's means.[15] On the contrary, the capitalist system is nourished by consumption; therefore, it tries to raise the level of satiation of individuals, and is successful in doing it. The difference between the known religions and capitalists system brings to mind the following questions: which is more to the benefit of people, lowering their level of satiation or raising it? Which one contributes more to their happiness? The per capita income in Turkey is about $3,000; would Turkish people be happier if their per capita income increased to $30,000? Why are the suicide rates very high in rich countries? Is it because their per capita income is high? What is the target per capita income in the European Union? Is it $60,000 or $300,000? If the per capita income in the EU reaches $300,000, will it be enough? How will people spend so much income? Is there a limit to how much people can consume? The US, Canada, Europe and Japan constitute about 11 percent of world population, but consume about 59 percent of the world's output. Can we expand this level of consumption to everyone on earth? If it were possible, would the world's resources and ecological balances be able to support it? If it is not possible, can affluence and poverty peacefully coexist? The world is

---

15 Let us take some examples from the Koran: "Consume not in wastefully and hastily," Surah 4:6; "do not act extravagantly; He does not love the extravagant," Surah 6:141; Surah 7:31; "… and do not squander wastefully, squanderers are brothers of Satan," Surah 17:26.

not capable of supporting even the present level of consumption. Where will civilization be going by increasing the level of consumption with great passion, by destroying nature and depleting natural resources? Perhaps most important of all: how will material hunger and happiness be reconciled?

We believe it is important to note another point here: many cultures and religions counsel people to share, and to care for others' consumption, as well as one's own consumption.[16] How can we incorporate deriving satisfaction from feeding and clothing other people, in our current understanding of the capitalist economic system? Of course, the economics of our day has an answer to this question. Capitalist theory believes that people do contribute with an expectation of a return. The return does not have to be a monetary or material return. It could easily be a moral or intellectual reward. On the other hand, in many cultures or religions, one should *give* without expectation of any reward. That is, in many different cultures and religions, people must serve others, offer food, shelter and clothing to those in need without expecting any return. One must do well because it is good simply to please God, without expecting any return. It is usually believed that doing *well* with an expectation of a reward has no value at all.[17]

The Results of these Assumptions

Today, the conclusion that the capitalist economic design best serves the interests of human beings is based on the very basic assumptions we have stated above. If these assumptions are not valid today, the conclusions reached will not be dependable also. For example, if there is a level of satiety for individuals, many of the conclusions reached by economic science will not be relevant to real-life cases.

Currently, the world is not able to support even the present level of consumption of the human race. As the gap between rich and poor widens, the need to increase the levels of consumption of the poor is also increasing. The world must be in search of economic systems that will present a solution

16 It brings to mind one of the quatrains of Ahmet Yesevi, who has influenced the culture of a great region from Central Asia to Hungary in Europe: "Lonely, poor, orphan; give joy them all/Tear your dear heart, sacrifice whole/If you find food give it to them/I've heard from God to tell these all."

17 In many religions, especially Zoroastrianism and Islam, God gives bounty to the rich to test them. They must share it with others, especially the poor. Wealth does not have to be material; it can be moral or intellectual.

to the hunger for material goods that we observe in the developed world. We must find ways and means to make people happy at lower levels of material consumption. There is an increasing awareness among scientists that we need to find ways to convert material hunger into moral satisfaction.[18] Perhaps the most important barrier we are facing in designing sustainable economic systems is the capitalist assumptions about the material hunger of individuals.

As we have shown above, our economic system today assumes that the road to happiness must be built on levels of consumption. On the other hand, consumption and ownership alone are not sufficient to secure happiness. Working itself can also be a source of happiness. Broadly speaking, we may say that people need to develop their means to be happy, that is, people must develop tastes, traits and habits to make themselves happy. If people do not develop or construct these, then ownership and consumption of goods will not be sufficient to make them happy. People's development of tastes and their appreciation of culture and the arts; of the enjoyment of company and of friends; of being benevolent, frugal, sacrificing and optimistic; or of not being prodigal, selfish and pessimistic can all be some examples for developing the means to become happy.[19] If we were to define broadly people's tastes, the meaning they assign to life and their belief structures directly influence their happiness. Developing these tastes, approaches and beliefs requires an effort by people. For these reasons, economic systems cannot be separated from educational, cultural and belief systems. That means that economic system should not be studied and evaluated independently of other systems. These systems are all social systems and their interaction must be taken in consideration.[20] At this stage, we face a very important point: if, in the capitalist system, education and cultural activities are organized and guided by money (profit) they are bound to be insufficient both in quantity and quality. We will try to explain this when we take up *externalities* in a later chapter.

To summarize, in capitalist market economies, the free markets guide production to meet the choices of consumers. In these free market economies, those who can satisfy consumers' choices better will make bigger profits; those who cannot do so will face bankruptcy. The system is based on meeting the personal choices of consumers. For that reason, companies in the capitalist

---

18 M. Mitchell Waldrop, *Complexity: The Emerging Science at the Edge of Order and Chaos*, New York: Simon and Schuster, 1993.

19 What we have listed here are the qualities of "good people," as described in most religious systems.

20 Jaroslav Vanek's most recent book is *The Unified Theory of Social Systems* (2000) <http://ecommons. library.cornell.edu/handle/1813/642>.

system must be consumer or customer oriented. Capitalism views this property of the system as the symbol of respect paid to the customers. In fact, due to this characteristic, capitalism has a lot to teach socialist systems. But, in the capitalist system, only the choices of consumers who have incomes or money are respected. Only they become active customers. In addition, the motive behind "customer orientation" is not serving people; it is maximizing profit. In capitalism, people are not the end; they are just a means to make a profit.

The Dilemma: Producing and Consuming People

As explained above, the perceptions of labor and the customer in capitalism conflict as if they were different entities. In the production process, people are a factor of production, a cost factor, in fact, rivals whose interests conflict with the interest of the capitalist owners. In the production process, people need to compete with other factor inputs like machinery and robots in order to be employed. As technology develops, the capabilities of machinery and robots increase. That is, competition with machinery and robots is getting ever more difficult. People need to develop new talents in order to compete. When they fail to do so, we see mass layoffs of workers in order to reduce costs and increase profits. Unemployment is emerging as the most important problem both in developing and developed countries.

On the other hand, when it comes to the area of consumption, people with money or income to spend suddenly becomes *kings*. The system must meet the kings' choices and desire to make profit. The more money they have, the more important the customer becomes. But, in reality, the labor in production and the customers are the same people. Laborers, when they earn their income, become customers. When you fire your laborers to save costs, you are in fact losing your customers. Of course, the relation does not have to be direct. Your customers may not be *your* laborers; but they are the laborers of other producing units. Thus, in economic systems, laborers are customers at the same time.

There is a point to keep in mind here: people are the purpose, the ends, of economic systems. All such systems are developed to serve people. The economic systems developed must function for the benefit of people, both in their production and consumption phases. We need to develop economic systems that will find ways to make people happy both in production and consumption. We must improve our systems to contribute to people's happiness. People do not derive satisfaction only from consumption; they derive satisfaction from production also.

Other Belief Systems' Perception of People

As we have stated above, both capitalism and socialism are belief systems. However, belief systems are more commonly associated with religions, which try to direct people to the *right path*, to the behaviors that are considered *right*. Even though what is considered to be *right* differs somewhat in different belief systems, many of them resemble each other. One of the common beliefs in different systems is a belief about human nature. In almost all belief systems, it is accepted that humans are inclined towards what is right and what is straight. Perhaps we could say under this assumption, religions try to guide them to what is right and what is correct. Capitalism claims that realism requires not ignoring the imperfections which still cling to human nature. In that sense, religions are realist also. They accept the fact that among people there are good and bad individuals. In some religions, people in essence are good. God has created them good. But every individual has a *ruh* (spirit) and *nefs* (self). Although the spirit seeks glory, the self is inclined to worldly satisfactions. Satan tries to deceive the self to create mischief. The Creator will reward those who do good deeds and punish those who go astray. The conviction is that a person has a spirit which is in harmony with goodness, and a self which is obsessed with selfish desires.[21] In the Zoroastrian religion, there is a great war between light (representing goodness) and dark (representing badness). People must take their position in this fight with their free will. In the end, good will be triumphant and all bad will disappear.

What we want to state here without going into too much detail is that religions are also realistic and state that there are people with good or bad conduct. But religions aim at finding what is good in people, and guiding them to that goodness. Religions are based on the faith that this is possible. This is where the capitalist orientation differs from other religious beliefs. Capitalism develops systems assuming that people are craving material satisfaction, that they are never satiated and that they seek only their own interest. In fact, capitalism guides people in the direction of its assumptions and is proud of its successes. The other religions try to make people shy away from material hunger, and to get away from seeking only self-interest. The other religions urge people to consider the well-being of others, to be content with what they have, to cooperate and share, to seek fairness and righteousness. The approach of the other religions reflects people's aspirations and is more sustainable.

---

21 Our point here may have some resemblance to Sigmund Freud's psychoanalytic theory. According to Freud, the "id" represents the uncoordinated instinctual trends and the "super-ego" the critical and moralizing function of mind; the "ego" finds itself simultaneously engaged in conflict between the "id" and "super-ego".

Summary

Capitalism sees people as self-oriented beings who seek their own interest, who view work as a burden, and whose satisfaction depends on their level of consumption and as beings who can never be satiated. Our capitalist theory today has been trying to prove that people are serving the society as a whole by seeking their own selfish interests. Capitalist theory has adopted this effort as a mission. The system developed under the assumptions made claim that the prices determined in free markets will guide the economy in such a way that the prices will clear all the markets, and full employment of all resources will be realized. Under this system, the resources will be allocated according to people's choices.

These claims of the capitalist theory do not get realized in actual practice. The gap between the poor and the rich is widening. Full employment is far from reality; in fact, unemployment is becoming one of the most important problems everywhere. Markets are not guided according to the wishes of all the people, but directed by those who have cash to spend. Capitalism lacks ethical concepts such as *fairness* and *equality*. Recently, people's demand for *fair* trade instead of *free* trade has been increasing. Hunger for material consumption is damaging the natural environment: rivers, lakes and oceans are polluted with the wastes and emissions of factories, rainforests are being depleted, glaciers are melting, the ozone layer is thinning, and the seasons are changing. With the tremendous power obtained by controlling the media, the capitalist system is harming cultural values, corrupting and reshaping people in the image defined by its assumptions.

In the capitalist system, human beings must compete with the other factors of production in order to be employed in a job. Human beings are considered as any one of the means of production. As a means of production, human beings are viewed as cost factors decreasing the profits of companies. Capitalism is in search of finding ways to decrease labor costs and may lay off thousands of people to increase its profits. But the labor cost in production is the income of the people employed. Decrease in labor costs would mean a decrease in the income to spend.

On the other hand, capitalism is customer oriented. A person who is able to earn income to spend is a prospective customer for capitalism. Such a customer is considered to be king. But, only the people who have money to spend are kings. It is important to recognize that the laborer in production and customer in the markets are the same people. Any economic system designed to serve human beings would have to search for ways of making them happy both in the process of production and in the markets.

In my opinion, in the twenty-first century, humanity will be able to create a better economic system, a better world to live in by considering the aspirations of the people, and by supporting the economic systems with cultural, educational and belief systems.

3

Competition:
The Driving Force of Economics

O citizens of the world! Live in harmony and concord. Be organized and cooperative.

(Rig Veda 10.191.2, p. 215)

Have we lost our honor; why should we compete? We artisans are cooperating in our town!

(Anatolian artisans)

Participants in economic operations display various types of behavior. These behavior types may present a wide spectrum from competition to challenge, from challenge to mutual aid, from mutual aid to mutual support, from mutual support to cooperation. The nuances between the types of behavior are very important. For example, when we consider challenge behavior, challenging a rival is very different from challenging oneself to achieve a goal. A person can challenge himself. The behavior types have another dimension also, namely the objective of the behavior. The behavior of individuals may have a personal objective or communal objective. Different systems impose different objectives on personal behavior. Some systems require self-sacrifice without personal reward. In some systems, people expend effort only if they anticipate sufficient remuneration or reward.

The basic behavior in capitalist systems is to compete to seek one's own interest. People compete with others in their personal interest in order to outperform them. In capitalist environments, competition is the prerequisite of success and the foundation of economic growth.

Capitalism and Competition

Competition is the driving force of capitalism. For that reason, the economic system of capitalism is designed as a competitive free market economy. According to the capitalist belief system, in competitive free market economies, the competition among people, among firms, among countries, among trade blocs, and world-wide is the foundation of economic success and economic development. Competition is the driving force behind all innovations and all advances. Competition in the markets increases the efficiency of economic activities and results in cost reductions. Competition enables the economic system to serve the people. These are the claimed virtues of competition in capitalist systems.

Competition is a broad and comprehensive concept. In any competition, the competitors are rivals. Each party in a competition has its own objectives to achieve. The only way to achieve your objective is to *defeat* your rivals. Companies compete with each other in order to sell their products to customers. They try to outperform other companies by designing and producing products that better meet the needs and tastes of their customers. This is a very important feature of competition. In competing with others, producers must be customer oriented. In a competitive environment, each customer of their own free will and choice decides to purchase products and services that best suit their taste. Therefore, in a capitalist system, "the customer is king" because of the competition among the producers. The capitalist, in order to make a profit, must serve the king. There is no other way to make a profit. However, this feature of capitalism does not make it people oriented; that is, the aim of capitalism is not serving people. Only those people with money to spend are kings; they are the potential customers. Those people with no money to spend have no place in the capitalist system.

In the capitalist system, the money that customers spend to purchase goods and services can be considered to be their *economic votes*. With their economic votes, they express their economic choices. From this point of view, some people consider capitalist market economies to be systems of economic democracy. However, this is not the way economic democracy is defined in its broadest sense. True economic democracy would have to embrace all the people, not only those who have purchasing power. Still, we can state with confidence that due to competition among the producers to satisfy the consumers, customers decide what is produced in capitalist economies.

Once we know what to produce, the new questions become "who will produce?" and "who will participate in production?". These questions are also answered in terms of competition, and the answers are somewhat related to each other. The producers who can produce the required products and services at the lowest cost will produce. Currently, many firms have their products made in South-east Asian countries since they are able to produce the products at a cheaper rate. The producers, on the other hand, compete with other producers to get the orders from the companies to produce their products. In this competition, in order to produce at the lowest cost possible, the producers would have to decide what *factors of production* to use – that is, how much labor, how much machinery, and what robots to use. The producers must decide how much and what type of labor will be employed. This is an area where laborers must compete with each other and with machinery and robots whose capabilities are increasing rapidly due to advances in technology.

Competition has been so well accepted as a way of conducting business that there are no other imaginable alternatives. In the corporate strategy to serve the missions of companies and to achieve the objectives of companies, competitive strategy has been the single strategy the firms follow.[1]

If such competitive behavior is implemented in its purest form, without any concessions, it must be merciless. Those who are successful get their rewards; those who lose must face the consequences, which are sometimes very harsh. In capitalism, failing firms go bankrupt. For capitalism to be efficient and to function well, failing firms should not be saved from the consequences of their failing. In reality, the failure of firms are not economic losses. Economic wealth does not disappear. Only the ownership of wealth changes. Everyone in the capitalist system should be ready to face the results of their decisions. They would have to consider the amount of risk they would face due to any decision they made. This fact alone, the fear of bankruptcy, is one of the reasons for efficient functioning of the system.

But sometimes the consequences of firms' failures may be very harsh. Society may not be able to face the damaging effects of firms' failures.

---

1   Michael E. Porter's highly acclaimed strategy book, *Competitive Strategy*, has been one of the most important references for strategy formulation: Porter, *Competitive Strategy: Techniques for Analyzing Industries and Competitors*, New York: Free Press, 1980. Porter's well-known "Five Forces of Competitive Position" model is often recommended to enhance the competitive position of companies. In these models, the "Five Forces" are competitive rivals, new market entrants, supplier power, buyer power, and product and technology development. That is, the entire business environment is viewed as a competitive environment.

Government may step in to save those citizens who are hurt very badly. But this kind of government interference has a bad influence on the capitalist system. It changes the rules of the game. Expectations about government interference may create opportunities for some profiteers or provide incentives for risk miscalculations.

For people in production, failure means either losing one's job or not finding a job; this is a very dismal scenario for the individual and their family. It is not humane to accept such a fact. Therefore even in the most pitiless forms of competition, some socio-economic systems are developed to heal the wounds of unemployment.

Differences in Practices

Various countries implement the rules of competition differently. Capitalism uses the purest form of competition, assumed to be the basic form of economic behavior among people, firms, countries, and the trade blocs. The reasons for the differences in the implementation of competition lie mostly in cultural differences and variations in value structures in different countries. For example, it is usually claimed that in Japan, cooperation rather than competition is widespread among employees, and among the firms various forms of collaboration exist. Only in the international markets do Japanese companies engage in competitive behavior, with foreign companies. The *keiretsu* type of organization helps companies to cooperate or collaborate in various areas,[2] while MITI (The Ministry of International Trade and Industry) has helped companies to improve their competitive position against the foreign competition.[3]

Turkish culture does not regard competition to be proper behavior, either among people or firms. Cooperation and collaboration are traditionally accepted as being more virtuous.

---

2   A *keiretsu* is a set of companies with interlocking business relationships and shareholdings. It is a type of business group.
3   The Ministry of International Trade and Industry was one of the most powerful agencies in the Japanese government. It was created just after the Second World War in 1949 by the mission of coordinating the economic policies of government agencies and industry. Its mission included increasing export competitiveness of Japanese industries. It served its purpose by providing protection from import competition, technological intelligence, help in licensing foreign technology, access to foreign exchange, and assistance in mergers. In 2001, its role was taken over by the newly created Ministry of Economy, Trade, and Industry (METI).

Other Types of Behavior

Different types of economic behavior present a wide spectrum of conduct. As we have mentioned before, the spectrum includes conflict, competition, challenging, helping, sharing and collaboration. In addition, exploitation and plundering may also be considered as types of economic behavior. In fact, the types of behavior are so difficult to define that trying to find their place on a spectrum may not be appropriate. Let us take competition and cooperation. We can define them to be on different ends of a spectrum. But on the other hand, these two types of behavior may be interpreted differently in a different environment in which competition and cooperation may support each other.[4]

Not long ago, many companies would try to develop systems to create competitive environments and to increase the competition between the employees working in a company. The systems created were based on the belief that rewarding success would motivate people to do their best to outperform others. In fact, many companies and even universities would take pride in creating a competitive environment in their workplaces and classrooms. People used to make fun of it, as revealed by the following dictum: If a manager is to hire a secretary, the best way is to hire two. One of them will certainly beat the other. And she is the secretary the manager needs. Today, competitive environments in the workplace are facing serious questions. Now many companies realize that team spirit in a cooperative environment serves the company's objectives better.

In the competitive environment created in workplaces, people may behave selfishly. They may hide some of the information to use for their individual success. Their interests and the interests of the company may not coincide. In their own interest, people would try to make themselves indispensable to the company. In order to make themselves indispensable, they might not help to train others to acquire capabilities needed by the company. In an era that acclaims *learning organizations*, such individualistic employee behavior could create barriers to learning. Learning organizations need collective aspirations.[5]

---

4   The two behavior types were combined in one by Brandenburger and Nelebuff: Adam M. Brandenburger and Barry J. Nelebuff, *Co-opetition: A Revolutionary Mindset that Combines Competition and Cooperation – The Game Theory Strategy that's Changing the Game of Business*, New York: Doubleday, 1996.

5   Peter M. Senge claims that learning organizations are "organizations where people continually expand their capacity to create the results they truly desire, where new and expansive patterns of thinking are nurtured, where collective aspiration is set free, and where people are continually learning to see the whole together": Senge, *The Fifth Discipline: The Art and Practice of Learning Organization*, New York: Century Business, 1990.

During the last decade or two, companies have been searching for behavior types other than competition in the workplace. The most popular of these has been the *team concept*. Many companies have started to focus on creating team spirit in their workplaces. They have reorganized their activities in teams and managers have become coaches. In some cases, team members have even elected the team captains. In some implementations, the entrepreneurs and managers assumed the role of the team trainers. These managers started stressing the fact that no one alone can win a victory, that to win a victory teamwork was needed. They believe, therefore, that the job of the manager is to induce motivation, determination and confidence in the team in order to be victorious. The environment that is being created by the concept of team spirit is contradictory to the competitive environment of the capitalist system. Success is elevated from individual success to team success, and competition is elevated from personal competition to competition among teams.

As the character of competition differs in different industries, the team contest differs in different sports activities. Football, basketball, or synchronized swimming may require different forms of contest. So the pursuit of team spirit, team contests and team behavior has created a virgin area of development for management practices. In the field of management, many believed that there might be some lessons to learn from successful trainers. This increased the popularity of successful trainers and made them members of the "management gurus" club. These trainers started giving conferences all around the world to enthusiastic managers.

It can be said that the most important aspect of creating team spirit in a contest environment is converting the competitive behavior among members to support of each other for the success of the team. The team has a well-defined objective. Each member of the team expends all of their effort to achieve the objective. The effort is to eliminate the weaknesses and capitalize on the strengths of all the team members. But, even in the team approach, some players must be better than others in order to get into the team. For that reason, the team approach may not be able to eliminate all competition among the players. In any case, team behavior is a rich enough concept to contribute significantly to the development of alternative behavior types in companies.

It is quite well accepted that cooperative or supportive behaviors are superior compared to competitive behavior in the workplace. But the cooperative or supportive environment does not develop by itself in a company. Companies must make conscious efforts to create such an environment. That is, the corporate culture must be built on such a cooperative foundation. Some company actions and the environmental conditions can make it difficult for laborers to have a cooperative and supportive attitude, forcing them to be competitive. The mass layoffs that have become very common recently are damaging the efforts to create cooperative environments in companies.

In their labor downsizing operations, some companies do try to benefit from the competition among their employees. After they calculate how many employees to lay off, they announce that they will use "success criteria" to decide who will go and who will stay. As unemployment rates increase, work stress and competition among employees increased also. People start to work later hours; they sacrifice their social lives. In Japanese, there is a special word for death from overwork: *kaoroshi*. The fear of losing one's job is one of the reasons for overwork.[6] In the previous chapter, we claimed that economic systems should try to make people happy both in the process of production and in consumption. Keen competition among employees limits what can be done to make people happy in the process of production.

In a competitive environment, outperforming the competitor companies would require creating comparative strengths in some important factors. These factors are called "key success factors" in strategy formulations. These important factors can be the factors the customers consider important, or can be the weaknesses of the competitors. Creating comparative strengths in factors that customers assign importance to, forces companies to improve their products and the services they provide. The idea of better customer service is gaining importance today, and is crucial in developing better economic systems. Customer-oriented marketing has become a dictum in the capitalist system in the last decade or two. But, on the other hand, if the competitive strengths developed are not in the areas that are important to the customers but rather aim at the weaknesses of the competitors, the strengthened competitive position of the company may result in the exploitation of the customers.

Competition in Anatolian Culture

Competition has never been an acceptable way of conducting one's affairs in Anatolian culture. During the Ottoman period, in addition to being considered annoying, competition was actually outlawed. The practice was of classifying products according to their quality and assigning a sale price to them on this basis (the *narh* system). For example, products brought to Istanbul used to be

---

6   John Micklethwait and Adrian Wooldridge, _The Witch Doctors_, London: Mandarin, 1997, p. 232.

taken to *kapans*[7] in order to assess quality and price. There, the merchandise would be classified according to its origin and quality, prices would be assessed and the products would be distributed to the artisans and merchants according to the size of their operations and customer bases, and the merchants would sell the products at the determined prices. There would be *narh*s (pre-determined prices) for the products produced by the artisans according to the quality of the raw materials they used. This system aimed at standardizing quality and price. Of course, the major aim was serving the customer with a fair price. In Istanbul, three *kapan*s along the Golden Horn were the most important: the flour *kapan*, the honey *kapan* and the oil *kapan*.

The *akhi* organization form that flourished in Anatolian lands provides one of the best examples of solidarity among artisans. In fact, *akhi* organizations aim at unifying commercial and moral principles in economic life. Let us mention some of the characteristics of *akhi* practices that have existed since the thirteenth century in Anatolia. In those days, the *souks* were divided into groups of shops selling the same types of merchandise. These divisions were called *arasta*, for example, the garment *arasta*, the shoe *arasta*, the copperwork *arasta*, and the leatherwork *arasta*. All the shops selling similar products were lined side-by-side in an *arasta*. There was no competition among the artisans and tradesmen in an *arasta*. It is commonly said that in an *arasta* a tradesman who had the first sale (making *siftah*) would not accept the second customer and would send him to his neighbor if his neighbor had not made his *siftah*. The society did not respect earning more than one needed. Artisans would donate a portion of their earnings to the common chest, called *orta sandığı*, which contained the common savings of the artisans in the *arasta*, and was intended to help anyone in financial distress. If an artisan faced a financial difficulty, his neighbors would try to help him to solve it. If their effort was not sufficient, the artisan in distress would get help from the *orta sandığı*. If the means of *orta sandığı* were not enough, the *yiğitbaşı* (the overseer of the *arasta*) would declare the bankruptcy of the artisan by firing a gun. Firing the gun was a message to inform everyone that no one should annoy that specific artisan in order to collect outstanding credits. *Topu atmak* (firing the gun) meant clearing the artisan from the financial obligations that he was unable to meet. Even today in the daily language in Turkey, *topu atmak* is used as a slang to mean "gone bankrupt." *Akhi* associations and practices served the people of Anatolia for more than six centuries.

---

7   *Kapans* were wholesale marketplaces such as big *souks* for distribution of merchandise to artisans and traders.

Even in the present day, tradesmen in Anatolia find it very difficult to accept competitive behavior. We had a very interesting experience of it. One of our students prepared a Master's thesis in 1994 on the privatized retail outlets of a major state-owned holding company. Over 300 shops, located in small towns all over Turkey, had been making losses for at least for five years; the shops were privatized in 1993 by transferring ownership to the employees of those shops. Early in 1994, Turkey suffered one of the worst economic crises in its history. In spite of the crisis, the privatized shops became very profitable. The student's thesis was supposed to determine the factors behind the shops' success,[8] and was based on a survey of the shops using a questionnaire. Two of the questions caused serious problems. The first one was: "What kind of competitive tools did you use that contributed to your success?" We expected answers such as "I made announcements on the town loudspeaker," or "I used leaflets," and so on. The answers were surprising: "One would have to lose his dignity in order to compete," "We are not corrupted so much that we could compete," or "In our town we artisans support each other."

The second question that created a problem was also interesting. The answers given indicate the importance of culture and beliefs in the perceptions of individuals. The question was "What kind of changes occurred in your standard of life after earning a good income?" A typical response was "One should not change his life standards after making money." Yes, in Turkish, there is an expression *sonradan görme*, which is a kind of insult to someone who spends extravagantly after making a fortune.

In fact, both competitive and cooperative behaviors are part of human nature. People compete in some fields and show cooperative behavior in others. The aim of both of these behaviors may be to gain benefits or other motives than benefits. Capitalism assumes that competing for one's own interests is the only behavior that is relevant in economics. Yet, most of the belief systems adopted by the majority of the world's population throughout history advise cooperation and altruism instead of competition for self-interest. Cooperation and altruism are also the types of behavior advised by all current religious belief systems. Below we want to give examples from two religious books: the Vedas and the Koran. As far as we know, the Vedas are the oldest religious texts; on the other hand, the Koran is considered to be the last one by its advocates. One could easily find many similar examples from other religious texts.

---

8   Gaye Gencer, *An Experience in Privatization: Transfer of the Retail Outlets of Sümer Holding to its Employees*, Master's Thesis, Boğaziçi University, 1995.

Economic Behavior in the Vedas

The Vedas, known to be the religious texts of India from 4,000 years ago, recommend sharing, mutual goodwill, cooperative work, and mutual support in order to attain happiness. We will present just a few examples from the Vedas:[9]

> *O mankind! I bind you together towards one*
> *objective – the welfare of man. Toil together with*
> *mutual love and goodwill. May you share the*
> *comforts of life equally. May you accomplish your*
> *work with mutual accord and finally may you, in*
> *the pursuit of your ambition at all times, engage in*
> *working together with goodwill!*
>
> *(Atharrva 3.30.7, p. 224)*

> *O citizens of the world! Live in harmony and concord.*
> *Be organized and co-operative.*
> *Speak with one voice and make your resolutions*
> *with one mind.*
> *As our ancient saints and seers, leaders and preceptors*
> *have performed their duties righteously,*
> *similarly, you will not falter to execute your duties …*
>
> *(Rig 10.191.2, p. 215)*

The advice of the Vedas is also seen in other common religions of our times, which also recommend mutual aid, mutual support and sharing. Most of their belief structures do not uphold competitive behavior.

Propositions of Islam

In a competition, competitors are considered to be rivals. Rivals compete in order to win. When one of the competitors wins, the other necessarily loses. The competitor who loses may be harmed or damaged. If he is an employee, he may lose his job; if it is a company, it may go bankrupt. That is, in short, the competitor who loses may suffer. In Islam, one should not make any other suffer. People have no right to inflict injury on others. In interpersonal relations, *hak*

---

9   *The Holy Vedas: A Golden Treasury*, Pandit Satyakam Vidyalankar (ed.), New Delhi: Clarion Books, 1998.

(right, justice, truth and privilege) is very important. No one should confiscate the *hak* of any other. God does not forgive those who have confiscated other people's *hak*.[10] For these reasons, Islam does not approve of competition; instead it induces people to compete for serving the people. In short, we may call it "competing to serve," which is a very different concept from competing for one's self-interest. There are others who are also competing to serve, but each one does their best in serving. And the service of each one does not weaken the service of others. If one competes to serve, there would also be no loser. In fact, in order to compete to serve, one may have to cooperate and collaborate with the others who are competing to serve also. The important thing is there is no rival in such a form of behavior. I want to show just a few examples about the kind of behavior the Koran exhorts people to adopt:

> *... and of them is he who is foremost in deeds of goodness by Allah's permission. This is the great virtue. (Surah 35:32)*

> *And everyone has a direction to which he should turn, therefore compete to do good works. (Surah 2:148)*

> *For every one of you We appoint a law and a way, and if Allah had pleased He would have made you all a single people, but that He might try out in what he gave you, therefore strive with one another to compete to virtuous deeds. (Surah 5:48)*

Under the Islamic principle of *hak*, the economic models developed are based on cooperation rather then competition. One of these models is the *mudarabah* type of economic organization to carry trade or production activities. *Mudarabah* is the partnership of capital and labor. In these types of companies, the capitalist (*rab-el-mal*) provides the financial capital of the company, and the laborer provides the human capital. The company thrives to generate income. According to the *mudarabah* contract, they share the income at predetermined percentages. Since the principle of sharing the income is predetermined, both capital and labor have a common objective and they both expend their efforts to maximize the income. That is, they cooperate in every possible way.

In economic life, the "competing to serve" type of behavior is customer-oriented behavior. Today, the importance of being customer oriented is well known. Perhaps one of the factors behind the breakdown of the Soviet socialist system was the absence of any customer orientation. The "competing to serve"

---

10 This can also be interpreted as "abused other people's rights."

principle in Islam is not only customer oriented, it also requires self-sacrifice in serving. The "competing to serve" recommended in Islam requires serving people even if they do not have money, and as such, is a constructive rather then destructive action. As was the case in *akhi* associations, "competing to serve" would require cooperation among companies, not competition. In interpersonal relations, the principle of "competing to serve" certainly requires cooperation and mutual support. Another aspect of the principle is that it would require challenging oneself to do good deeds, which in return may provide chances for self-actualization and happiness. Perhaps this is the source of the happiness of people when they are self-sacrificing. In fact, what Islam says is very similar to the sayings of the Vedas. We may take a verse from the Vedas to see the similarities of the teachings:

> *Following the path of self-sacrifice,*
> *May you render service to humanity.*
> (*Sama 63 s.256*)

Conclusion

Capitalism claims that people compete in their own self-interest. Just thinking that this may not be true is thought to befit not economists but dreamers. According to the belief system spread by capitalism, competition among people and among companies ends up in serving the society as a whole. According to the capitalist theory, this is a fact supported by scientific methodology. Capitalism is successful and victorious, and competition is a prerequisite of this success.

On the other hand, contrary to the teachings of capitalism, most past and existing religions advise people to help each other, to cooperate and collaborate. As a mode of conduct, competition in one's self-interest, which is a prerequisite of success in capitalism, is replaced by "competing to serve" in religious wisdom. In the religious conduct of affairs, such aid and support are not only the obligations of the rich to the poor, they are the necessary form of behavior in production and in all economic activities.

The main problem with capitalist thought is that it considers that capitalism's success depends on a kind of behavior which integrates competition and self-interest. But this integration may mean success at the expense of others, of society and of nature and the environment. Perhaps for this reason, with the spread of capitalism's implementation in the world, poverty is also spreading, unemployment is increasing, income distribution is deteriorating and the environment is suffering. Competing based in self-interest is creating a new type of people who are autistic, detached from the wider society and selfish. On the other hand, the major belief systems of the world are trying to create a type of people who are outward oriented, altruistic, competing to serve, and respectful of society and nature. This second type will help humanism to spread all over the world.

4

The Market Guidance of the Economy

Markets in our culture are a totem; to them can be ascribed no inherent aberrant tendency of fault.

(John Kenneth Galbraith)[1]

In this and the following chapters, we will try to explain how markets guide the economy in theory and practice. In this chapter, we want to present the assumptions and the models of the theory; and in Chapter 5, we want to explain real-life cases that do not meet the assumptions and their expected results.

The Competitive Market Economy

Markets are spaces where goods and rights are traded. Markets existed and were organized in all places, and at all times wherever there was trade. Throughout history, markets and fairs developed in secure places, and providing security to markets and fairs was accepted as a sign of sovereignty. Caravan routes connected the markets and fairs. Yes, markets existed in all economies, but the concept of a "free market economy" was developed by the classical economists, starting with Adam Smith in the eighteenth century. The system that is called the free market economy is a well-defined, very specific economic system. Free market economies are guided by the prices determined in the markets by the behavior of buyers and sellers each acting in their own interest and competing with one another. So the prices reflect the preferences of all the participants of the markets. They do not reflect any one individual's choice. For that reason, it is said that an "invisible hand" guides

---

1   John Kenneth Galbraith, *A Short History of Financial Euphoria*, New York: Viking Penguin, 1990, p. 24.

free market economies. And this guidance works for the best interests of the society if the markets are free and perfectly competitive.[2]

The opposite of a free market economy is one which makes price decisions outside the free markets. In our previous chapter, we explained that in the Ottoman Empire some authorities fixed prices and competition was banned. Even today, in spite of all the efforts made toward liberalization of the markets, governments often control some prices such as petroleum and agricultural product prices. In the Ottoman Empire, price setting was called *narh*; today in Turkey we have a special word for price increases set by the authorities: *zam*. In a free market economy, there is no room for *narh* or *zam*. But, in Turkey, *zam* is a frequently used word. Government makes *zam* on petroleum prices; municipalities make *zam* on public transportation prices. And, quite often, companies make *zam* on their products. Sometimes the public at large becomes furious at the *zam*s following one another, and screams: "Don't we have anyone to control these prices?" In free market economies, there would not be anyone to control prices. In fact, in free competitive markets, no one should be able to influence prices by their will.

Another form of fixing prices outside the free markets is practiced in socialist economies. In the Soviet socialist economic system, the supposedly *informed* bureaucrats working in the central planning offices fixed prices. The pricing decisions reflecting political choices may or may not have depended on short- or long-term plans made in the planning offices. Some political decisions may have reflected day-to-day choices. In spite of that, in the current understanding, the opposite of the currently prevalent free market economy system was the centrally planned Soviet socialist economic system.

As Adam Smith did, the classical economists studied the two extreme types of markets: the markets of perfect competition and monopolist markets. The conclusion reached by the classical economists is very clear: In order to serve

---

2   Paul A. Samuelson, who is known to be an advocate of the competitive markets, describes the benefits and costs of competitive behavior in the markets very clearly:

Society would be lucky if the conditions for absolutely free entry of thousands of competitors hold in every industry. Why lucky? Because then the Invisible Hand would very clearly be determining the best solution to the how-goods-shall-be-produced problem. Perfect competition would then operate just like the ruthless Darwinian struggle-for-existence to ensure that each viable firm produced at minimum average cost, with the industry getting its goods produced at the rock-bottom total cost possible ... Alas, what makes all this so often inapplicable in real life is the fact that the cost curves may be decreasing to such a degree that, if each firm were somehow made to produce down the bottom of its U, we would find only a handful of firms in the industry and not the great number needed to keep perfect competition perfect (Economics, New York: McGraw-Hill, 1961, p. 540).

the public, the markets must be fully competitive, that is, conditions specified as fostering perfect competition should exist. The monopolist markets, which are the opposite of the perfectly competitive markets, end up exploiting people and society at the expense of the profits of the monopolists. Let us see how Adam Smith explains it:

> *The monopolists, by keeping the market constantly under-stocked, by never fully supplying the effectual demand, sell their commodities much above the natural price, and raise their emoluments, whether they consist in wages or profit, greatly above their natural rate.*
>
> *The price of monopoly is upon every occasion the highest which can be got. The natural price, or the price of free competition, on the contrary, is the lowest which can be taken, not upon every occasion indeed, but for any considerable time together.*[3]

In free markets, prices are determined by the joint decisions of the buyers and sellers in the market. Both the sellers and buyers act according to their free will, without any influence of others. According to the assumptions made, when the prices increase sellers supply more goods to markets, but at high prices buyers demand less. When sellers are unable to sell their goods they reduce their prices. If the prices decrease buyers demand more, but sellers supply less to the markets. Under these assumptions, prices on the market reach an equilibrium level. The equilibrium price has an important aspect: it clears the market. That is, under such a price, everyone who is willing to sell at that price would sell, and everyone who is willing to buy at that price would buy. There would be no excess supply or demand on the market. This equilibrium price is the joint decision of the buyers and sellers in the market, and they reflect the preferences of all participants in the markets.

The type of competition defined by the classical economists suited their time very well: farmers took their produce to the markets, artisans sold their produce in the markets, service people performed their services there. The economists following the classical teachings had to define the market conditions appropriate for the development of economic theory much more rigorously. They specified the assumptions that would lead to the formation of prices on the markets, prices that would be able to guide the economy for the benefit of the whole society. What they defined was the assumptions of efficient markets. For markets to be efficient, the competition in these markets

---

3   Adam Smith, *The Wealth of Nations*, New York: The Modern Library, 2000, p. 61.

would have to be perfect competition. According to the assumptions made, for perfect competition there would have to be very large numbers of buyers and sellers, there would have to be full information on everything relevant to markets, there would have to be no transaction costs, and each participant of the markets would have to be small enough not to influence the market. Economists showed that under these conditions a common price would develop, which could guide the economy to the benefit of society. In John Kenneth Galbraith's words, "The first requirement of the classical system, as everyone is aware, is competition. In the design of the system this was fundamental and, if it was present in a sufficiently rigorous form, it was also sufficient."[4] Again, as everyone knows, the assumptions of classical economists are not fulfilled by the realities of our time.

In real life, it became very clear that the competitive markets, as defined by classical economists, disappeared very quickly in time. Today, companies have grown so much that in one way or another they strengthen their monopoly position in the markets they operate in, and start managing their prices. Realizing these facts, economists had to define new market structures and tried to understand how they could operate to serve the public at large. The markets they studied were *oligopolistic* markets and *monopolistic competition* markets. But even today, the virtues of free market capitalism are defended on the grounds established by the classical economists.

As we have stated above, the opposite of the free market economy is understood to be the centrally planned economy. In such planned economies, production decisions are made within the framework of centrally structured economic plans. During the twentieth century, the preference, the choice between the free market economies and the planned economies, changed quite frequently. Until the world economic depression of the 1930s, free market economies were popular in the West. During the depression, countries had to redefine the amount of government intervention needed in their economies. After the Second World War, the world rapidly moved towards increased government intervention in economies, and central planning became quite popular. Not only countries, but also companies developed planning agencies and departments to make their decisions in the framework of a long-term plan. In those years, countries like the United States adopted free market economics, the Union of Soviet Socialist Republics established a socialist economy based on central planning, and others, one of them being Turkey, established a *mixed*

---

4   John Kenneth Galbraith, *American Capitalism*, New York: The New American Library, 1952, pp. 17–18.

economy system. In mixed economies, the private sector coexisted with the public sector in production and distribution. Mixed economies had planning agencies, but the plans were only binding for the public companies, while they only provided incentives to the private sector. The idea of the mixed economy model was to eliminate the weaknesses of the public and private sectors, and to benefit from the strengths of each one. The important thing is that every economic system has its strengths and weaknesses. And their strengths and weaknesses depend on the conditions and objectives of the economy. It would be an error to expect an economic system to solve all the economic problems of any country at any time. But today, unfortunately the capitalist free market economy model is being promoted globally as a universal solution.

After 1980, the promotion of the capitalist free market economy entered a new phase and became transformed into a kind of coercion. The World Bank and the IMF put great effort into expanding the free market economy model in all developing countries. The transition from government-controlled economies to free market economies was called *liberalization*. Very similar policies were recommended to all developing countries, as if the uniform recipe provided would cure any kind of economic problem these countries were facing.

The year 1990 was a turning-point for reshaping the world and for the establishment of a *new economic design*. In that year, the Berlin Wall was torn down, uniting the two Germanies as a single government and a single economic system; the free market economy system. In 1991, the Union of Soviet Socialist Republics collapsed politically and economically. These two events, which were not expected even a few years earlier, created such a vacuum and intoxication that the events were interpreted as the victory of capitalism, instead of the failure of the Soviet type of centrally planned economy. With the confidence this created about the virtues of the capitalist free market economy, free markets and free trade started receiving wide acceptance everywhere in the world. Early in 1995, the General Agreement on Trade and Tariff (GATT) was signed, liberalizing international trade in goods and services. For the implementation of the GATT, the WTO (World Trade Organization) was established. In fact, this was the foundation of a *new economic design*, which was now in the process of development. Under the *new economic design,* all goods and services would be traded in the international markets without any barriers. This meant the creation of a single global market for goods and services.

But, at the existing stage, it would be an error to claim full liberalization of the markets in the world economy. As we will explain below, in market economies there are four major markets: the goods and services markets, the capital markets, the foreign exchange markets, and the labor markets. The GATT liberalized only the goods and services markets, and it is only these markets that are globalizing. And, for some goods, the GATT will be implemented in a step-by-step form. In capital markets, there are two forms of capital flows among countries. One form is direct foreign investment, and there has been a tremendous amount of brainwashing in claiming the benefits of direct foreign investment. Currently, almost all countries welcome direct foreign investment, hoping that it will contribute to their development. On the other hand, short-term capital flows among countries seem to have created great problems in developing countries (in terms of capital flows, these countries are called "emerging markets"). Short-term capital flows provide funds to developing countries so that they can consume more than they are producing. Thus, as these funds move into a country, they provide a false feeling of abundance. But if these funds suddenly leave the country, that country's economy collapses. After the 1990s, we have seen an increasing number of economic crises in developing countries, mostly caused by the flows of short-term capital. For that reason, short-term foreign capital is called "hot money" in daily use, and its entrance and exit in some countries are controlled.

In the *new economic design*, the mobility of labor is not welcome. If we consider two types of human resources, physical and intellectual laborers, in many countries there is no barrier to the free entry of intellectual laborers. But almost in all countries there are strong barriers to the entry of physical laborers. The interesting thing is that, in spite of all the efforts to liberalize the free flow of goods and services, there is no consideration of the free mobility of labor in the *new economic design*.

In short, as we have explained before, after the declaration of the victory of the free market economies after 1990, the capitalist free market economy system has transformed itself to a belief system, into a new religion. In this new religion, there is a claim and a belief that the free market economy system will serve the people at large, everyone, whether in the underdeveloped, developing, or developed countries. But on the contrary, since the establishment of the *new economic design* in 1994, poverty has increased in the world, the gap between the rich and the poor has widened, unemployment has increased and natural resources depleted at a pace not observed before.

> *As for lifting the global poor, The U.N. Development Program's 1999 Human Development Report revealed that the gap between the wealthy and the poor within and among countries of the world is growing steadily larger. It blamed inherent inequalities in the global trade*

system for this situation. Even the U.S. Central Intelligence Agency concurred. In its Global Trends, 2015 report, the CIA maintained that globalization will create an even wider gap between regional winners and losers than exist today. [Globalization's] evolution will be rocky marked by chronic volatility and widening economic divide ... deepening economic stagnation, political instability, and cultural alienation. [It] will foster political, ethnic, ideological, and religious extremism, along with the violence that often accompanies it. Such is already the degree of wealth concentration that the world's 475 billionaires are now worth the combined income of the bottom half of humanity.[5]

It is interesting that the discrepancy between the promise and the reality did not have any significant effect on the belief in the virtues of the capitalist religion. Since capitalism has converted itself into a religion this is interesting, but not surprising. Still today the belief persists that the prices determined in free markets, in a competitive environment, will be able to guide economies to provide the best solutions to the economic problems of humanity. This belief is expanding and getting stronger.

Markets and Prices

Market economies are guided by prices determined in the markets. As we noted above, classical economics defines four different markets in the market economies: goods and services markets, foreign exchange markets, capital markets, and labor markets. In each market, prices develop under the rule of supply and demand. These prices respectively are prices of goods and services, foreign exchange rates, interest rates, and wages. These prices, as determined in their respective markets, guide the economy in free market economies. The decisions on the allocation of income to consumption and savings, allocation of consumption to different products and services, what will be produced in what amount, how much will be invested in machinery and equipment and human capital, how much money will be raised to make the investments and to finance the customer: all these decisions are guided by the prices determined in the markets. Now let us turn to each one of the markets to observe the assumptions and conclusions of the theory.

---

5   International Forum on Globalization, *A Report of The International Forum on Globalization, Alternatives for Economic Globalization*, San Francisco, CA: Barrett-Koehler, 2002, p. 30.

GOODS AND SERVICES MARKETS

Economic theory is built under the assumption that both supply and demand are under the influence of prices. It is assumed that more would be demanded at lower prices, less would be demanded at higher prices. On the other hand, at higher prices more would be supplied, while less would be supplied at lower prices. Similarly, when the prices increased, more would be supplied but less would be demanded; and when the prices decreased more would be demanded but less would be supplied. As it is seen, as the prices increase or decrease, the supply and demand are affected in opposite directions. This, then, guarantees that there would be an equilibrium price. This is called the *demand and supply rule*. Under the demand and supply rule, the equilibrium price clears the market. That is, there would be no seller in the market who is willing to sell but cannot at the equilibrium price; and, there would be no buyer in the market who is willing to buy but cannot at the same equilibrium price. This is the indication that the preferences of the participants of the market fully reflect to the prices. To its believers, this fact is the source of *sacredness* of the market mechanism.

If we consider the rule of supply and demand for various products in the market, the increase in the demand for a product causes the prices to increase; this increase in the price would induce the supply, and the equilibrium would be reached at a higher price and quantity. Let us take a different case. Let us assume that the costs of production of a good decrease. This will induce the sellers to supply more at the given price, but for buyers to buy more, the sellers will have to reduce their price, and the equilibrium will be reached at a lower price but higher quantity. As these examples indicate, the preferences of the people, changes in production technology and savings in costs will all be reflected in the prices in the markets properly. This is the way prices are determined in the markets, and this is the way the prices developed in the markets guide the economy. This is the creed of free market economics.

FOREIGN EXCHANGE MARKETS

Let us now examine how foreign exchange rates are determined in the foreign exchange markets. When exchange rates fall and domestic currency appreciates, the demand for foreign currency will increase. This is because foreign products will become cheaper compared with domestic products and more will be imported. On the other hand, when the exchange rates fall, the supply of foreign exchange will decrease. This is because exporting will be less attractive, and lower export earnings will mean less domestic currency and income. To summarize, as the foreign exchange rates decrease, the demand will increase but the supply will decrease, and as the foreign exchange rates increase, the demand will decrease but the supply will increase. Again, the supply and demand rule will lead to the equilibrium exchange rates. In fact, the equilibrium exchange rates will also balance foreign trade. But, unfortunately, this conclusion is only correct if the demand and supply of foreign currency comes solely from foreign trade markets. But, foreign exchange is not only a means of payment in foreign trade. Billions and billions of dollars of foreign currency flow among countries each day simply to earn money. This kind of foreign exchange floating among capital markets are known as short-term capital, or "hot money." The flows of short-term capital among countries also create a demand and supply of foreign exchange. That is, the total supply of foreign exchange in a country is the sum of foreign exchange earnings (exports) and the short-term capital inflows; and, the total demand of foreign exchange is the sum of foreign exchange spending (imports) and the outflow of short-term capital.

In a particular country, if the foreign trade deficit is financed by the short-term capital inflows, there will be no pressure on foreign exchange rates to increase in order to equalize the foreign trade deficit of the country. The opposite is also true. If a foreign trade surplus finances short-term investments in other countries, there would not be pressure on exchange rates to decrease to equalize foreign trade.[6] When there is no pressure on exchange rates to make corrections, we may say that in some cases the demand and supply rule does not work.[7] In fact, this has been another source of problems for the developing countries. Developing countries' capital markets are called "emerging" markets. Emerging markets provide very profitable opportunities for "hot money." In general, interest rates are high in these markets partly to compensate for the risks involved. When "hot money" moves into these markets, the supply of foreign exchange increases, and the increase in supply decreases the exchange rates. Decreasing exchange rates increase the gains of "hot money." The increase in gains invites *more* "hot money" to come. The flow of more "hot money" further reduces the exchange rates and further increases the gains of the "hot money." The "hot money" entering the country finances the foreign trade or current account deficits of the country since the domestic currency appreciates in value. This is called the "high interest and low exchange rate"

6   For a more rigorous analysis, we would have to consider foreign direct investments and foreign borrowing and lending.
7   The demand and supply rule works for the total demand and supply but, as we will explain below, there is a tendency in the capital markets to develop vicious cycles that usually end with a market crash.

cycle. This vicious cycle, or spiral, is not sustainable; it usually ends with a financial crisis. This spiral has been at the heart of most of the financial crises faced by developing countries. We will return to this in a later chapter. For the time being, it is sufficient to note that the free market economy claims that exchange markets will reach an equilibrium that will reflect the choices of the people. This is the creed of the capitalist free market economy system, which usually fails.

CAPITAL MARKETS

Now, let us see how the demand and supply rule determines interest rates in capital markets. Economic science considers interest to be the *time value* of money. Those who save their money, then loan it, and get it back with interest at the end of the loan term. This interest is compensation for the individual who saved and thus deferred consumption for a term. In Irving Fisher's words:

> The rate of interest ... is based, in part, on a subjective element, a derivative of marginal desirability; namely, the marginal preference for the present over future goods. This preference has been called time preference, or human impatience.[8]

According to the rule of demand and supply, when interest rates increase, individuals will postpone spending more of their income because they will get a chance to consume more in the future. This will increase the supply of money that can be loaned in the capital markets. On the other hand, the increasing interest rates will reduce the demand for loan money, because borrowers will have to reduce their consumption more in the future. Part of the demand for loan funds will come from investors. When interest rates are high, the demand of investors will be low, and their demand will be higher when the interest rates are low. This follows because, according to an assumption of economics, as the amount of investment increases, the return from the additional investments would decrease. Again, as it was the case in other markets, the supply and demand rule will lead to an equilibrium interest that will clear the capital markets. If the interest rates on the market are above or below the equilibrium interest rates, there will be a pressure on the market rates to move toward the equilibrium rate.

Let us assume that peoples' propensity to save increases. In such a case, lenders in the capital markets will supply more funds at the same interest rate.

---

8   Irving Fisher, *The Theory of Interest*, New York: Augustus M. Kelly, 1961, pp. 61–2.

This will force the interest rates to fall. Take another assumption: let us assume that there is a technological advance increasing the profitability of investments. In this case, investors will demand more funds in the capital markets. This will force the interest rates to rise. Again, the changes in preferences, in the form of technological changes, are reflected in the interest rates developed in the capital markets. These are the beliefs of the capitalist free market economies.

We would have to mention here that the real-life scenario is not as simple as the assumptions made by economic theory. For example, economic theory assumes that everyone has full information relating to the decisions they are making. But we all know that, especially in the capital markets, participants make their decisions with partial information. Another point is that the relevant economic theory was developed under the assumption of certainty. That is, until very recent times, the risks relating to the decisions were assumed not to exist. The theory of interest was developed for an environment in which there is no risk. On the other hand, we all know that the future bears a significant amount of risk. We can never be sure about the outcomes of our decisions, especially in decisions relating to transactions in the capital markets. In capital markets, the borrowing and lending decisions' outcomes will be realized in the future. Capital market transactions involve interest rate risk, inflation risk, foreign exchange risk and risk of default. These risks would need be accounted for in the theory. Over the last 40 to 50 years, there have been significant developments in the areas of finance relating to the measurement of risks. Financial institutions claim that financial decisions are made after considering the risks and returns of the decisions. It is assumed that in order to accept taking such risks, individuals would have to be compensated. This compensation is called the "price of risk." And, under some assumptions, financial models have showed that the capital market (financial markets) determines the price of risk and this price reflects the consensus of the participants in the financial markets.[9] This finding in finance theory was a relief to the advocates of the free markets. But there is a problem here also. Both the time value of money (interest rate) and the price of risk are determined in a single market – the capital market. This may be a significant limitation in determining the equilibrium interest rate and equilibrium price of risk. Those who believe in the virtues of the free market economies claim that capital markets are able to determine the equilibrium interest rates, and in case of disequilibrium, the market forces will make the necessary corrections.

---

9 One of the most popular models relating to the price of risk is the "capital assets pricing model" (CAPM).

LABOR MARKETS

In the labor markets, workers sell their labor. For thousands of years, slaves were traded just like any other product in the goods and services markets. Prices in the slave markets used to reach equilibrium according to the demand and supply rule. When the supply of slaves decreased, prices would go up, and if the supply of slaves increased, prices would go down. Market forces would help to determine equilibrium prices for slaves.

In capitalist economies, workers sell their labor as an input of production.[10] According to the capitalist belief system, people allocate their time to work or leisure. The time allocated to work is the supply of labor. It is assumed that work is a burden and the wage earned is the bliss, that is, compensation for that burden. On the other hand, employers provide the demand in the labor market. They purchase labor to use in production just like any other production factor. The wages paid by the employer are considered a component of the cost of production. That is, for the employer, the wages paid are the burden and the profit-yielding products produced are the bliss.

When wages increase, it is assumed that the supply of labor will increase. That is, workers will allocate more time to work. But, when wages increase, the employer will employ less labor since the costs of production will increase; that is, the demand will decrease. On the other hand, if wages decrease the supply will decrease and the demand will increase. Again, the demand and supply rule will operate to reach an equilibrium wage. If the wages deviate from the equilibrium wage, market forces will correct them.

Very strict assumptions are made in relation to the labor market mechanism. As we have mentioned above, the basic assumption is the claim that working is a burden. This assumption may suit the old days when labor was mostly physical labor. Perhaps carrying stones and breaking them, building pyramids and the like would not be pleasing the laborers. But attitudes about work must have changed as physical labor changed to skilled labor, and skilled labor changed to intellectual labor. In case of skilled labor and intellectual labor, working itself may be bliss. Working may provide someone a chance to prove themselves, and provide the means for self-actualization. Another point is that the opposite of working is being unemployed. Losing a job may be much more than loss of income. Some one who has lost their job may lose self-respect.

---

10 In labor-managed market economies, and in workers' cooperatives, human labor is not bought or sold. The workers are entitled to the produce of their labor.

In theory, it is also assumed that people do not have a target income to earn by selling their labor. If there is a target income and if the wages increase, the supply of labor may decrease. People would reach their targets by working less. The opposite is true also: if wages decrease, people would have to work more to reach their target. That means that when wages decrease the supply of labor may increase. People's spending or payment obligations usually provide such a target income to earn. In spite of all these questions, the advocates of free market economies believe that free labor markets would determine an equilibrium wage.

The Globalization of Markets

Another aspect of the markets is the fact that they are organized as national, international and global markets. At different historical periods, each one of these market organizations received popularity in line with the objectives of the dominating countries. The major empires in history benefited from free trade within their boundaries and accumulated great fortunes. Colonial empires were able to accumulate wealth by exploiting their colonies. The emergence of nation states introduced a new concept to trade. These nation states provided incentives for exports but at the same time implemented economic sanctions on imports to protect their domestic industries. As cited by Galbraith, during the mercantilist era, the line of thought was that it is always better to sell goods to others than to buy goods from others, for the former brings a certain advantage and the latter inevitable damage.[11]

In this mercantilist period, extending from the mid-fifteenth to the mid-eighteenth centuries, the nation state's main economic objective was to enrich the state. They believed that their foreign trade needed to produce a surplus in order to accomplish it. This period in history was called the period of mercantilism, or merchant capitalism. While the economic design of the period was structured to serve the merchants, the claim was that of serving the national interest. In Galbraith's words:

> The merchants in the mercantilist era did not like price competition. The obverse, such as agreements or understandings between sellers as to price, grants of patents of monopoly from the crown for a particular product, a monopoly of trade with a particular part of the world, the

---

11 Johann Joachim Becher, a German exponent of mercantilist thought, quoted in John Kenneth Galbraith, *History of Economics: The Past as the Present*, Penguin Books, 1987, p. 39.

prohibition of competitive production and sale of goods in the colonies
of the New World, served the merchants' interest. And so serving, they
were then seen as the national interest.[12]

Mercantilist policies bear a great resemblance to the policies of our times. Many countries today try to benefit from liberal foreign trade to increase their exports but revert to import restrictions to protect their domestic production. Countries implement quotas, tariffs and compensating taxes to restrict imports. Economic theory developed some concepts to excuse these import restrictions; the infant industry argument being one of them. The infant industry argument states that strategic investments need protection during their period of infancy, since they would not be able to face international competition until they grow strong.

Today, it is claimed that the world is becoming one single market, with the implementation of globalization policies. Globalization's proponents believe that the liberalized markets and worldwide competition in these markets will increase the welfare in the world. Therefore great efforts go into liberalizing the world's trade. The creation of the GATT and the establishment of the WTO were the major steps in the direction of globalization. However, all around the world, there is a growing amount of resistance to the imposition of globalization. This will be examined in a later chapter.

Parities Among the Prices

We have reviewed the determination of equilibrium prices in four types of market. These prices guide the economy in the free market economies. It is not just that prices balance the supply and demand on the markets, but also the relations among the prices influence the direction of the economies. For an economy to accomplish its objectives, the relations among prices in the markets must suit the goals set for that economy. For example, let us assume that individuals prefer to consume less at present in order to consume more in the future. That is, they are willing to postpone their consumption. This attitude will increase the loan funds in the capital markets and reduce the interest rates. This decline in interest rates will stimulate investments and increasing investments will increase production in the future. That is, declining interest rates will guide the economy to higher levels of production and income.[13] On

---

12 Galbraith, ibid., p. 40.

13 We have simplified the case here. The reality is more complicated then the explanation here. For example, the reduction in current demand may reduce prices and reduce the attractiveness of

the other hand, if the opposite is true, the national income growth will slow down. What is important here is that the prices developing in the markets will reflect the current preferences of the individuals, but these preferences may not be consistent with their or the economy's long-term objectives and aspirations. The society may desire higher economic development in the global competitive environment. And this objective may require more investments. That is, the short-term preferences of individuals may create long-term conditions inconsistent with the objectives of society.[14] For that reason, many countries provide incentives to economic agents to alter their decisions in the direction of national objectives. The incentive measures used are corrections on the prices determined in the markets. To illustrate our example, many countries provide low-interest loans to investors to induce them to invest more.

The relations among the prices that are determined in the markets are even more important in an open economy, that is, in a globalized economy. In open economies, different countries or economic blocs have different currencies. When the currencies used in trade and investment differ, exchange rates and foreign exchange markets enter the scene also. In such an environment, two parities would have to hold among the prices and interest rates in different countries. These parities are the *purchasing power* parity and the *exchange rate* parity. The purchasing power parity requires the foreign exchange rate to move in such a way as to guarantee the purchasing power of any two currencies to remain the same. The interest rate parity, on the other hand, requires foreign exchange rates to move in such a way to guarantee that an investment in any two currencies would yield the same return. These two parities imply a dynamic balance between inflation and the exchange rates on the one hand, and interest rates and exchange rates on the other in a country's markets. And, if these balances hold, the dynamic balance between inflation and the interest rates would hold.[15] The advocates of free market economies and those who believe in the virtues of the market mechanism assume that the market mechanism and the demand and supply rule would establish these parities as well as the balances among prices in a country. In real life, the imbalances between prices in individual countries and the lack of parities between the prices of any two

---

future investments. The declining interest rates may increase current consumption rather than increasing investments. But although simplified, our example makes some sense in the context of our current observations. The high propensity to save in Japan has reduced interest rates, helped investors to expand their time horizons, and helped Japanese economy to flourish.

14 In fact, current economic thought has eliminated such a consequence by assuming that the individuals are rational decision makers; and thus, their short-term and long-term preferences would be consistent. But this is also an assumption; not a reality.

15 Since the interest rates in a country also include the price of risk, if the risks in two currencies are not symmetric, this balance may not hold.

countries are very common. The most common imbalance is the vicious cycle of *high interest–low exchange rate* that we observe in developing economies. This vicious cycle causes a local currency to appreciate artificially. The consequences of this artificial appreciation of the local currency are increasing current account deficits, the eventual unbearably high cost of "hot money," and consequent economic crises. Lack of parities is not only the problem of developing countries. The US has been claiming that China has been intentionally keeping its currency, the Yuan, undervalued, and the undervalued Yuan is claimed to be hurting the US economy.

Prices Determined Outside the Markets

Capitalism recognizes the four markets we analyzed above and believes that the prices determined in these markets will reflect the preferences of people and guide the economy to the benefit of society as a whole. There are economic systems that do not regard the market system, so they use alternative systems that rely on price fixing outside the markets, in spite of the existence of the markets.

In the Soviet socialist system that existed in the USSR before the 1990s, production and distribution decisions were made centrally, mostly in planning departments, without regard to the markets. In such a system, people had money to spend but there were no goods in the shops. That is, the prices did not clear the market and they were not equilibrium prices. However, long queues in front of the shops are not only the scene in socialist economies. In many countries where market prices are not respected, people may line up in front of shops in order to buy products at prices lower than the equilibrium prices. Usually in those countries, black markets develop to balance supply and demand. As governments fix prices for consumers to benefit from low prices to serve social purposes, consumers pay equilibrium prices in the black markets. Usually in such cases, the beneficiaries are not the consumers but the black market operators. This may indicate that price controls may not be the best way to serve social objectives.

On the other hand, market prices do not reflect the social benefits and costs of production and consumption. Therefore, governments may need to interfere and correct market prices to bring equilibrium prices to socially desirable levels. In fact, this kind of intervention may be desirable from an economic point of view. Taxes levied on cigarettes and similar goods that inflict harm on society, provide a good example for correcting market prices.[16] On the other hand, governments may provide subsidies to reduce the prices of some goods that indirectly benefit society in order to increase their supply. We will discuss similar cases in Chapter 7.

Summary

Free market economies are guided by the prices established in the markets. These prices are determined in four markets: in goods and services markets, the prices of goods and services; in capital markets, interest rates and the price of risk; in foreign exchange markets, exchange rates, and in labor markets, wages. According to capitalist teaching, the individual choices of the participants of the market (buyers and sellers) made in their own interest end up in serving society as a whole. The equilibrium prices determined in the markets satisfy all the buyers and sellers in the markets. Equilibrium prices clear the market. This is the heaven on earth promised by the capitalist creed.

This heaven may be a heaven promised by capitalism, but it is nothing more than a promise. Unemployment rates are increasing in most countries, the gap between rich and poor is widening, the world's resources are being depleted, and the environment is facing a great threat. The preferences reflected in the prices are only the preferences of those who have money to spend. The system is serving only the privileged members of society. The market economies have an inherent aptitude to create crises. The market crises faced in many countries have resulted in great economic and social costs. The markets do not reflect some social and ecological costs and benefits to the prices. For that reason, the environment is being polluted; and some social goods that would help humanity to advance are not produced in the desired quantities. In short, free markets do not guide economies towards the aspirations of mankind.

On the other hand, in many cases, government interventions in prices and the fixing of prices outside the markets do not serve any purpose. When the equilibrium prices developed in the markets do not reflect the choices of society and are not expected to lead to the aspirations of the people, it is better to use indirect measures such as taxes and incentive measures rather than interfering with the prices themselves.

---

16 Taxes levied on cigarettes may have the objective of generating tax revenue for the state.

The First Concession
of Market Economies

*Everyone has the right to work, to free choice of employment, to just and
favorable conditions of work and to protection against unemployment.*
(The Universal Declaration of Human Rights)

As we have explained in the previous chapter, the claim of the free market
economy is that the equilibrium prices developed in the markets will reflect the
preferences of the people. The prices determined in the markets by the demand
and supply rule will clear the market; every seller who would be willing to
sell at that price will sell and all the buyers who are willing to buy at that price
will buy. There will be no excess supply or demand in the market. If we look
at the case from the point of view of the labor market, this claim would mean
there would not be any unemployment. In other words, everyone willing to
work at the equilibrium wages in the market would find employment, and
all employers would find labor they needed. The market will reflect the free
choices of the laborers and employers.

In spite of the strong belief about the sacredness of the market system and
the demand and supply rule, after the Industrial Revolution, as the labor class
was in the process of formation, it was observed that employers were able to
exploit workers, paying them subsistence salaries and forcing them to work in
extremely inhumane working environments. It was concluded that free labor
markets could not determine wages properly. So free labor markets and the
demand and supply rule were abandoned in the determination of wages. This
was the first concession of the capitalist economy in its devotion to the free
market system. The reason for this concession was not theoretical but practical.
The demand and supply rule did not produce an outcome in the labor markets
that was socially acceptable; in fact, it created miserable working conditions.
The outcome did not meet the aspirations of people: wages were very low,
working conditions were very bad, and child labor was common. In spite of

the fact that wages were at subsistence level, there was still unemployment. All these conditions disturbed society's conscience.

In fact, the main reason for the failure of the free labor market was that it did not meet the theoretical assumptions. In theory, it is assumed that no laborer or employer would be able to influence the market. But this was not so in the labor market: employers could easily influence the market in seeking their self-interest.

A different system, as it will be explained below, known as the collective bargaining system was designed to solve the problem. But it is interesting to note here that in spite of all the efforts spent and the concessions given, after the globalization and liberalization of trade, the world is facing problems similar to the those that emerged after the Industrial Revolution. Under globalization, multinational companies have their products produced in countries where labor is cheap, and sell them in markets where demand is favorable. It is usually claimed that globalized companies are paying about 14 cents an hour as a wage, providing very unhealthy working conditions, and exploiting child and female laborers.[1] When wages increase in the country where the companies base their production, the companies move to other countries where labor is still cheap.

Wage Determination in Labor Markets: The Collective Bargaining System

The reasons for the existence of unfair wages in free labor markets were investigated, and the cause was identified. The cause of the misery created by unfair wage determination was not a basic failure of the free markets, but had to do with the specific character of the labor markets. In the labor markets, the strengths of labor and the employers are not balanced: the employers are strong, since they have the money; but the laborers are weak, since they need the money.[2] Because of this imbalance, employers were able to set the rules of the game and impose wages to maximize their profits. The remedy prescribed aimed at creating a system that equalizes the strengths of the employer and employees in setting wages.

---

1   Walter LaFeber, *Michael Jordan ve Yeni Kuresel Kapitalizm* [*Michael Jordan and New Global Capitalism*], trans. Aysel Morin, Istanbul: Cep Kitapları, 156/21 (Yüzyıl Dizisi), 2001, pp. 121–2.
2   On the contrary, in free markets all the participants, buyers and sellers, should not be strong enough to influence the market.

The system put in place was the collective bargaining system. That is, wages, which are among the prices guiding the economy, were not to be determined in the free markets, but were to be bargained for at the table by the employer and representatives of the employees. To equalize the bargaining position and strengthen both employers and employees, they were provided with the right to form and join trade unions.[3] Workers were able to increase their bargaining power by forming or joining trade unions, and employers were able to form and join their own unions. Employee unions were not only to bargain for suitable wages, but also to seek the interests of the employees by improving the working conditions in the workplaces. Similarly, employer unions were to seek the collective interests of the employers.

The establishment of such employee and employer unions was not found to be sufficient to balance power at the collective bargaining table. The employers were still much stronger financially, and the workers were comparatively weak due to widespread unemployment everywhere. Or, seen another way, the employers needed the laborers to increase their profits, but laborers needed the money to be able to meet their basic needs. The formation of trade unions did not adequately repair the weak position of the laborers. A solution was found to repair this imbalance in their relative bargaining powers; both parties to the bargaining process were each given a deadly weapon: labor was given the right to strike, and to the employers the right to lockout. If the bargaining process did not reach satisfactory results, either the employees or employer could inflict great damage on the other. Either strikes or lockouts would certainly harm the company.

Although the collective bargaining system is designed as a remedy, it has great potential to inflict great harm, on not only the employer and employee but also on the third parties that depend on the operations of the company in question. If a company's operations stop by declaration of a strike or a lockout, the customers, the suppliers, the environment, and society as a whole may suffer. This is not just. These third parties, who are not represented, and are not parties to the bargaining process, may suffer the consequences of the bargaining process. Today, the concept of the "stakeholder" is gaining importance. It is commonly agreed that companies should not only serve their stockholders but also must serve the interests of their stakeholders. The concepts of stakeholder responsibility and corporate ethics are expanding their boundaries. The

---

3   Today, the right to establish unions is considered to be one of the basic rights of human beings. Article XXIII.4 of the Universal Declaration of Human Rights states that "Everyone has the right to form and to join trade unions for the protection of his interests."

stakeholders of companies include the stockholders, workers, customers, suppliers, the distributors, the public, the environment, and government. The company has responsibility to protect and enhance all their interests.

Since the collective bargaining process could harm innocent stakeholders in many countries, certain services or professions, such as medical services and doctors, educational services and teachers, are denied the right to strike or lockout.

Problems of the Collective Bargaining System

The collective bargaining system has serious problems even in a capitalist economy where everyone seeks their own personal interest. One of these problems may be that the labor unions may not serve the interests of labor, but only the interests of their union members. The ratio of laborers who are trade union members is quite small. Even if we consider the rate of unionization to be sufficient, the collective bargaining system brings no solution to the problems of that faction of labor that cannot find employment, or unemployed laborers. Today, the mental and physical requirements of work have been rapidly changing. The concept of "human capital" is gaining importance. Therefore trade unions would have to expend effort to train laborers and invest in human capital development.

The capitalist system considers the collective bargaining system to be a system that fits well with its philosophy. For a capitalist, a laborer is a means of production, just like machines and robots. Labor is also a cost factor, just like the other means of production. Therefore, to maximize profits, costs must be minimized as much as possible. If it reduces the capitalist's costs, machines and robots must replace laborers. This capitalist view of labor also suits very well the basic philosophy of the collective bargaining system, which considers the employer and labor to be rival parties whose interests conflict. Both parties see the collective bargaining system as a zero-sum game: whatever the employer gives is seen as a gain for the laborers at the former's expense. The less the employer gives, the higher the profits. That is, in this system, one party's gain is seen as the loss of the other party, as if better working conditions would not increase the size of the cake to be shared. Since the pursuit of self-interest is so ensconced at the heart of capitalism, the fact that motivated employees would increase the total income to be shared is not even noticed. On the other hand, today, intellectual labor is increasing its importance. This fact requires a new vision in companies: a vision that considers all the participants of production to share a common destiny, a vision that everyone shares a common purpose in companies. Companies in the twenty-first century must learn to share the fruits of their joint production. This change in vision would increase the motivation of all participants in production and improve the competitive position of a company.

As we have stated above, if the employer and the workers' union cannot reach an agreement, not only they but also all who are affected by the operations of the company in one way or another lose out, and even the society at large suffers. This is not just. It is not moral to inflict burdens on people who are not parties to the conflict.

As we have mentioned above, today, new concepts are emerging relating to the objectives of companies. One of the most significant of them is the *stakeholder* concept. Stakeholders are all groups that have an interest in the operations of a given company.[4] They are the stockholders, employees, customers, suppliers, retailers, banks, those who live in the neighborhood, the immediate environment and government, that is, all who affect or can be affected by an organization's actions. There is a growing belief that companies should not only serve the stockholders but also serve all their stakeholders. That means that companies should not only seek profit, but should contribute to the satisfaction and well-being of all its stakeholders; in capitalist parlance, they should serve the interests of the stakeholders also. The stakeholder concept is expanding fast and gaining increasing acceptance. But the present state of understanding still leaves much to be desired. Currently, serving the stakeholders' interests is accepted not for the sake of serving them, but in order to increase the profits of the companies. That is, currently, stakeholder responsibility is not the end but a means to reach the real end, namely, profitability. At this stage of development, companies have started to believe that they must be just and equitable in their relations with all the stakeholders and serve them all equitably. Companies have started to view stakeholder responsibility as a prerequisite of long-term profitability.

It is a difficult task to reconcile the stakeholder concept and the collective bargaining system. Contrary to the stakeholder concept, the collective bargaining system ignores the employers' and workers' responsibilities to the other stakeholders. Under the stakeholder concept, firms try to find ways to harmonize the interests of all the stakeholders and try to create synergy in the

---

4   In a more rigorous definition, stakeholders are persons, groups, organizations, or systems that affect or can be affected by an organization's actions.

services they provide. But on the other hand, the collective bargaining system sees the employer and workers as rivals in the negotiations and does not consider the other stakeholders at all. In spite of everything, the development of the stakeholder concept can be understood to be interrogation of the capitalist system; at least, it opens the mind to question the long-believed virtues of capitalism. The stakeholder concept carries hope for the development of new systems that may have a chance to serve humanity better than capitalism.

The Balance of Power in Other Markets

The lack of balance of power in the labor markets between the buyers and sellers was the main cause of setting aside labor markets and formulating a different model to determine wages. Keeping this in mind, we need to ask if a balance of power exists in the other markets between the buyers and sellers. If the balance of power does not hold, what are the consequences of it? What are the problems that need solutions? The twenty-first century must find answers to these questions.

If we take a look at the product markets, the companies that produce and sell their products, and the consumers, are they equal in strength? Can the producing and marketing firms influence market conditions? Do they have a chance to limit supply to increase their profits? Can they exploit the customers? Do conditions change in different industries? Can pharmaceutical companies, for example, serve to fight HIV and other diseases better?[5] The results reached by economic theory are based on the assumption that perfect competition conditions exist in all markets. But the balance of power between buyers and sellers is not a fact, it is an assumption. Economic theory studies well the perfect competition and monopoly cases. It comes to the conclusion that monopolies exploit the customers by reducing supply in order to increase profits. The theory claims that perfectly competitive free markets will serve humanity. But perfect competition is an assumption, which does not hold true in actual life. In actual life, companies can neither be called monopolies nor competitive firms. Each company has a varying degree of monopoly position due to their product differentiations. Under globalization, product differentiation is the rule. And, product differentiation means the ability or power to influence the markets.

---

5   In a World Trade Organization meeting in Doha, African countries pleaded for the suspension of some intellectual property rights for a given period in order to help the fight against the HIV epidemic, but no action was taken.

Another trend is the increasing emergence of mergers and acquisitions between companies. Mergers and acquisitions usually increase the monopoly position of companies. For that reason, under these realities of life, laws to eliminate unfair competition and laws to protect consumers, have increased in importance. For the implementation of these laws, many countries have developed agencies and organizations to protect the interests of consumers. It is a well-known fact that if the rights of consumers are not protected, they may be easily exploited by emerging monopolies or by companies whose monopoly position is getting stronger. In the process of liberalization implementations, many state-owned companies were privatized in many developing and developed countries. In most of these privatizations, especially in the energy, transportation and telecommunications industries, public monopolies were converted to private monopolies. These private monopolies ended up being more harmful than the public monopolies they replaced.[6] For those reasons, agencies like an Office of Gas, Telecommunication and so on are created, to protect the public from exploitation by the companies whose monopoly power has increased. The important thing is that all companies today have some degree of monopoly power and have chances to exploit the people. The claimed virtues of capitalism and its recent form, globalization, are based on the assumptions of perfect markets. But, on the other hand, the solutions to current economic problems are still sought in terms of the old liberal market economy assumptions. The dominant claim still is that if each one seeks their own interest in a free market economy, the results will be in the interest of society at large.

Today, the most important tool for companies to bolster their monopoly positions is the ownership of trade-related intellectual property right (TRIPS). Trade-related intellectual properties are rights like designs, printed circuits, brand names, patents, copyrights, and geographic indicators. In the *new economic design*, these rights are strictly protected. The protection of these rights is one of the duties of the World Trade Organization established by the GATT (General Agreement on Trade and Tariffs). The main rationale for the protection of these rights is the research and development expenditures (investments) needed for the development of these intangible assets. The claim is that if these assets are not protected properly, such investments would decrease and the world would be deprived of their benefits. This would mean a slowdown in the welfare development of the world. We will address the issue of TRIPS later, when we discuss the *new economic design*. But it is sufficient to note here that, in many of the world's belief structures, limiting the use of intellectual

---

6   J. Wikers and G. Yarrow, *Privatization, An Economic Analysis*, Cambridge, MA: MIT Press, 1988.

properties only to those who created them (if indeed they could credibly claim that they did so in intellectual vacuums) would not be acceptable. In many belief structures, the conviction is that these kinds of fortunes granted to individuals and organizations are the gifts of God, which assign duties rather than privileges to the people and organizations so honored. According to these creeds, these fortunes must be used not only to the benefit of the individuals or organization that have developed them, but must be used for the benefit of society.[7] The intellectual properties that individuals and companies possess are also gifts in their possession. These gifts must also be shared with those who do not have them.

In my opinion, exercising monopolistic power to seek benefits at the expense of others would not receive any acceptance in these religious belief systems.[8] There is an urgent need for a new system that will share the costs and the benefits of intellectual properties, instead of the current capitalist system that allows for the creation of monopoly rights and the exploitation of people for the sake of profit maximization.

Similar to the product markets, the imbalance in the relative power of the participants is no different in the capital markets. Most of the financial markets theory is based on the assumption of *efficient markets*. One of the requirements of the *efficient market hypothesis* is that in the capital markets, neither the buyers nor the sellers can influence the markets. In the actual life cases, big sellers and big buyers can easily influence or manipulate the capital markets in their own interests. Small and unprotected players in the market may suffer a lot from these types of behavior. Securities and Exchange Commissions or Capital Market Boards in various countries try to do their best to eliminate price manipulations. Another problem in the capital markets is the asymmetry in

---

7   In Zoroastrianism, one of the most ancient verses in the Avesta is Ahuna-Vairya. The second and the third lines of this verse are: "The gifts of 'Vohu Man' come as reward for deeds done out of love for the Lord of Life; Ahura's Kshathra surely cometh down on him who serves with zeal his brothers meek." This is interpreted to mean, "Our riches may consist in bodily strength or in wealth and worldly power; may they consist in spiritual insight, or in Divine Wisdom; – whatever they be, God hath bestowed them upon us not for our benefit, but that we may share them with our brothers and that the world be made richer through our possessing these gifts": I.J.S. Taraporewala, *The Religion of Zarathustra*, Tehran: Sazman-e-Faravahar, 1980, p. 36. Similarly in Islam it is believed that the poor have a share in the wealth (physical, intellectual and moral) of the rich: "And seek by means of what Allah has given you the future dwelling, and do not neglect your portion of his world, and do well to others as Allah has done well to you. And seek not corruption in the earth; surely Allah does not love the corrupters" (Surah 27:77); "And in their wealth to poor and the outcast had due share" (Surah 51:19).

8   In the holy Vedas, God says: "I am the one who strikes with a deadly weapon the big exploiters. As the lightning strikes the furious clouds, I strike these fattening blood-suckers so hard that they are thrown far away across the bright sky" (*Rig* 10.49.6 s:70).

information possessed by those who have relations with the companies (the insiders) and the rest of the participants in the markets. In capital markets, there are special regulations relating to the transactions of the insiders to eliminate any possible exploitation. This also shows that the prices determined in the markets cannot automatically guide the economy in the interests of society at large. Systems are needed to protect the interests of all the participants in the markets. The assumptions of the economic theory and the realities of the markets do not coincide. But, the virtues of the capitalist system are defended on the basis of conclusions reached by using the limiting assumptions in the underlying theory.

Conclusion

The free market economy asserts that the prices determined by the free will of the participants in the markets guides the economy in the interests of all individuals in society. Starting with the Industrial Revolution, it was witnessed that the conditions in the labor market were far from producing results that would meet the expectations and the aspirations of the people: labor was exploited and worked for a subsistence level of income under very inhumane working conditions. These conditions were clear indications that the free market economy was not able to function in the labor market. Therefore, a different system, the collective bargaining system, was developed to determine the wages that would be considered to be *fair wages* by society. It was concluded that the wages determined by the collective bargaining system, rather then the free labor markets, would provide guidance to the economy. This is the first and the most significant concession of the capitalist free market economy. But this concession brings up two important follow-up questions that require answers.

The first is: are the other markets – product, foreign exchange and capital markets – immune from the problems faced in the labor markets? Don't some of the participants of those other markets have power to influence these markets in their own interests? Are the assumptions of the economic theory about markets satisfied in these other markets? We know very well that the assumptions of the capitalist free market economies do not hold true in the real world. For that reason, capitalism was not able to increase prosperity and not able to eliminate, or even reduce, poverty all over the world. The twenty-first century will have to find solutions to the problems created by the free market economy implementations around the world.

The second question relates to the solution created in the labor market to solve the problem of free market failure, that is, the collective bargaining system. Is this system, developed to solve the problems of the previous century, expected to provide answers to the problems of our current one? Don't the realities of the twenty-first century and the aspirations of the people require a better system? In our opinion, assuming labor and employers to be opposing sides with opposing interests does not meet the realities of the present century. The twenty-first century will have to create a better system in the labor markets for wage determination, one that will meet the aspirations of humankind. The system developed will have to see labor and the employers as *partners* rather than *rivals*.

6

Misguidance of the Markets and Crises

But one thing is certain: there will be another of these episodes and yet more beyond. Fools, as it has long been said, are indeed separated, soon or eventually, from their money. So, alas, are those who, responding to a general mood of optimism, are captured by a sense of their own financial acumen, This it has been for centuries, thus in the long future it will also be.

(John Kenneth Galbraith)[1]

How lucky you are in Turkey, you can walk on the street!
In Chicago if you walk on the street you would be hit by a car, if you walk on the sidewalk you would be crushed under a banker committing suicide.

(Merton Miller, in one of his speeches in Turkey)

In Chapter 4, we saw that in capitalist economic theory, prices developed in the free markets guide the economy in the interests of society. This is the widespread belief shared by the adherents of capitalist thinking. According to the theory, the prices developed in the free markets perform their guidance function so perfectly that the prices reflect the free will and preferences of all the participants of the markets in reaching an equilibrium that clears the markets. This is the theory. On the other hand, when we consider reality, we do not reach the same conclusions. In this and the following chapters, we will explain the shortcomings of markets in fulfilling their duties. In this chapter, we will consider the problems created by the market structures and the supply and demand conditions. We will take three issues into consideration. The first two issues relate to the market structures. In capitalist theory, the assumption is that

---

1   John Kenneth Galbraith, *A Short History of Financial Euphoria*, New York: Viking Penguin, 1990, p. 110.

in each market a price is determined by the supply and demand in that market. But, in real life, the foreign exchange rates (the price of foreign exchange) are determined by the supply and demand generated in two different markets: the foreign trade market and the capital market. That is, one price is determined in two markets. On the other hand, in the capital market, two different prices are determined: the time value of money (the interest rate) and the risk premium. That is, one market determines two prices. The third issue relates the structure of demand and supply. Capitalist theory assumes that current prices influence demand and supply. In real life, both current prices and price expectations in the future influence demand and supply.[2]

Problems in Exchange Rate Determination

According to economic theory, the supply and demand for foreign exchange in the capital markets determine the equilibrium exchange rate that clears the market. And, as discussed in Chapter 4, it is believed that this equilibrium exchange rate guides the economy in the interests of society. The conclusion of the theory would be correct if foreign exchange was directly a source of utility for the individual. That in turn would require people to derive utility by holding foreign exchange, and to trade according to the utility created. In other words, the conclusion of the theory would be correct if foreign exchange was one of the products consumers directly consumed. In reality, foreign exchange creates utility for individuals indirectly. Foreign exchange is a means of payment in the foreign trade market and an investment instrument in the capital market. Therefore, the demand and supply for foreign exchange originates from both foreign trade and capital markets.

In foreign trade markets, demands for imports and the supply of exports create demand and supply for foreign exchange. Those who export goods and services are sellers in the foreign exchange markets. On the other hand, the goods and services importers are purchasers of foreign exchange. The foreign trade deficit of a country indicates excess demand for foreign exchange. If there is no other supply of foreign exchange, the excess demand for foreign exchange would push the exchange rate up. The rising exchange rate would reduce imports and increase exports and the exchange rate would reach equilibrium. Attaining equilibrium would mean the elimination of the foreign trade deficit.

---

2   In technical language, the theory assumes that demand and supply are a function of prices; but in reality, demand and supply are a function of price and expected changes in price, holding all other variables constant.

Part of the demand for foreign exchange originates from the capital markets. In the capital markets, it is possible to borrow in foreign exchange, lend in foreign exchange, invest in local financial instruments by selling foreign exchange, and invest in foreign financial instruments by buying foreign exchange. The supply and demand for foreign exchange in capital markets may result in a deficit or a surplus. If the exchange rates increase, borrowing in foreign currency gets expensive. This is because the borrowers would have to pay back the debt and the interest by purchasing foreign exchange at a higher price. Similarly, if the exchange rates increase, the gains of foreigners investing in local instruments decrease, again because they would be able to convert their invested capital and earnings back at a higher price. This would reduce the supply of foreign exchange in the capital market. On the other hand, if the exchange rates decrease, borrowing in foreign currency gets cheaper and the investment in local instruments by selling foreign currency increases. This, of course, increases the supply of foreign currency in the capital markets. Thus, the supply and demand for foreign exchange in the capital market may not be in equilibrium; that is, there may be a deficit or surplus.

The interesting thing is that if the shortage or surplus in the foreign trade market is balanced with the surplus or deficit in the capital market, the total demand and supply will be in equilibrium. But, this is an equilibrium achieved at the expense of imbalances in the two markets in question; that is, in the foreign trade and capital markets. This, as it will be explained below, may become a source of a dynamic disequilibrium, which is the main reason for the financial crises experienced in developing countries.

The trade deficit of a country is an indicator of its overvalued currency. The opposite is also true. The trade surplus is an indicator of a local undervalued currency. When a country's currency is overvalued, its exporters may suffer great losses. But, importers may benefit. The crucial point is that when there is an inflow of short-term capital (so-called "hot money") into a country, and if this inflow finances the trade deficit, there would be no pressure on foreign exchange rates to increase for the sake of a correction. The inflow of "hot money" into a country may develop a vicious *high interest–low exchange rate* cycle, which is one of the main reasons for the crises observed in developing countries since the liberalization in the capital markets. Let us shortly explain how this vicious cycle develops and turns into a financial crisis.[3]

---

3   The explanation here will not be a rigorous analysis, but just explanatory, but covering the common observations.

Usually, interest rates are high in developing countries due to high risk factors. Market risks, such as inflation, interest rate and foreign exchange risks, are high in developing countries. In addition, when the *high interest–low foreign exchange* cycle starts working, devaluation and financial crises risks also increase. High interest rates in a country will attract short-term financial capital ("hot money") to that country.

The "hot money" flowing into the country will be converted into domestic currency and will be invested in government securities to benefit from the high local interest rates. The increase in the supply of foreign exchange will depress the exchange rates and cause the domestic currency to appreciate.

This will have the following consequences both on foreign trade markets and the capital markets:

- In the foreign trade market, imported goods and services will became cheaper and exported goods and services will become more expensive. This will cause a deficit in the foreign trade accounts of the country. The deficit in foreign accounts will mean excess demand for foreign currency in the foreign trade market.

- In the capital markets, the gains of "hot money" will increase. In addition to the high interest earned on investing in government securities, "hot money" will earn an additional return from the currency exchange. The increasing gains of "hot money" will invite *new* "hot money" into the country, which will close the deficit in the foreign trade market.

- Decreasing foreign exchange rates will also decrease the cost of foreign exchange nominated borrowing. Importers will import their goods and services by borrowing abroad. This will postpone the demand for foreign exchange by the importers. This will further depress the foreign exchange rates and increase the inflow of "hot money" and increase the trade deficit.

Depending on the price elasticity of imports and exports and the interest rate elasticity of "hot money" and the foreign borrowings, this vicious cycle may converge or diverge. In most cases, the cycle has not been converging to equilibrium but has diverged, ending up in a financial crisis. The increasing foreign trade deficit causes the current account deficit to increase. Many economists studying financial crises after 1990 claim that if the current account deficit of a country is more than 5 percent of the national income, the country is likely to face a future financial crisis.

We can derive the following conclusion from our short explanations above. If the currency of a country is overvalued, there will be no pressure on the foreign exchange market to force it into equilibrium, since the trade deficit will be financed by the "hot money" coming into the country and the market will reach a dynamic balance where the currency of the country continues to appreciate in value. The question is, under the developments in the other markets, in which direction will this dynamic balance move? More specifically, the following questions await answer:

- As the "hot money" flows into the country, will it be able to reduce the interest rates in order to reduce the attractiveness of the country for the further influx of "hot money"?

- As the foreign exchange gets cheaper, will the domestic prices go down faster to reduce the attractiveness of imports?

The answers to these questions depend on the environmental conditions. But general observations indicate that the interest rates do not go down to reduce the amount of "hot money" entering the country, and the inflation rates do not go down as much as the decrease in the exchange rates. The experience of Turkey just before the 2001 crisis supports these observations. This can be explained as follows: the foreign exchange entering the country increases the supply of foreign exchange, but since it finances the trade deficit, or current account deficit, it does not increase the amount of savings in the country. Since the supply of savings in the capital market does not increase, the interest rates would not go down. Additionally, the domestic interest rates incorporate a domestic risk premium and are under the influence of the *debt-interest* vicious cycle experienced in developing countries. Under the *debt-interest* vicious cycle, the interest burden of debt increases so much that the government starts borrowing in order to pay the interest on the existing debts. Domestic risk and the risk faced by foreign investors differ when foreign exchange rates are pegged. Domestic investors face an inflation risk but foreign investors do not face an exchange rate risk when the exchange rates are pegged. For these reasons also, the general observations are in line with our theoretical explanations above.

It is necessary to mention another simplification in the theory, one which also causes the theory and practice to diverge. The theory assumes that supply and demand in the capital markets is a function of the interest rates. Under this assumption, the interest rates reach equilibrium. But in real life, investor behavior in capital markets is influenced not by only the level of interest rates but also the expectations of interest rate changes in the future. The theory claims that if the interest rates are high, the amount of loan funds increases; and if the interest rates are low, the amount of loan funds decreases. In capital markets, the expected decrease in interest rates increases the supply of loan funds because the capital gains of investments would be expected to increase. Especially for short-term investors (the providers of funds in the capital market), capital gains are a very important part of their investment returns. As we have mentioned above, the interest rates are usually high in developing countries due to the high-risk premium. If the interest rates were expected to decline, the inflow of "hot money" would increase. The increase in the inflow of "hot money" increases the supply of foreign exchange; this would depress the foreign exchange rates, thus contributing to the functioning of the *high interest–low exchange rate* cycle. These explanations show that the market mechanism in developing countries may not help to correct the overvaluation of the domestic currency, and might contribute to a vicious cycle that may end up with a financial crisis. This vicious cycle can be explained as:

- overvaluation of domestic currency,

- influx of "hot money" to finance the current account deficit in the country's balance of payments,

- increasing expectations for the currency to further appreciate, and

- further influx of "hot money" into the country to finance the increasing current account deficit.

This vicious cycle is not a sustainable one. As the current account deficit increases and this is financed by increasing the amount of inflow of "hot money," sooner or later the currency devaluation expectations increase. The authorities may devalue the currency by stepping in, or the markets may do it themselves. In case of a devaluation, the "hot money" invested in short-term instruments in the country would suffer big losses. It is the same for those who have borrowed in foreign currency and have short foreign exchange positions. As the devaluation expectations increase, the anxiety of the "hot money" and those companies whose foreign exchange positions are short increases. Any investor or borrower attempting to save themselves before the others would trigger a rush to the foreign exchange markets. This converts itself into a mob behavior and then develops into a crisis.[4] In developing countries, a market crisis easily turns into an economic crisis, and the countries suffer big losses.

It is important to note one point in order to eliminate any misunderstanding. There would not be any problem if the domestic currency appreciates due to improved competitive advantages. In fact, this would be desirable. If the domestic currency appreciates due to efficiency gains and an improved competitive position, the country would not face a current account deficit. In the above analysis, we were concerned with the overvaluation of domestic currency. When a currency is overvalued, the inflow of foreign exchange finances the current account deficit, which is mostly caused by the foreign trade deficit. Here we need to add another dimension to our analysis. If the foreign trade deficit is caused by imports of investment goods, there may not be a problem. But common observations indicate that it is not such investment goods but the increasing demand for consumption goods that are the main cause of foreign trade deficits.

The cost of the failure of the markets to reach equilibrium exchange rates is not the only cost of the possible crises the country may face. When the local currency appreciates, the financial gains of the "hot money" flowing into the country may become so high that it could be considered pure robbery. The Turkish experience is a good example. In the year 2002, although the inflation rate in Turkey was around 31 percent, the dollar exchange rate increased by only by 9 percent. That is, the Turkish lira appreciated in value about 20 percent. The same year, the interest rates on government bonds and treasury bills were around 64 percent. In such an environment, "hot money" invested in Turkey for a year earned more than 50 percent. No country, no economy, no firm can pay such a high price for "hot money," that does not contribute to production, coming into the country. This was just robbery. The $15.5 billion of "hot money" invested in Turkey financed the trade deficit of mostly consumer goods. The cost to the country was around $8 billion. The case was even worse the next year. In 2003, the Turkish lira still appreciated in value, and the interest rates still did not decrease. The "hot money" invested in Turkey earned about a 60 percent return. The trade deficit in 2003 was about $22 billion and it was financed by additional "hot money" entering the country. This exploitation of a country by "hot money" cannot be defended by the alleged virtues of the free market economy. Many developing countries have faced similar exploitation.

---

4   An exceptionally good explanation of the development of market crises is available in John Kenneth Galbraith, *A Short History of Financial Euphoria*, New York: Whittle Books, 1993.

Many countries had high inflation problems and tried to curb their inflation using models developed under capitalist theory. One of the models recommended by the International Monetary Fund (IMF) was using the exchange rate anchor. In this model, the increase in exchange rates was limited by a percentage determined by the expected decrease in inflation. This model failed in many countries, including Turkey. When the inflation rate did not decrease fast enough, the local currency appreciated in value. This appreciation started the vicious cycle that we have explained above. The IMF model for controlling inflation is one of the major causes of the crises experienced in South-east Asia in 1997, the crises experienced in Turkey in 2000 and 2001, and the crises experienced in Latin American countries often. Today it is a well-known fact that as "hot money" flows into a country, people feel as if everything is going fine, since they consume more than they produce. It is a euphoria that governs all economic actions. But when the "hot money" escapes the country, it destroys the economy, and leaves behind a complete wreckage. For that reason, some countries have developed regulations to eliminate or reduce the undesirable effects of short-term capital flows in and out of their countries. The financial crises that have been experienced in many countries are the result of the malfunctioning of the market economy as we have explained above.

Interest Rates and Price of Risk

In Chapter 4, we explained how the free capital markets determine interest rates; that is, the time value of money. The market mechanism is expected to work as follows: the supply of loan funds will be high when the interest rates are high, and will be low at low interest rates. On the other hand, the demand for loan funds will be low at high interest rates and will be high at low interest rates. The supply and demand rule will produce an equilibrium interest rate. This equilibrium clears the market; everyone who is willing to borrow at this rate will borrow and everyone who is willing to lend at this rate will lend. Under the free will of the borrowers and lenders, no one will be left unsatisfied. When we were discussing the short-term capital flows among countries, we also added a new dimension, stating that the supply and demand for funds are also influenced by expectations of increase or decrease in interest rates in addition to the level of the interest rates. In real life, both the level of interest rates and the expected increase or decrease in interest rates will influence the supply and demand for loan funds in the capital markets. Although the real-life cases are more complicated than the simplified assumptions of the theory, we may say that the market mechanism can determine an equilibrium interest rate. But, the expectations of increase or decrease in interest relate to the future and cannot be certain. For that reason, there is an element of risk to consider. Risk is a complicated subject; the free market theory was unable to find any meaningful answers to it for a long time. Still, the subject is not fully understood and accounted for in the theory.

The fact[5] that everyone accepts is that the interest rates that develop in the capital markets give not only the *time value of money* but also include a *risk premium* to account for the market risks involved. That is, when an investor in the capital markets invests funds in an instrument (a bond, bill, or any security), he would be exposed to various risks. He may lose part of the money invested or its expected return. That means his return may not be the return he expected. He may well incur a loss. For a very long time period, the capitalist theory was not able to incorporate the risk element in the models developed. In theory, the risks were disregarded and certainty assumed. During the last 50 years, theoretical developments in finance theory reached some meaningful conclusions in incorporating risks into financial decisions. But these conclusions were reached under some strong assumptions. We have come to a theoretical understanding that the capital markets determine both the time value of money and the risk premium of capital assets. The most popular one of these theoretical models is the Capital Assets Pricing Model (CAPM), structured under the *efficient market hypothesis*. The CAPM has shown that the return expected from any investment in any security in the market is the sum of the time value of money and the risk premium of the security. The risk premium of the security is the price of risk in the market multiplied by the risk of the security relative to the market.[6] When you take a risk you are compensated by its price. The greater the risk, the more compensation you need. Although the assumptions of the model are strong and limiting assumptions, the model received very wide acceptance. The conclusion of the model was so much welcomed that four economists who have contributed to the development of the theory at its different stages earned the Nobel Prize.[7] This wide acceptance was not surprising; the conclusion of the model was a victory for the free market mechanism and capitalism. The free capital markets not only determined the time value of money, but also the price of risk. This is important. Until the CAPM model, though, economic theory had to assume certainty, and in real life there is no certainty.

---

5   It is rather a belief; not a fact.
6   The CAPM model states that $Rj = Rf + \beta j \, (Rm - Rf)$.
7   Franco Modigliani received his Nobel Prize in 1985, and Harry Markowitz, William F. Sharp and Merton H. Miller shared the award in 1990.

But it is important to state an important point here: the virtue of the demand and supply rule comes from the fact that it directs prices towards equilibrium. As we have explained for the product markets above, as the prices of products increase the supply increases, but the decrease in demand pushes the prices down in the direction of the equilibrium. The same may not be applicable for risks in certain cases. When the price of risk increases, the market interest rates increase; the increasing interest rates would increase the risks of the borrowers; the increasing risks of the borrowers would push the risk premium up still more. A vicious cycle may develop here that causes the interest rates to increase to levels hard to justify. Turkey has suffered from such a vicious cycle since 1989. Respecting the market forces, the Turkish government paid about a 32 percent inflation-adjusted interest rate on government securities. If we consider the time value of money to be 4 percent, the remaining 28 percent was the risk premium. This is an unseen and unjustifiable level of risk premium. It may mean the probability of government default is 22 percent. It does not make sense to expect such a default. Yet, such a high real interest and risk premium inflicts so much damage on the economy that it certainly increases the risks of the government's obligations. No producer, company, or country would be able to pay this high interest by using their income; they would have to pay it by giving up their assets. This has been the case for some developing countries such as Mexico, which met its obligations through *debt-equity swaps*.

The source of risk is the lack of knowledge of the future. Both real and financial investments incorporate risks. The CAPM has received such acceptance that the conclusions of the model claimed to be applicable to real investments also. Since most of the real investments are not made often and repeatedly, the conclusions of the CAPM model may not be applicable to them. Real investments have different types of risks; risks arising from the uncertainties relating to the outcomes of the operations of the investments. The sales revenues of investment in an operation, for example, may not be realized as expected. These kinds of risks are called "operational" risks. On the other hand, financial investments have market risks. Market risks include inflation risk, foreign exchange rate risk, devaluation risk, interest rate risk, and default risk.

The market risks assumed by domestic investors and the foreign investors may not be the same; that is, they may not be symmetric. For domestic investors, the inflation risk is important. Inflation will eat up the value of their investment and the interest they earn. For that reason, when the inflation risk increases the interest rates go up also. On the other hand, the inflation risk is not relevant for the foreign investors. For them, the foreign exchange rate risk is important.

They would have to convert their capital and earnings into their own currency. When the inflation risk and foreign exchange rate risks differ, the risk premiums will have to differ also. This is the case when exchange rate controls are used as a tool to curb inflation. In the free market system, exchange rates would be left to float in the market. But in an inflationary environment, floating exchange rates may make it difficult to control inflation. For that reason, exchange rate controls have been used as a tool to bring inflation under control. Exchange rate controls take various forms, for example, using fixed exchange rates, pegging exchange rates, anchoring exchange rates and using crawling pegs. In all these forms, exchange rates are allowed to increase at rates lower than that of inflation. It is hoped that cheaper imports would reduce production costs, and in order to compete with imported products, local producers could not increase their prices. Unfortunately, these hopes do not materialize in most of the real-life cases. The main problem is that when exchange rate controls are used, inflation risk does not decrease but the foreign exchange rate risk is almost eliminated. Since the local interest rates incorporate inflation risk, foreign investors benefit from high interest rates without taking any risks. This was what happened in Turkey when IMF-guided stabilization programs were used. As mentioned above, foreign investors were able to earn extremely high returns for their investments in Turkey, much more than 25 percent in most of the cases.

When a developing country faces the *high interest–low exchange rate* vicious cycle, the most important risk is the devaluation risk. As the local currency appreciates in value, the trade deficit and the current account deficit enter an increasing trend. Many economists believe that this trend is not sustainable. If the current account deficit exceeds 5 percent of the national income, a correction in the value of the currency would be needed. This is done either intentionally by the authorities, or by a rush in the foreign exchange market. Since devaluation is very costly to foreign investors using short-term capital ("hot money") and those companies with short positions in foreign currency, a crowd behavior in the form or rush would be inescapable. When there is a rush to get foreign exchange, the exchange rates go sky-high. This usually leads to a financial, and then to an economic crisis.

The free market economies have not been able to solve the problem of market crashes and economic crises. The world has been experiencing market risks nearly once every 30 years. But since the overwhelming and unquestionable acceptance of the capitalist system as the victorious economic system, the frequency of such market failures and economic crises have increased.

Market Gains

The most significant delusion of the free market economies is the belief that markets may generate income or cause loss. This is not an error of economic theory but is the result of the transformation of capitalist economic theory into a creed or a religion. But this delusion has cost humankind dearly for many centuries, with the accompanying market clashes and economic crises. For example, this delusion played a significant role in the global crises of the 1930s.

First, we should indicate that markets are the places where exchanges take place. In an exchange, one value is exchanged for another. That is, when you give something of value, you get another thing of value. If the transaction takes place of the free will of the parties, for either one of the parties the value of the thing obtained is more than the value given away. In the markets, if the medium of exchange is money and if the transactions take place under free will, for a buyer the value of the purchase is more than the price he is paying; similarly, for the seller the value of the thing he sells is less than the price he charges. Both the buyer and the seller gain from the exchange. The gain of the buyer is called "consumer surplus" in economic theory. But these are gains; they are not incomes.

Let us take the stock exchanges in hand: when a stock is sold at a price, the buyer would expect the stock to be more valuable than the seller believes; the seller on the other hand believes that stock is worth less than the price he is getting. The buyer gets an expected *unrealized gain* when he buys the stock. He buys the stock with an expectation that the market will realize the real value of the stock, and he will realize his unrealized gain. If the stock is not sold at a price higher than the price he paid, his gain would not be realized. The gain only comes by sale. In other words, in order to realize a gain, one would have sell the stocks and leave the exchange. But, as we have mentioned above, this is a gain, not an income.

Now let us take a trading session. Let us note somewhere the total amount of stocks and the total amount of money all the participants of the market have at the beginning of the session. Let us say there is "X" amount of money and "Y" amount of stocks. Let us assume the stock exchange index has increased by 10 percent. The stock exchange bulletin will announce that the exchange has resulted in a 10 percent gain in that session and this announcement will be repeated in the television news. In spite of the gain in exchange, at the end of the session the amount of money and the amount of stocks of the participants will not change: Still there will be "X" amount of money and "Y" amount of stocks at the end of the trading session. Neither the amount of money nor the amount of stocks have changed; in fact they cannot change. What has happened is that only the value the participants assigned to the stocks which have been traded has changed, and this change is reflected to the transactions. Those who sold their stocks must have thought that the real value of the stocks is less than the market price, and those who bought must have thought that the value of the stocks is more than the market price. Those who realized their gains are investors who sold their stocks at higher prices than they previously bought them. But those sellers who bought their stocks at higher prices previously have incurred losses. Those who have not traded have not realized gains nor realized losses. No one could know what the prices would be; therefore no one could predict what the gains and losses will be in the future.

In summary, the 10 percent increase in the stock index may have caused some of the traders to gain or lose, but there is no *income* generated for anyone. The real wealth of society is the same before and after the trading session, only the wealth has changed hands, and some people assign more value to the wealth they have. In transactions, some investors may have incurred a gain or a loss. The same would be true if the trading session resulted in a 10 percent or any amount of decline in the stock index.

In an economy, the actual production of goods and services is the only way to generate income. Income cannot be generated by exchanging wealth. Unless you produce, you cannot consume. Assume you have great amount of gold as wealth. You cannot consume gold for your breakfast. Someone would have to produce bread, cheese and butter; others would have to produce tea or coffee and many other products or services that you may consume. You must be able to purchase these products or services in order to have your breakfast. You may use your wealth as a means of payment for consumption goods. But in that case, someone else must be willing to own or hold that wealth. The important thing is that you cannot have income unless you produce something and you cannot consume unless you or someone else produces the things you need for consumption.

Let us return back to our stock exchange case. Common stocks give to their owners the right to get dividends from (the incomes of) the companies. The income generated through the operations of a company is the difference between the revenues it earns through selling its products and services and the payments it makes for the material inputs it gets from the other entities. This difference is called "value added" in economics. Value added is the total income generated by the factor inputs of the companies. Therefore the value added is the total of wages paid to laborers, interests paid to debts, profit, and taxes paid to government. The dividends the stockholders get are their share of the profits of the company. That is, a dividend is an income, supported by the same amount of goods and services produced. For that reason, the value of a common stock is accepted to be the present value of all the future dividend payments.

The most significant delusion of the free markets is the belief that it is possible to create income by market transactions: earning money by exchanging money. This delusion was the cause of many speculative rises in the markets and the final unavoidable crash and the misery it has caused in society for many centuries.

Behind the speculative rises in the markets lies the expectation of gains from market transactions. John Kenneth Galbraith describes speculative episodes:

> *The price of the object of speculation goes up. Securities, land, objects d'art, and other property, when bought today, are worth more tomorrow. The increase and the prospect attract new buyers; the new buyers assure a further increase. Yet more are attracted; yet more buy; the increase continues. The speculation building on itself provides its own momentum.*[8]

John Kenneth Galbraith has studied the recurrent speculative episodes in history starting with the "tulipomania" speculation in tulip bulbs in 1636–1637, in Amsterdam, Holland. He tried to determine the common factors behind the speculative behavior and the final burst of the bubble created by this speculation. We can summarize Galbraith's conclusions as follows:

- The speculative episodes accrued are the results of mass insanity.

- Speculative episodes observed since the tulipomania in 1636–1637 have caused clashes once every 20 years.

- Due to extreme brevity of financial memory, financial disasters are quickly forgotten.

---

8   Galbraith, *A Short History of Financial Euphoria*, p. 3.

- After forgetting these financial disasters, people come to think that there are new opportunities arising in the markets. Since people associate money with intelligence, and since money is the measure of capitalist achievements, euphoria develops to capture the opportunities.

- People are encouraged by the conviction that markets cannot make mistakes. This is supported by faith in the inherent perfection of the markets and the belief that *"markets ... are theologically sacrosanct."*

- As the result of this financial delusion *"Fools, as it has long been said, are separated, soon or eventually, from their money."*[9]

Galbraith asserts that, "one thing is certain: there will be another of these episodes and yet more beyond." The reason is "Recurrent speculative insanity and the associated financial deprivation and large devastation are ... inherent in the system." Yet still people have faith that markets are inherently perfect. We can say that mathematical and rational models developed in theory cannot understand financial behavior. That is why a new area of finance, behavioral finance, is emerging in collaboration with psychology.

Conclusion

The capitalist economic system strongly believes in the faultlessness of the free market mechanism. There is an unshaken trust in the functioning of the demand and supply rule. We should admit that free market economies deserve praise since they respect the free will of the people. Developments in the world since the 1980s have helped us to witness the failure of the systems that did not respect the free will of the people. The dissolution of the USSR, where production decisions were made in bureaucratic structures, is a good example of these failures.

But the market mechanism has many limitations and shortcomings also. We need to understand these shortcomings very well in order to be able to serve people better. Market mechanisms must be used in a way to reach the objective of serving humanity. In using the market mechanism, we need to benefit from its strengths and repair its shortcomings. What is wrong is the glorification of the market mechanism, while ignoring its shortcomings.

---

9   Ibid., p. 110.

The market mechanism's main strength is its respect of people's choices, though currently, only the choices of those who have the means to purchase are regarded. We may be able to find ways to enlarge the coverage of the people whose choices matter. The market mechanism has many shortcomings that we have discussed above. The inherent weakness of the mechanism is that it may foster euphoria in some markets and vicious cycles that lead to financial crises. These deficiencies of the mechanism require solutions.

Today, as capitalism is transforming itself into a religion, the markets have become sacred also.[10] Ignoring the shortcomings of the market mechanism, and not taking the necessary corrective actions, have inflicted great damage in society and have caused great pain. Some of these costs have been apparent in the form of significant market clashes, which have destroyed the lives of millions, while others lived in silence, accepting this fate.

---

10 "Markets in our culture are a totem; to them can be ascribed no inherent aberrant tendency or fault": ibid., p. 24.

7

Costs and Benefits that are not Reflected in Markets

The World Resources Institute's mission is to move human society to live in ways that protect Earth's environment and its capacity to provide for the needs and aspirations of current and future generations. Because people are inspired by ideas, empowered by knowledge, and moved to change by greater understanding, WRI provides – and helps other institutions provide – objective information and practical proposals for policy and institutional change that will foster environmentally sound, socially equitable development.

(Mission statement of the World Resources Institute <www.wri.org>)

The sun and the moon follow a reckoning. And the herbs and the trees do adore [Him]. And the heaven, He raised it high, and He made the balance, do not transgress the balance.

(Koran, Surah 55:5–8)

Free market economies are guided by the prices that the markets determine. In the previous chapter, we have explained the difficulties encountered in the markets in reaching equilibrium prices. We have discussed these difficulties under the topics of "Problems in Exchange Rate Determination," "Interest Rates and the Price of Risk" and "Market Gains." We have also illustrated that these difficulties have prevented the system from reaching equilibrium prices the way it is defined in the free market theory. We have also shown that disequilibrium in the markets have been the main cause of the widespread crises and great depressions experienced throughout the centuries. In this section, we argue and illustrate that these prices cannot guide the economy in a manner that will generate welfare for society as a whole (or for the citizens of the world), even if we assume that the prices determined in the markets are the correct equilibrium prices.

Prices that are determined in the markets may guide the economy to serve the benefits of society only if they reflect all the costs and benefits incurred, including social costs[1] and social benefits.[2] In the profit-oriented capitalist system, only the direct costs and benefits to firms are reflected in the market prices. That is, social costs and benefits are not reflected. This has two important consequences: if social benefits are not reflected in the prices, society is deprived of some goods and services since they are produced in insufficient quantities; on the contrary, if the social costs are not reflected, the system leads to the overproduction of some goods and services. Overproduction of goods with unaccounted social costs results in social and environmental pollution, and depletion of natural resources.

Social Costs not Reflected in Markets

In free market economies, acting of their own free will, buyers and sellers create the demand and supply in the markets. Demand and supply determine the equilibrium price, which clears the market. These prices developed in the markets reflect the choices of the market participants. The economy is guided by these equilibrium prices. That means the economy is guided by the free will and choices of buyers and sellers for the benefit of the society. This is the primary assertion of the free market economy. However, in reality, the participants' individual choices might not be to the benefit of society as a whole, due to the presence of social costs and social benefit that are not reflected in the prices.

SOCIAL COSTS

According to the demand and supply rule in the capitalist system, those who supply goods and services to the market sell their goods and services until the cost of the last unit to be sold is equal to the revenue to be gained from that sale.[3] But the rule also states that the price that is established in the market must be above the average cost of production. These two complementary rules determine the amount of goods and services supplied to the market by the producers. Hence, production costs influence the amount supplied to the market. As previously stated, when costs decrease, more goods and services are supplied at the same price level; while the amount supplied will be less

---

1   Social costs are costs to society which are not reflected to the producers as losses.
2   Social benefits are the benefits to and gains of society which are not reflected to the producers as incomes.
3   In technical terms, the marginal cost should be equal to the marginal revenue.

at the same price level in the case of an increase in the costs. The costs, which are referred to here, are the costs that are directly incurred by the suppliers (producers). However, there are also costs that are not borne by the suppliers but are reflected to the society at large. Costs of environmental pollution, social pollution, deforestation, global warming, and ozone depletion are some examples of these types of costs, which accrue to the society but not to the suppliers. These economic costs are referred as "externalities" in economics. Externalities are only a part of the total social costs that may accrue to society. Social costs also include costs such as the negative impact of some goods and services on the culture and the ethics of society. These types of social costs are called cultural and social pollution.

Today, there is an increasing awareness of environmental pollution. The magnitude of the environmental costs are much larger than their previously assumed levels. Costs such as poisonous gas emissions, water waste and noise pollution created by production plants do not accrue to the companies producing them, but to society. The cost of natural resources used as raw materials, such as water and forest products, are much lower to the companies than they are to society and the environment. When the externalities are not considered, the system produces excessively and this results in huge costs to the environment and society. Global warming and climate change are threatening the world, and ozone layer depletion is influencing human health badly. The world is losing arable land and about 80 percent of the rainforests are already lost.[4] These are mainly the consequences of overproduction resulting from the miscalculation of costs and from not considering the social costs of production. Gradually, the balances of the world are changing, and may end up in a vicious circle leading to total destruction.[5]

There is also an increased awareness of the social costs related to the consumption of some products, for example, "recreational" drug use. As widely acknowledged, the production costs of drugs are very low, while social costs are very high. Since the social costs do not accrue to the producers, very large amounts of drugs are produced. When the supply is restricted, the production and trading of drugs yield generous profits, making the business a highly attractive one. Even though very strong sanctions are put on drug trading, it is

---

4   For more information, refer to the report by Catherine Cotton, "Buying Destruction", Amsterdam: Greenpeace International Publications, 1999 <http://archive.greenpeace.org/forests/forests_new/html/content/docs.html>.

5   In the Koran, it is stated: "And the Firmament has He raised high, and He has set up the Balance [of Justice], In order that ye may not transgress [due] balance" (Surah 55:7–8).

almost impossible to control it. This is what one should expect under the profit motive of capitalism.

We must admit that there are many goods and services which have harmful effects on the health and culture of society, whose social costs do not accrue to their producers and sellers. The market mechanism is unable to reflect the social costs of these types of goods and services to production and trade.

Furthermore, it is very difficult to measure social costs. How can you measure the cost of increasing cases of cancer due to air pollution? How can you measure the cost of the spreading use of drugs among teenagers? It may not even be possible to agree on a common definition of social costs. Cultures of different societies may display significant differences in their perception of social costs. Some social and cultural costs, which are perceived to be significant in certain societies, may not even be perceived as social and cultural costs in others.

SEEKING REMEDIES

Since the markets ignore the social costs, prices determined in the markets are lower than what they would be otherwise. Then the production and consumption of that product increases, and thus the magnitude of the destruction inflicted on nature, society and the world increases. Remedies to this grave problem are mainly searched for along two different platforms.

At the national level, levying additional production and sales taxes, restricting consumption, and designing preventive regulations and sanctions are some of the remedies aiming to reduce the level of consumption of these high social-cost products. Taxes levied per unit of production directly increase the marginal cost and decrease the amount of production. Sales taxes, on the other hand, increase prices, and therefore may be expected to decrease demand. But, for sales taxes to decrease demand, consumers must be sensitive to prices,[6] which may not be the case for many products. Sales taxes on alcoholic drinks and tobacco may be examples of products for which consumer demand is not sensitive to prices. The sales taxes produce significant amount of revenue for governments. Therefore, governments may have a conflicting objective in levying taxes on these kinds of high social-cost products: collecting taxes versus reducing consumption. Provisions relating to the installation of purification

---

6   In economics terminology, the "price elasticity" of demand must be high.

systems for water wastes in production plants and provisions for solid wastes are among the examples of preventive regulations.

These remedies designed for the national level do not produce sufficient results to protect the world from accelerating pollution due to the inherent nature of capitalism. The objective of firms in capitalism is not to preserve nature or improve social conditions; it is to make profits. Ignoring social costs is an attractive means of increasing profits. For this reason, serious difficulties are encountered in the application of remedies designed at the national level. Companies do whatever they can to circumvent the regulations. Depending on their cost-benefit analysis, they may even be ready to pay sanctions rather than invest in environmental protection required by regulations. There are many controversial problem areas: for example, sulfur dioxide emissions, and the use of cyanide in production, remain unresolved after many decades. Moreover, national provisions remain inadequate to address the issues, which go beyond national boundaries. For example, in the case of nuclear waste, some producing countries have even devised formulas for transferring their radioactive waste to developing countries, which face problems and difficulties in the enforcement of their environmental laws. In such cases, the countries that suffer the consequences of pollution are not the countries producing these wastes but the poor countries. Some social costs are global in nature. The costs of natural degradation due to excessive consumption in rich counties may be borne by other countries all around the world.

The second platform where remedies are sought is the international platform. There is an increasing international awareness of global warming, the greenhouse effect and climate change caused by carbon dioxide emissions. Great efforts have been made in order to provide an international solution to high levels of carbon emissions. We observe very little success in these efforts since some countries still take positions on these discussions from the point of view of their national interest. Some countries still do not understand the fact that we are sharing the same planet and that the planet is in danger. Since this is a life and death case for the world, we want to review the course of developments in the hope of finding a solution on the international platform:

- In the United Nations Intergovernmental Climate Change Meeting that took place in May 1990, it was declared by leading meteorologists that the global climate was warming and that this development would lead to undesirable consequences.

- At the World Climate Conference in November 1990, participating countries reached a decision to study and take measures on climate change.

- In June 1992, more than a hundred heads of state participated in the first international Earth Summit convened in Rio de Janeiro and signed the Convention on Climate Change.

- Countries agreed to limit their greenhouse gas emissions and decrease them in the year 2000 to the levels of the beginning of 1990.

- In the year 1995, countries which signed the Convention, decided that the measures taken individually by the countries were not sufficient and agreed to form a Protocol to reduce greenhouse gas emissions.

- In the meeting held in Kyoto in December 1997, the Kyoto Protocol was signed. The Kyoto Protocol is an agreement under which industrialized countries will reduce their collective emissions of greenhouse gases by 5.2 percent in the period 2008–2012 as compared to the year 1990.

- Kyoto Protocol was opened for signature on March 16, 1998, and closed on March 15, 1999.

- The Kyoto Protocol came into force on February 16, 2005, following its ratification by Russia on November 18, 2004.

- As of November 2007, a total of 175 countries and other governmental entities had ratified the agreement. The United States, although a signatory to the Kyoto Protocol, neither ratified nor withdrew from the Protocol. The signature alone is purely symbolic, as the Kyoto Protocol is non-binding on the United States unless ratified. The United States was, as of 2005, the largest single emitter of carbon dioxide from the burning of fossil fuels.[7]

As can be seen above, the capitalist system, under the guise of national interests, cannot forego the interests of the companies, even at the cost of

---

7   <http://en.wikipedia.org/wiki/Kyoto_Protocol#Objectives>.

inflicting great damage to the ecological balance. Today, global warming still continues to be a very severe problem, the world climate is changing and glaciers continue to melt.

Human Beings as a Cost Factor

In the capitalist system, production costs consist of the payments which are made to the factors of production. Factors of production are traditionally defined as land, labor and capital. Production is assumed to be a function of labor and capital in the theoretical analyses. In other words, capital and labor are used in order to produce goods and services. Labor and capital are obtained from the labor and capital markets at prices which form in response to supply and demand. In practice, capital is obtained from the capital markets in two different forms, namely, debt and equity. Companies pay wages to the labor hired, and they pay interest for debts they acquire. Equity owners run the companies in their own interest to earn profits. Profits are determined by deducting the expenses (incurred costs) from the revenues. That is, in a capitalist enterprise, the costs of material inputs, wages paid for labor employed and interest paid on debt used are deducted from revenues to determine the profit of the capitalist owner. That means, in the capitalist system, wages paid to labor are a cost element that needs to be reduced in order to increase the profit of the capitalist owner. To secure this profit maximization of the capitalist owner, the capitalist system provides him the right to run the company in his own interest. Thus, the capitalist system is a system which assumes employees (labor) to be a cost factor and utilizes employees as a device to increase the profits of the shareholders (capital).[8] From this point of view, the interests of capitalist owner and labor conflict in the capitalist system. Shareholders try to decrease labor costs in order to increase their profits. On the other hand, employees try to increase their welfare by winning more wages.

In reality, the wage paid to a laborer is his income that he spends and his spending makes up the revenues of firms. Reducing labor wages reduces the revenues of firms indirectly.

The capitalist and socialist systems resemble each other in this respect. The socialist system also starts with the presumption of a conflict of interests

---

8   Jaroslav Vanek calls this the "negative sign syndrome" and believes it to be the source of the failure of the capitalist system: Vanek, *The General Theory of Social Systems* <http://ecommons.library.cornell.edu/handle/1813/642>.

between labor and capital. The only difference is that in the socialist system the capital is owned by the state. This presumption is not in conformity with the value structures humankind has been developing over thousands of years and with contemporary developments in value structures. Most belief systems and contemporary developments perceive capital and labor to be in unity and recommend their cooperation.

From a scientific perspective, it is possible to perceive labor not as a cost factor but as a production factor which will receive a share from the revenue generated. When viewed from this perspective, the costs of the goods and services produced by companies become only the costs of materials acquired from firms and the interest paid on debts acquired from the capital markets. When the cost of goods and services are deducted from the sales revenues, the income generated by the company is obtained. This income can then be shared between the employees and the shareholders. We are not proposing an alternative system here. We only want to demonstrate that different systems can be established using scientific methods. It is important to note that if we accept labor as a production factor, which shares the income generated, then labor and capital are no longer competitors, but they are directed to cooperate to increase the income that they will be sharing. In this case, employees also must participate in the decision-making process of the company, together with the shareholders.[9] More importantly, society as a whole will benefit from this cooperation also. In such a system, units of production and employment will be at higher levels since production costs will be less.[10]

Actually, there are systems which do not treat labor as a cost factor. The labor-managed market economy model[11] is one such system. We have briefly explained this model in an earlier chapter. This model depends on obtaining all capital (debt plus equity) from the competitive capital markets by paying market interest and the sharing of the resulting income by the employees. In this case, only the employees have a right to participate in the decision-making process. Similarly, output and employment will increase in this system since the costs will decrease.

---

9   Today, participative management is advocated in contemporary management science.

10 The technical explanation for this expectation is that marginal revenue should be equal marginal cost for maximization of the income that will be shared between capital and labor. Units of production are expected to increase since the marginal cost will be less and the marginal revenue remains the same.

11 Jaroslav Vanek, *The General Theory of Labor Managed Market Economies*, Ithaca, NY: Cornell University Press, 1970.

Another example of a system which does not treat labor as a cost factor, is *mudaraba*, which, along with *murabaha*, *muşaraka* and *vouch*, is an Islamic economic institution.[12] Murat Çizakça defines *mudaraba* as the partnership of shareholder and entrepreneur.[13] In our opinion, *mudaraba* can be defined as a partnership of labor and capital in its context. The provider of labor is called *mudarıb*, while capital provider is called *rab-el-mal*. In this partnership, providers of labor and capital receive a predetermined share from the income generated. This predetermined rate is subject to agreement between the parties. In the case of loss, providers of labor would lose their labor while providers of capital would lose their capital. Providers of labor are not responsible for the loss of capital. Such a system relies on increasing the total income generated from production (value added), which are in line with the macro-economic objectives of countries. One of the main economic objectives of a country is maximizing the national income. The contribution of each economic unit to national income is the value added generated by that unit.

In a free market economy, the labor cost of production and the social cost of labor significantly differ in the case of unemployment. In economic theory, in a production unit, the employment decision is made according to the rule of marginal costs and benefits. That means the wage of the last person employed should be equal to the contribution that person makes to the revenue of the company.[14] This wage paid to the last laborer hired is the cost of labor that determines how many laborers the company will employ. On the other hand, again according to economic theory, there is no (that is, zero) economic cost of employment in an environment where there is unemployment. In economics, cost of a resource in a specific use is the revenue foregone from the best alternative use. Revenue foregone from the best alternative use is called the "opportunity cost." If labor is unemployed, there is no revenue from its alternative use. From a macro-economic point of view, that is, if we consider the interest of the country, if there is unemployment, the social cost of labor in that country is nil. Employing a person in a job will mean addition to income without sacrificing any income, since that person was not employed before. There are some other economic concepts defined in economic theory leading to the same conclusion, for example, the linear programming model. This model uses mathematical techniques to allocate scarce resources to production in order to maximize an objective function. In the optimum solution, the model assigns costs to the

---

12 Murat Çizakça, *Comparative Evolution of Business Partnerships*, Leiden: E.J. Brill, 1996, pp. 3–9.
13 Murat Çizakça, *A History of Philanthropic Foundations*, Istanbul: Boğaziçi University Press, 2000, p. 262.
14 In technical terms, the wage of an employee (price of labor in the market) should equal the marginal revenue of their production.

scarce resources that are used in maximizing the objective function. These costs are called "shadow prices." It is a mathematical fact that any input that is not fully employed (that is, if there is unemployment) has zero shadow prices. Using everyday terminology, if there is unemployment of labor in a country, socially labor has zero cost.[15] Benefiting from the linear programming model, we may state that the welfare of the economy cannot be maximized if we assign a cost to labor. That also means that if there is unemployment, the participative and revenue-sharing models we described above are more appropriate.

The present form of capitalism can be defended on the grounds that labor markets are not fully competitive, that collective bargaining, not perfect competition, is effective in the determination of wages. Wages determined under collective bargaining practices are not market wages, and since they are above the market wages, unemployment is the natural cause of it. According to capitalist theory, there would be no unemployment if the free market economy rules were applied: that is, full employment will be achieved in all the markets. When full employment is reached in this way, labor costs to companies would be the same as their *alternative costs* and *shadow costs*. This defense is the strongest evidence for the inconsistency between the free market economy and the aspirations of humanity. This is because equilibrium wages would be realized at levels lower than the current ones, and many employees would have to struggle for survival with these lower wages. For this reason, the collective bargaining system was developed due to the ineffective functioning of the market mechanism. However, the collective bargaining mechanism has created a new set of problems and issues, as we have mentioned in previous chapters.

Costs and hazards of unemployment are not only economic; they are multi-dimensional. Unemployed people may feel depressed, their families might break apart, the education of their children may deteriorate, and even their inclination toward crime may increase. The greatest destruction unemployment wreaks is on the personal identity of the unemployed. Unemployed people lose their self-confidence and their zest for life.

It is worth noting that unemployment has become one of the most significant problems of our times. Unemployment is among the most significant problems in the US, in Europe and in developing countries. It seems that it will be the most significant problem in the future as well. Capitalism considers labor as a

---

15 In linear programming, the contribution of the factors of production to the objective function is measured by "shadow prices." The "shadow price" of an input factor is positive if it is used fully, and zero if not utilized fully.

cost item. Labor must compete with machines and robots to gain employment. Machines and robots are becoming more and more skillful, displacing labors' jobs and functions in the process of production. Perhaps we should come to the understanding that labor is not a means of production, it is the goal of production. Capitalism and expanding globalization cannot satisfy people's employment aspirations. The Universal Declaration of Human Rights can be perceived as a reflection of the aspirations of people all over the world. Article 23, item 1 of the Universal Declaration of Human Rights states that: "Everyone has the right to work, to free choice of employment, to just and favorable conditions of work and to protection against unemployment."

Social Benefits

Similar to the social costs that are not reflected in the markets, there are social benefits that are not reflected either. The buyers in the market will base their purchasing decisions on the benefits that they themselves derive from the products they purchase. They would not consider the benefits that society gains when they buy a product or service. For a buyer to purchase a product or service, the price of the product or the service purchased must be lower than the benefits that accrue to him.[16] On the other hand, the consumption of some goods or services creates benefits to society in addition to the benefits that they create for the consumer. Services such as education, culture and health are among the most significant examples of this. In their purchasing decisions, individual consumers only consider the benefits that accrue to themselves; they naturally ignore the benefits that accrue to society. Consequently, the supply and consumption of educational, cultural and health services will be lower than they might be. This is the reason for the free or subsidized provision of educational, cultural and health services.

The twenty-first century will be a century in which the importance of human capital will increase and investment in human capital will be one of the most significant concerns of societies. In order to increase the value of human capital, societies will need to make significant investments in educational, cultural and health services.[17] Expenditures on educational, cultural and health services are not expenses but rather investments in human capital. Leaving

---

16 In technical terms, the marginal utility of consumption received from each product must be proportionate to their prices. In other words, for each product consumed marginal utility obtained for each amount spent must be equal.

17 It is currently believed that gross domestic product (GDP) is not sufficient to measure the well-being of people. For that reason, since 1990, the Human Development Index has been

these investments to the decisions of those who have the resources and handling these investments within the market mechanism will deprive humanity of the most significant form of capital, which is human capital. In the capitalist system, educational, cultural and health services are increasingly privatized and left to market mechanisms.[18] These privatizations contain a significant threat. Governments advocate and promote privatization by decreasing the quality of the public services in the areas of education, culture and health. There is even a technical term for reducing the quality of public services in order to induce privatization: "privatization by indirect means."

There is another advantage to providing education publicly. Those who receive these services using publicly provided resources will be indebted to society and will assume responsibility for the further development of human capital. These services are society's investments in individuals. When society provides the investment, it also has a right to the fruits of these investments. Intellectual property[19] created through these investments can be claimed to belong to society. On the contrary, in the current globalization movement, intellectual property is individualized, with all the income from the intellectual property belonging to the individuals. On the other hand, most belief systems advocate that material and spiritual privileges provided to individuals by the Creator are not their own property and assign them the responsibility to share them with others. This concept will later be elaborated upon when the *new economic design* is analyzed.

The number of consumed goods and services whose benefits not only accrue to the individual purchasing it but to society in general is actually more than one realizes. People want to live in nice environments, where welfare is widespread, income is equitably distributed and consumption opportunities are more equal. Even this claim seems to be contrary to the value structure of capitalist system. On the other hand, this is an opinion which is shared by most of the belief systems and religious systems all around the world; in fact, this is a claim which is widely supported even in our times. It is a common belief in many cultures that any affluent person cannot have inner peace, or sleep easily, if there is one who must go to bed hungry. The capitalist system

---

used instead. This index considers life expectancy, literacy, education and health standards in addition to GDP. The index was developed by Nobel Prize winner Amartya Sen.

18 How supervision systems will be utilized after privatization of these services should also be considered. Governments have a very important duty of supervision, generally, in the services which are monopolistic in nature and in strategic sectors. For that reason, supervisory authorities are created.

19 Intellectual property includes copyrights, patents, trademarks, industrial designs, printed circuits and geographical indicators. Trade-related intellectual property rights are under protection on the TRIPS Agreement.

has perceived these as types of altruistic considerations, claiming that they are in the domain of social considerations.

Conclusion

In summary, under its widely acknowledged assumptions, the market economy's principles provide correct guidance to the economy only when all the costs and benefits are fully reflected in market prices. Costs and benefits are costs and benefits that accrue to the buyer and seller and also the costs and benefits to society resulting from the production and consumption of goods. If all the costs are not reflected in the prices, supply and consumption will increase. This increase in supply and consumption can cause irreparable harm to the environment and nature. On the contrary, if all the benefits are not reflected in the prices, demand and consumption will be lower than the levels actually required. Social costs and social benefits are among the costs and benefits that are not fully reflected in prices. Distortions caused by this are among the most important problems to be resolved in the twenty-first century.

Currently, our planet is facing a serious threat due to the overconsumption of many products. The greenhouse effect is leading to global warming, glaciers are melting, the path of the Gulf Stream current is shifting, the ozone layer is depleting, and rainforests are being destroyed. As a result of all this, nature is fast losing its ability to regenerate itself. The consequences are worse than previously supposed.

In addition, opportunities for realizing people's aspirations are jeopardized due to our devoted adherence to the market mechanism and privatization, which inhibits the provision of educational, cultural and health services at the levels desired.

All these weaknesses and limitations of the market system are due to its lack of ability to account for social costs and benefits. This does not mean that the market mechanism is a system that has failed. The market mechanism has virtues as well. At least individual choices are reflected in the prices in the markets. The Soviet socialist system failed because it could not reflect individual choices in production and consumption. However, there is also a need for increased awareness about the weaknesses and limitations of the market mechanism. The market mechanism should be applied in a way that reflects the aspirations of societies in regards to production and consumption. This is an important mission to realize in the twenty-first century.

Demand and Production:
The Theory and the Reality

*The cause of human suffering is undoubtedly found in the thirsts of the
body and in the illusions of worldly passion. If these thirsts and illusions
are traced to their source, they are found to be rooted in the intense desires
of physical instinct ... If desire, which lies at the root of all human passion,
can be removed, then passion will die out and all human sufferings will
be ended. This is called the Truth of the Cessation of Suffering.*

(The Buddha)

In previous chapters, we have stated that the prices determined in the free
markets by the supply and demand rule, under the free will of the participants
of the markets, guide the free market economies. The goods and services
supplied in the markets are the goods and services produced by the production
process and demanded by consumers. Economics has a special treatment of
production and demand. Production of goods and services and the demand
for these goods and services are studied under the production and demand
models to which we now turn.

We need to recall the economics assumptions about the markets that we
pointed out before: economic theory assumes the perfect competition to exist in
the markets.[1] Only if the perfect competition criteria are met may the markets
lead to equitable prices – prices that would not lead to exploitation – and
guide the economy in a way desired by society. Let us specify the conditions
the markets need to satisfy in order to be classified as perfectly competitive
markets. There would have to be large number of small buyers and sellers on

---

1 Perfect competition is an economic model that describes a hypothetical market form in which
   no producer or consumer has the market power to influence prices. Perfect competition would
   lead to a completely efficient outcome. Perfect competition leads to a market equilibrium in
   which all resources are allocated and used efficiently to serve the interest of the society.

the market, each of them so small that its actions could have no significant impact on the market prices. In economic terminology, the participants are "price takers." Goods and services traded on the markets must be identical; that is, there would be no product differentiation. All buyers and sellers would have to have complete information on all relevant facts about the market. There would need be no barrier to entry; that is, all participants would have to have access to products and production technology, plants, and all the means needed. So any participant of the market may enter or exit at their free will. There would have to be full mobility of resources. All buyers and sellers would have to act independently in seeking their own interest: there would be no collusion or no cartels. The prevailing economic theory is constructed on these hypothetical assumptions and the conclusions of the theory are relevant only under these assumptions. Under these assumptions, the prices determined in the markets will guide the economy in the interest of the public at large.

Demand Theory in Economic Science

Demand theory studies the factors affecting the demand of buyers, and how these factors influence demand. In its study, economic theory benefits from the models it develops, again under some assumptions. Using these models, economic theory tries to reach some conclusions.

Economics assumes that people consume in order to increase their utility. This is the basic assumption of the economic theory of demand. In order to consume, people need to buy goods and services. This desire to buy creates the demand for goods and services. Getting or increasing utility is the result of two acts. The first one is purchasing, the second one is consumption.[2] The demand theory does not separate these two acts. It assumes that purchasing something results in consumption and this consumption increases utility. But, for many products, purchasing and consumption may differ significantly. There are such goods and services that just purchasing them may not be sufficient for consuming them. The act of consumption may require the development of talents and tastes to get utility. Anyone who has cash can buy a CD and listen to it, or go to a concert. But he may not be able to derive satisfaction or utility if he has not developed his appreciation or tastes accordingly. We may claim that the utility derived from consumption of a good and service may depend on the amount of investment in one's ability to consume. And this investment may be

---

2   Since capitalism creates its own type of people, today's people buy irrespective of consumption. They derive utility just from the act of purchasing.

personal, social, or cultural investment. In fact, there may be cases where the social and cultural investment made in the individual may increase his utility by reducing the amount of consumption of some products or services.

In economic theory, most of the products consumed cease to exist; they vanish, like eating an apple. But, in real-life cases, there are products that increase in amount or quality as one consumes them. Perhaps the consumption act itself converts them to investments in ability to consume. Perhaps, the act of consumption is not instantaneous but long-lasting, and may even grow in time. The important thing is that perhaps cultural settings may determine what will happen to the products consumed.

In real life, the marketing function very well knows the difference between the act of purchasing and the act of consumption. They try to manipulate the perceptions of people in order to increase the demand for the product.

Another important point to mention here is that we do not have to buy many of the things we consume or things we get utility from. These things may naturally exist, may be bought by others, may be produced by others, or may be provided by the society we live in. We may get utility from a decent environment, beautiful nature, happy people around us. In fact, we may not be getting utility from consumption if we are *not* surrounded by such an environment. But economic theory ignores most of the sources of utility and satisfaction that are not traded in the markets. Because of this ignorance, in order to produce goods and services that are traded in the markets, the system may pollute, destroy, or demolish the environment. The destruction of the environment itself may create new demands for products like clean water and clean air. These help capitalism to flourish: capitalism grows as it creates solutions to the problems it creates. The social environment is not hurt less by capitalist motives of self-interest. As the income gap between rich and poor widens in the society, social pollution increases also. Increasing poverty in society creates many social and health problems, for example, more frequent epidemics. These again can be a source of opportunity by creating demands for new products and services. Capitalism may convert these demands to profits. Let us continue our tour of demand theory.

Assumptions of Demand Theory

In demand theory, consumers are assumed to derive utility from consumption. In economic parlance, utility is a function of consumption. The theory assumes a specific functional relation to exist between consumption and utility. In order to understand the strengths and the limitations of the theory, it is important to understand the assumptions about the relation between consumption and utility derived from consumption. The theory is based on two basic assumptions:

- The utility derived from the consumption of a product increases as you consume more of it. The more you consume, the higher the utility you get. That is additional consumption of any product contributes positively to the utility obtained.[3]

- As more of a product is consumed, its contribution to the total utility decreases.[4]

As we have explained in Chapter 2, the first assumption above means that people never reach a consumption saturation point. This assumption defines the individual as perceived by capitalism as someone who is always craving for more.[5] The prototype of capitalism is perhaps the basic problem behind most of the problems the world is facing. But, these are the assumptions made in the demand theory as we will explain.

In demand theory, under these assumptions, the utility map of an individual is obtained. Basically, these maps show that, as the level of consumption increases, the utility the individual derives from consumption also increases. The limit to the utility individuals will be able to reach is determined by the amount of money they have – which is called the "budget of the individual." People will allocate their budgets to the purchase of different products in such a way to reach the maximum level of utility.

There is an implicit assumption here also. It is assumed in the theory that, in the purchasing transaction the products received are a source of utility, that is, bliss; but the price paid is disutility, a burden. And, it is assumed that the price

---

3   In technical terms this assumption means the marginal utility of consumption is always positive.

4   In technical terms this assumption means the marginal utility decreases as the consumption increases.

5   There is an assertion that the most important job of the twenty-first century is that of determining how to convert the material hunger of men into moral satisfaction.

and the utility are not interrelated. The theory does not consider any relation that may exist between the price and the utility derived from the product. In actual life, the price itself may be a source of utility. People may take pride from paying a high price for especially prestigious goods. That is, the price paid in some cases may itself be bliss. The price on the market may have other functions than just being a burden on the consumer budget. The price of a product may be a very reliable source of information about the quality and the attributes of the product.

Under these assumptions and under the model built, these are the conclusions of the economic theory of demand:

- In the optimum budget allocation, the consumer will get the same amount of utility when he spends his last bit of money on any product available.

- If the price of one product is to decrease, the real income of the consumer will increase since they will be able to reach the previous level of utility with less expenditure and will have additional money to spend on any other product of their choosing.[6]

- The increase in the real income of the consumer will grant them a chance to purchase more of the products they purchase. That is, they would be able to buy more of the product whose price has not changed.

- When the price of a product declines, the product becomes cheaper compared to others; therefore the consumer will buy more of that product.

As we see, the conclusions of the economic theory are quite logical: when your income increases, you purchase more, and when something gets cheaper, you buy more of it. Economic theory recognizes some exceptions to these conclusions. When the income of an individual increases, he would be tempted to purchase less of inferior products; and when the price of a luxury good decreases, he may buy less of it. These are the conclusions reached by economic theory, under the above assumptions, using the scientific approach. If the assumptions change, the results would also be expected to change.

---

6   Real income indicates a constant level of purchasing power.

Utility and Needs

Economic theory defines goods and services to be the source of utility for consumers. Goods and services are bought to satisfy the needs. That is, behind the utility derived from goods and services lies the needs of the individuals. In scientific studies, it is claimed that there may be a hierarchy of need. Unless the needs at the lower levels are satisfied, the upper-level needs may not be important. The hierarchy of needs was ranked by acclaimed American psychologist Abraham Maslow as follows:

1.   physiological needs,

2.   safety needs,

3.   love and belonging needs,

4.   self-esteem needs,

5.   self-actualization needs, and

6.   curiosity and expression needs.

This hierarchy of needs provides strong insights to the structure of needs. But it is a simplification of the complex nature of human feelings and emotions, which may change not only in their types but also in their intensities. Needs may vary from simple likes, to wants, desires, addictions, and passions. The feelings that lie behind the needs are like a stormy ocean. It may be very difficult to set rules for emotions and needs. Sometimes pride, honor, or dignity may not have any meaning for people living in poverty, who cannot even feed themselves. But on other occasions, pride, honor and dignity may be more important than life or death.

The focal point of the analysis of demand should not be the products and services assumed to be consumed, but the needs they satisfy and the emotions they meet in human beings. The source of demand is these needs and emotions. Today, an understanding of these is the guide to product differentiation. Customers may pay more for environmentally friendly products, or if they believe that those who produce the product are paid a decent wage. Customers may prefer the products of socially responsible firms. The way to understand demand is via understanding the customer's emotions, needs, values and faith. The emotions may range from affinity to hate and disgust. When you try to meet and satisfy them, they may intensify and become violent. More important than all, exorbitant consumption may be a source of shame. Some people may get satisfaction not from consumption, but from restraining themselves from consumption. In many religious faiths, the source of needs and desires is the *nefs*.[7] People are recommended not to obey the desires of the *nefs* and to control it. The ability to keep the *nefs* under control is considered the way to perfection. On the other hand, the focal point of attention of the capitalist system is the products and services in the economy. Companies make profits producing these goods and services, and consumers increase their utility by consuming them.

In our changing world, it may be more appropriate to view goods and services as the means to satisfy individuals' needs within their value structures. The same product of service may satisfy different needs and very different goods and services may satisfy the same need. An automobile may meet the transportation needs of one person, and the prestige need of someone else, and the rationality desire of another person. From this viewpoint, to give someone a book, a CD, or a theatre ticket would serve the same purpose.

If we were to generalize, the complex structure of individuals' feelings and emotions constitute their characters. This personality or character is an identity. Individuals try to be consistent in their behavior with this identity they find fit for themselves. In all their purchasing operations, they may want to attain a harmony between their identity and the identity of the products they buy; or they may want to enhance their identity with the products they consume. The relation between a product's identity and personal identity may also take various forms.

Currently, goods and services constitute an identity by means of their design, brand name, style and price. And design, brand name, style and price are the factors that influence customer demand. As there are great varieties of customer identities, there would have to be many product or service identities to fit customers' identities.

Here, we need to note a very important aspect of product and service prices. As mentioned above, economic theory considers the price of a product or service to be a burden the customer must bear in order to obtain that product or service. In recent developing market conditions, price is an integral part of the product's identity, not an independent factor to consider. The product's

---

7   In Islam, a person has a *nefs* (physical body, self and ego as opposed to spirit) and *ruh* (soul and spirit).

price must be in harmony with the other factors to contribute to the identity of the product. In fact, price has an additional function of conveying information about the identity of the product.

To summarize, in the developing world order, goods and services are made up of two components: the hardware and the software of the product. The hardware of a product is its tangible and functional structures. The software is its design, brand name, style, perceived qualities and similar properties that contribute to the image of the product. Both the hardware and software of products together make up the identity of the products. Goods and services which are very similar in their hardware may be very different in terms of their software. When people buy goods and services, they buy both of the components of the product. Either one of these two components would meet different needs of individuals. As we will discuss below, the hardware and software of the products are produced differently by different factors of production. In fact, the same producer need not produce them in the same place. Both of these components possess different competitive positions. Even if the hardware of products suits the perfect competition criteria of the market economies, their software may not fit those criteria at all.

As an example, let us take a shirt into consideration. Imagine that the prices of shirts range from 10 units to 450 units, depending on their identity and the image they project of the customer. A purchaser who buys an expensive, prestigious shirt pays for the prestige also.[8]

In short, buyers' demand for products is much more complicated than the way they are treated in economic theory. The conclusions reached by economic theory under the assumptions made are applicable only if those assumptions are relevant. The conclusions would change by changing assumptions. It is obvious that as world conditions change, the need to make changes in economic theory will increase.

---

8   The Nike shoe company designed its sport shoes in Oregon, manufactured them in Indonesia paying 14 cents an hour to woman laborers, and sold the finished product in the US for $49–125, which had cost $5.95 to produce: Walter LaFeber, *Michael Jordan ve Yeni Kuresel Kapitalizm* [*Michael Jordan and New Global Capitalism*] (translated by Aysel Morin), Istanbul: Cep Kitapları, 156/21, 2001 (Yüzyıl Dizisi), p. 103.

Production Theory in Economic Science

We have explained above that economic theory assumes that people derive utility from the consumption of goods and services. The way these goods and services are produced, the way the limited production factors are allocated to the production process, and the way the income generated from production is shared by the input factors are also in the domain of study of the economic theory.

FACTORS OF PRODUCTION

In economic theory, the production of goods and services is realized by the factors of production. Production units may be people, firms, or companies. The production units convert the raw materials, services and parts they obtain from other units into products or services. In other words, they produce their products by increasing the value of raw materials, services and parts purchased from other production units. This increase in value is called "value added." In economics, production means adding value to something, that is creating value. Naturally, this is applicable for raw materials, services and parts used in the process of production and also for the products produced. Raw materials, services and parts purchased in the process of production are produced in other production units of the economy. In a production unit, value added is created by the factors of production used in this unit. In economic theory, production factors are grouped symbolically under land, labor and capital. The two concepts we have tried to explain here – *production factors* and *value added* – are the key concepts upon which we will construct our arguments.

For further clarification of these key concepts, we need to highlight another aspect of them. The total of the value added created in all production units of a country constitutes the *national income* of that country. The value added of each production unit in a country is its contribution to the national income. In other words, the value added of any unit in the economy is the income generated by that unit. This amount of income generated is the income to be shared by the factors of production of that unit. The way this income is shared by the factors shows differences depending on the economic system they use. In the capitalist system, workers get their share in the form of wages, the lenders get their share in the form of interest, and the remaining amount of value added belongs to the capitalist (or entrepreneur) in the form of profit. In the capitalist system that we use today, wages and interests are the cost factors of production. When these costs are greater than the value added created by its operations, the production unit may incur a loss. When there is a loss it is the loss of the capitalist owner. It is believed that the driving force of the capitalist economy is the capitalist owner or entrepreneur's passion for profit.

Let us take an overview at the income-sharing mechanisms of other economic systems. In the communist system, value is created by labor and labor alone. For that reason, only labor is entitled to the income generated in the operations. In labor-managed market economies, capital is purchased from the competitive financial markets and whatever is left from the value added after the payment of interest belongs to labor as its income. Workers share their share of income among themselves according the quality and intensity of their involvement. In the Islamic *mudaraba* system, the value added is shared by the provider of labor (*mudarıb*) and the provider of capital (*rab-el-mal*), according to pre-determined ratios.

After these short explanations on the value added of the economic units, we can discuss the production model of each economic theory.

As mentioned above, in the capitalist system, the factors of production are symbolically considered to be land, labor and capital. Land in this classification represents the gifts of nature such as land, rain, climate and location. These may be natural features, or may be artificially created or developed. When artificially developed, they may take the form of investment. Labor represents the human factor, which range from the physical qualities to dexterity and mental qualities of human beings in production.

Throughout history, the participation of this human factor in production has changed in its form and content. For many centuries in history, workers were slaves who could be raised or purchased in slave markets. They were the type of investment like a machine in a production unit. The slave markets behaved similarly to the other goods markets; demand and supply determined the price of slaves. And these prices guided the economies. Today, slavery is somewhat abolished. People participate in production with their labor, which has come to mean the time spent by the human factor in the process of production. Depending on the economic system, the role of labor and the form of its participation in production differs. In the capitalist system, not slaves but the time of labor is traded; therefore labor is considered to be a cost factor.[9] In some economic systems, labor time is also believed not to be a thing

---

9   Jaroslav Vanek calls it the "negative sign syndrome" and believes that it is the source of many problems faced in capitalist systems: *General Theory of Social Systems* <http://ecommons.library.cornell.edu/handle/1813/642>.

to be traded in the markets. These systems believe that labor should take a share from the value added of the production unit. In the past 20–30 years, the attributes of labor are changing fast. A new definition of labor in the current capitalist system is "human capital", and as human capital, labor possesses a "portfolio of competencies" that is offered for sale. Labor competencies are developed by making investments in human capital. This investment in human capital is partly made by the production units and partly by labor itself. Labor sells appropriate competencies to those who need it. The sale itself may or may not depend on time duration. It is believed that the recent developments have given people greater power to control their labor. Of course these are relevant to mental labor.

When we look at the form of labor, it has changed in time also. Historically, labor meant physical effort; that is, labor participated in the production process by physical power: digging ditches, breaking stones, carrying loads and working in the fields. With the invention of the steam engine, brute power lost its importance as machines replaced people in many tasks. Labor had to develop new traits and capabilities in order to be employed. In the era following the invention of steam engines, labor skills and dexterity gained importance. Labor created employment opportunities for themselves by outperforming machines and equipment in jobs needing high skills and dexterity. Here we need to mention that labor in this era has become competitive with machines. As a cost factor, labor's contribution to production had to be cheaper than the contribution of the machines.

Recently, new dimensions are being added and are emerging in the competencies of labor. These are the accumulated experience, constructiveness, imagination, value structure, vision and creativity of the people. These competencies of the human factor in production units create the design, brand name, style and image that constitute the products' software. These new competencies of labor change the concept of using labor. Previously, when labor was used, the laborer's time end energy used to be consumed. But now, when a laborer works, he accumulates experience and knowledge, increases his imagination, broadens his vision, and contributes to his value structure. These increase his competencies. In the new production processes, labor may not be a cost, it may be *human capital* which increases through working.[10]

---

10 This was partly the case in the development of skills and dexterity. Artisans had to work for a long time to learn their traits. But its importance has increased when products were separated into hardware and software.

Let us turn to the production factor definition of economics: the third factor the economy defines is capital. Capital may represent assets such as machinery and equipment and physical space or money invested in the production unit. In the capitalist system, the capitalist provides the production units the funds they use in order to buy the factory, the machinery and the equipment. The owner of the production unit is the capitalist. As the owner of the production unit, the capitalist runs the production system in his own interest to earn profit: he makes all the decisions, and is the one who is responsible for the results of those decisions. Other factors of production are bought or hired somehow from their respective markets. After paying the prices of all input factors (factors of production), the capitalist owner is entitled to the company's profits The capitalist may share some of his authority with the managers he hires. But even in that case, the capitalist owner is the principal and the managers are agents who run the unit to serve the owner's interests. The principal and agents have interests that may conflict. *Principal and agent conflict* is an important issue in capitalist theory. In running the company in the owner's interest, production units may lay off labor. And, when there are mass lay-offs, the owner's profit may increase, but in many cases the value added may decrease. In the capitalist system, what is important is the capitalist owner's profit.

Economic science has defined some other production factors as times and needs have changed. The most important one is *entrepreneurship*. The definition of entrepreneurship has helped the capitalist economy to justify the profits the capitalist owners were seeking. As we have explained in previous chapters, economic theory has proven that the prices developed in free market economies guide these economies in society's interest. This means production proceeds at the minimum costs, and there would be no profit over and above the prices paid to the production factors. In such an environment, there would be no profit. But of course the markets must be perfect markets in the way the theory has defined them. In perfect markets, that is, the perfectly competitive markets, all the production factors would earn the incomes they deserve and there would be no profits. Profits in these markets are signs of exploitation. On the other hand, when entrepreneurship is considered as another input factor, one can easily claim that the profit of the production unit is the return to the capitalist's entrepreneurial skill. Entrepreneurship is a very important factor. It is one of the driving forces of economic growth and development. Innovations and the entrepreneurial spirit go hand in hand. Entrepreneurial skill is profit oriented. The profit motive feeds the entrepreneurial spirit. Under these assertions, profits we observe are not signs of exploitation but the return for entrepreneurial skills that serve the people at large. We can also consider these entrepreneurial skills as the return for the risk the entrepreneur assumes.

Another production factor is technology, which is the pool of all existing knowledge of production. Technology is somewhat similar to investments. Product, process and basic technology grow through investments in research and development. Those who develop technology by investments receive the ownership of their findings. Laws protect some of these ownership rights, such as through the patents obtained. As production factor inputs, these patents provide strong monopoly positions to their owners. These monopolistic positions also violate the assumptions of the perfect competition that is assumed to exist in the markets in economic theory. This has been quite an embarrassment for economic theory. But the economists who are the advocates of free market economies have eliminated the discomfort. Economists have claimed that investments in research and developments were the foundations of the economic advances. To promote the investments in research and development, their output – the patents – had to be protected. In their view, these patents and related rights introduced a new and a different type of competition, a competition which is also serving the interests of society.

In short, in capitalism, knowledge is not the common property of society, but is the private or corporate property of the capitalist who was instrumental in its creation. It is open for discussion whether the private or corporate ownership of this type of knowledge is serving the interests of the public or not.

Since we have explained the factors of production and the value added created by production, we may now study the production model of the prevalent economic theory and the results reached by using the model.

Production Function

Economic theory defines the production process as a "production function." There are two kinds of inputs to the production relation: the material inputs and the factor inputs (production factors). The output is the goods or services produced. But the production function is mostly defined in terms of production factors entering the production and the value added created. Therefore, the production function defines the value created by the production factors used. As we have said before, the production factors the economy considers are land, labor and capital. Since the amount of land is assumed to be fixed, the production function in economics defines the value created by labor and capital. As we have mentioned above, technology is an important factor in production. But, since technology develops in time, it is constant at any moment in time. Therefore the production functions are defined under a given technological environment. Economic theory tries to incorporate technological advances into the model when economic development is in concern.[11] In short, economic theory believes that the product produced is a function of the labor employed and the machinery (including robots and computers) used. Economic theory also makes important assumptions about the form of production functions, and reaches some conclusions under these assumptions. The most common assumptions made are the following:

- In the process of production, labor and capital are substitutable. They are competitive factors that can be used in production.

- Production increases as more and more labor and capital are used.[12]

- When the quantity of one factor is increased while the other is kept constant, the productivity of the factor, which is held constant, increases.[13]

Under these assumptions, the conclusion of the economic theory is: under the optimal solution, the last unit of money spent in the purchase of any production factor should produce the same amount of product. This conclusion is applicable to any of the production factors, whatever they may be. The amount of labor and capital to be used in production will be guided by this rule.

Putting this into everyday language, all this theory of production states is that labor and machines are rivals in the production process to minimize the cost of production in order to maximize the profits of the capitalist owners. Labor is a dispensable factor of production. Additional money to be spent for labor or capital should produce the same output. These rules are applicable not only to the final products, but also to any services including the administrative services of the production units. Today, machines are becoming more intelligent day by day; competencies of robots are increasing; computers are able to do jobs with the accuracy and speed once only found in labor. In the process of production, human beings must compete with them. In the process of production, if human beings cannot develop skills to do things that cannot

---

11 In these studies the general assumption is that, technological advance provides a chance to produce more with the same inputs. One topic well discussed is the labor or capital intensity of technological advances.

12 In technical parlance, the marginal physical product of each factor is positive.

13 In technical parlance, the marginal physical product of the factor held constant increases as the use of other factor increases.

be done by these fast developing machines, robots and computers, they face losing their jobs or experiencing wage cuts. This is one of the reasons for the increasing unemployment in the developed and developing countries.

Perhaps the main reason for the unemployment and income distribution problems we are facing is that we consider labor and machinery as competitive factors, that is, as rivals. If the laborer combines their talents with the rapidly increasing capabilities of machines, robots and computers; if they uses the increases in the capabilities of machines, robots and computers to expand and develop their own talents, they may be able to produce more by working less. That is, a system which does not consider labor and machinery to be rivals may give a chance to labor to share more of the income generated in production by working less. One possible way to accomplish this is by constructing a system in which laborers own the necessary machines, robots and computers. Labor-managed market economies may provide a solution also by reducing working hours to eliminate unemployment.

In a capitalist economy, in the near future, if robots alone accomplish production, if capitalists own all the robots, and if the laborers are unemployed, who will purchase the completed products? A system where the goods and services are produced by robots will be sustainable if and only if every one has free access to robots and the products. Perhaps capitalism will transform itself into such a system in the future.

Recent Developments in Production and Production Factors

As we have said before when we were analyzing the demand theory, today the definition of goods and services has changed dramatically. Goods are not the physical products that we had before. Similarly, services are not the discrete products we previously provided the customer. The products and services together are the things the customer receives, that is, the things that satisfy the needs of the customers. From this point of view, goods and services constitute a whole with their structure, design, image, fashion and price. This totality provides it a product identity. That is, products have an identity that integrates their hardware and software.

We can say that the factors that make up a product's identity are its structure, design, quality, brand name, image and price. All these factors must be in harmony and interact with each other to create a synergy that enhances the product's identity. All these parts are produced in the production process separately, but in harmony. They must be produced separately because the production factors producing them are different. If we are to simplify and generalize, the hardware and the software of the products are produced separately by different production factors. The production of the products' software is getting more and more important under the trends we live in.

Presently, the hardware and the software of the products are produced in different countries due their different factor endowments. The production factors for the products' hardware are labor, capital and know-how. As might be noticed, the factors of hardware production are very similar to the classical production factors we have described above, with one significant difference: the know-how. If we are to generalize, developed countries are rich in terms of capital and know-how. But both know-how and capital can be transferred to any country where the production is to be carried out. Labor, on the other hand, is abundant in some developing countries. China, India and many Southeast Asian countries are good examples of countries with abundant labor. Since labor is abundant and cheap in some developing countries and since it is costly and undesirable to provide free mobility to laborers, the hardware of the products are produced in those developing countries.

The production factors of the products' software are "intellectual properties" and the information channels. Intellectual properties are designs, patents, trademarks and images created by control of and dominance in the information channels. In the *new economic design*, all these intellectual properties can only be used by their owner and these rights are very well protected by the laws and the institutions of the new world.[14] These rights, their protection and the results of the protection are discussed in a later chapter. However, there are two important aspects of intellectual properties that need to be mentioned here. First, all these intellectual properties are produced and possessed by a human element in production. Second, the only way to develop intellectual properties is by making investments in human capital and technology. All intellectual properties are created by the creativity, constructiveness, imagination, visions, dreams, value structures and other capabilities of human beings. That is, the products' software is produced by intellectual properties like designs, patent, trademark and image; intellectual properties, on the other hand, are produced by human capital using their creativity, constructiveness, imagination, visions, dreams, value structures and other capabilities of human beings. Developed

---

14 Intellectual properties are protected by the TRIPS (Trade Related Intellectual Property Rights) agreement and the WTO (World Trade Organization) acts for the enforcement of the agreement.

countries are rich in the intellectual properties developed so far. These intellectual properties are well protected by the *new economic design*. Developing countries cannot imitate them. Therefore, the software of most products is still produced mainly in the developed countries.

It is important to note here that the production functions of designs, patents, trademarks and images are very different from the classical production functions, and the assumptions made for the classical production functions are not suitable for them. We cannot say that additional efforts would result in more intellectual properties. More than efforts, it is the creativity, constructiveness, imagination, visions, dreams, value structures and capabilities, and in many cases the inspirations and aspirations, of human beings that are important. Perhaps not the quantity but the quality of the efforts made is more important. Perhaps the more important difference lies in the consequences of using the production factors. In classical production functions, when a resource is used it vanishes; in the production functions of the components of product software, the use of the production factors augments them. Creativity or the use of creativity may increase the capacity to be creative.

The separation of the production of hardware and software of products creates new opportunities and consequences. With recent developments, the hardware can be produced at anywhere in the world. The General Agreement on Trade and Tariff (GATT), signed in 1995, provides for the free flow of goods and services among countries. There is keen competition for production of the hardware of products among labor-abundant countries. Therefore, labor's wages sink to subsistence level. Supranational or global companies buy or develop the software, provide global capital and know-how, get their products produced in the labor-abundant and cheap labor countries, and then transport their products to countries where the markets are the most lucrative. In this process, the developed countries benefit from the "global opportunities." Countries with the cheap labor get the chance to feed their people at subsistence level. Another consequence of this new production design is the increasing unemployment in developing countries and their increasing poverty. The movements of hardware production to the labor-abundant countries do cause an increase in the unemployment in developed countries as well.

Today, production of technology is a strategically important area of production. In this type of production, knowledge is used to create knowledge; also, the efforts expended do not vanish but accumulate in the form of experience. The production factors of technology production are the knowledge and the brainpower of the people involved. This brainpower itself is produced by appropriate quality education. We should also note that the field of technology is also expanding. We have started talking about the technology of quality assurance, technology of image building, technology of brand creation, and technology of design creation.

The software of products is creating very strong monopolistic powers for multinational companies, while the dominance of trademarks is increasing world-wide. The main production factor behind all productions, software or hardware, is the people with their different qualities and capabilities; that is, their intellectual power. This is the reason for calling the production factors of the product's software its *intellectual properties*. Under the present circumstances, a product's intellectual properties provide great monopoly powers to those who possess them. For the time being, the developed countries possess these properties, and this is one reason why the gap between rich and poor is still widening. On the other hand, there is no reason why the developing countries should not be able to develop or obtain the intellectual properties they need.

Production and Income Sharing

As we have explained above, production factors produce income in the production process. This income is distributed to the production factors in a way designed in the system. In the capitalist system, the income generated is not shared by the production factors in any equal way. The capitalist owner owns the company and the company is run for the owner's benefit. All other factor inputs are purchased from the respective markets by paying their market prices. Whatever is left from the income created by the operations after payments to factor inputs is the return to the capitalist owner in the form of profit.

The amount of labor to be hired and the amount of capital to be allocated for operations will depend on the productivities of labor and capital. Labor is employed by, and capital assigned to, the company as long as the productivity of the last unit is equal to the price of labor and capital. At equilibrium, the productivities of the last hired labor and the last capital assigned are equal to the wages and the interest in the markets. The theory claims that by doing so, the incomes obtained by laborers and capital will be fair and will exhaust the total income generated. That is, according to the theory, the payments they get in market prices will be their fair shares of the total income. The conclusion of the theory is correct if the production functions proposed have certain mathematical properties. For income distribution to be fair, production functions must have the property of *constant returns to scale*. In the theory, this property is assumed to hold.[15] In real-life cases, the production functions may have increasing returns to scale or decreasing returns to scale. In such cases, one cannot talk about the fairness of the income distribution function of the capitalist system.

The capitalist system's main problem is that of treating labor as any other item that is bought and sold on the market, and considering it a cost factor. The laborer shares a common destiny with the company. They develop talents the company needs, and would be hurt and lose their job if the company fails. But in the capitalist system, the laborer does not participate in crucial decisions relating to the company's fate. There are strong arguments favoring labor's participation in decisions involving their companies' operations. The principles of participation are also spelled out in some theoretical works. The claim is that labor must participate in decision-making processes according to their quality and intensity of involvement. Such a participation and sharing a common destiny with the company will increase labor's motivation and effectiveness.[16]

The increased importance of the human element and human capital in production relations have also increased the importance of sharing the fruits of production. When labor shares the fruits of the activities participated in, its motivation would also increase. A motivated labor force may produce many times more than that of an unmotivated one. In fact, not only sharing the fruits of the operations and pride in the company's successes, but also sharing the results of failures, would be expected to make a contribution to raising the motivation of the workers in the company. Designing an effective income participation system is perhaps the first step in creating a comprehensive participative system in the work environment.

Economic systems have different schemes for the distribution of the income generated in the production process. The capitalist system relies on the markets and purchases the factors of production by paying their market prices. But in practice, various kinds of income participation schemes are used. ESOPs (Employee Stock Ownership Plans) and executive profit participation schemes are just two examples. But, the theory does not provide for any participation scheme due to its high regard for the market system. The main aim in the

---

15 If the production functions are of the constant return to scale type, when inputs increase by a certain percentage the output increases by the same percentage also.

16 Here we are using the effectiveness concept instead of efficiency. We believe the efficiency concept suits better the machinery and equipment used, not the human element.

capitalist system is cost reduction. And production factors are considered cost items. At the other extreme, in the labor-managed market economy system, the production units are owned by labor and all the other factors of production are purchased from their respective markets. The labor-managed market economy system model does not have a sharing mechanism for all the production factors involved. The system believes that the workers own the enterprise and workers should share the fruits of their common and combined effort by reaching a mutual agreement. Since workers' competencies, their positions in the organization and the involvement in production process differ, designing a sharing scheme is not an easy task.

In Islamic production institutions, income sharing generated by the cooperation between capital and labor is the rule. In Islam, interest is forbidden (*haram*), but income and profit is praised (*helal*). Economic activities seek to create as much income as possible. Islam believes in the partnership of labor and capital in production. At the time of the establishment of the partnership, labor and capital agree on the principle of sharing. Each of the production factors agrees to a certain percentage of the income generated. This sharing scheme creates a common purpose and common objective. The more they gain collectively, the more each production factor will get. In case of losses, labor loses its toil and the provider of capital loses their capital. Labor is not responsible for the capital lost.

We have given just a few examples of schemes of distribution of the income generated by productive operations. It will be the task of humankind in the twenty-first century to design just, equitable and fair distribution systems that will increase the motivation of all participants of production.

Although economic theory assumes that work is a burden people must bear in order to earn an income, people do gain, or may gain, non-pecuniary incomes from their work. The work itself may be a source of satisfaction, meeting the various needs of people. The working environment, being a member of a team with a specific objective and challenges, and the status the work affords may grant individuals a great amount of satisfaction that can be hardly measured in monetary terms. The status of people in work may be a means for them to reach the identity they see as fit for themselves. When we were discussing the demand theory, we claimed that people spend money in order to reach the identity they visualize for themselves. The identity one obtains from one's work may be an identity possessed without making any payment for it. The Japanese economy has benefited from the non-pecuniary income provided by work status. It is a unique economic system, which is difficult to classify either as a strictly capitalist system or a socialist one, and which benefits from the cultural characteristics of its people. Japanese culture assigns a very high social status to managers, especially the top managers of enterprises. These positions are regarded as very respectable positions. For that reason, those managers do not reap the same financial rewards as their American counterparts. This also reflects the income distribution in the society. In Japan, the average income of the top 20 percent of the population is only 2.9 times of the average income of the lowest 20 percent. In the US, this ratio is 9.1.[17]

Summary

The assumptions made in the models developed by the capitalist system on demand and production and the results reached under these assumptions do not suit today's economic conditions and requirements. But these assumptions and models are used to support the assertion that the capitalist market system guides the economy to serve the people's interests as a whole.

Capitalist economic models are built on the assumption that all the products that are goods and services are homogeneous. The theory considers only the hardware of goods and services. Today, products have split into two components: hardware and software. The software – the design, brand name, perceived quality and style – make a significant contribution to the identity of the products. People buy products to enhance their identities. For that reason, the software of products is becoming more important than their hardware. In capitalist theory, the product's price is the burden to bear to obtain it, and it is an independent aspect of the product. But in the real world, the product's price is an integral part of it, that contributes to the product's identity. Similarly, capitalist theory assumes the price of the product to be at the focal point of competition; that is, the competitors compete on price. Following current developments, the competition is not on price but on the creation of a product identity that will most suit the customer's identity. In other words, the competitive factor today is in the product's software.

In terms of production, capitalist economic theory considers only the production of the product's hardware. In theory, the production factors are symbolically grouped under land, labor and capital. But with contemporary developments, the production of goods and services has also split into two.

---

17 Robert Locke, "Japan, Refutation of Neo-liberalism," *Post-Autistic Economics Review*, issue no. 23, January 5, 2004 <http://www.btinternet.com/~pae_news/review/issue23.htm>.

Products' hardware and software are produced by different production factors under different conditions. The hardware of products is produced by labor, capital and knowledge. Usually, multinational companies provide the capital and know-how, and the hardware is produced in countries where labor is abundant and cheap. The software of products is produced mostly in developed countries. The production factor of software production is human capital. In the *new economic design*, brand names, copyrights, designs and similar aspects of the software are under the protection of the TRIPS agreement. Products' software gives the producers strong monopolistic power. There is fierce competition in the production of hardware by the labor-abundant and cheap countries; but strong monopolistic powers are granted to the software producers and intellectual property owners. For that reason, the potential for income generation is low in hardware production and high in software production. Again, for the same reason, income distribution in the world is worsening instead of improving.

One of the failures of the capitalist economic system is the distribution of income generated by the operations of the factors of production. Labor is assumed to be a cost factor that must compete with machines that are gaining in intelligence, and with robots and computers. This puts a real strain upon the workers. The capitalist economy is not able to unite all the production factors under a common objective. If the production factors are united under a common objective, there will be a better chance to serve humanity. Income-sharing systems and plans may help to unite today's disparate production factors under a common objective.

9

What is the Objective: Profit or Income?

O mankind! I bind you together towards one objective – the welfare of man. Toil together with mutual love and goodwill. May you share the comforts of life equally! May you accomplish your work with mutual accord and finally may you, in the pursuit of your ambition at all times; engage in working together with goodwill!

(Atharrva Veda 3.30.7 s: 224)

The most important question humanity is now facing is what is the purpose of our economic activities? Is it making profit or generating income? Of course, the main objective of economic activities is to serve people. But the question is, is it serving people by generating income, or is it making a profit by serving people? Serving people, is it the end or a means to reaching the end of making profit? The answer to this question is very important, since economic systems are built to reach the objectives set for them.

In the capitalist system, the objective of companies is the maximization of their profit. That is, when capitalist companies decide how much to produce, how much labor will be employed, how much they will borrow, how much capital they will raise and the prices they will set for their products – in other words, in all their decisions – their criterion is maximizing their profits. However, maximization of profit may not, and usually does not, correspond to the maximization of the income generated by the operations.

Economic theory has a dilemma here. In macroeconomic theory, the economic objective of nations is believed to be the maximization of national income. A country's national income is the sum of the factor incomes created by the operating units in the economy. The sum of profits is only a part of it. Of course, from the macroeconomic point of view, maximization of national income is not the only objective. More equitable income distribution and the elimination of unemployment and poverty are the most often mentioned economic objectives. Besides these economic objectives, countries have educational, health care and many other social objectives. Still, from the economic point of view, the objective of increasing income is the most important objective, and one which also serves the other objectives set for the country.

In spite of the variety of objectives, the objective of maximizing national income is so well accepted that, until very recently, countries were ranked according to their per capita national income in international statistics as an indicator of their development level and affluence. When we say the US's per capita income is above $30,000, this indicates that people in the US are prosperous compared to those in Turkey, where the per capita income is around $6,000. Recently, other criteria – for example, the Human Development Index – have been added in determining the well-being of the people in various countries. But the important point is that when we look at economic objectives from the countries perspective, the national income is what is important; not how much profit companies generate in those countries.

One question is still relevant: is it a dilemma to state that the objectives of companies is profit maximization while the objectives of countries is national income maximization? According to the capitalist free market economic theory, there may not be a dilemma. Under the assumptions of the capitalist free market economy, with prices developed in the perfectly competitive markets, theoretically, all the markets are cleared and factors of production receive their fair shares from the output. If the profits are considered as returns to entrepreneurial skills, entrepreneurs will get their proper share from the income generated. So the competitive markets provide full employment and fair returns to all factors. There may not be the problem of generating more or less income. But in real-life cases, there is a dilemma, since profit maximization may not necessarily lead to income maximization. In fact, companies' decisions for profit maximization may well reduce countries' national income. These issues will be discussed below.

The Definition of Profit

The concept of profit has different meanings in economics and accounting. In daily usage, the accounting concept is used.

In economics, profit is the residual income left after payments are made for all the factors of production. As we have mentioned above, in free market economies, profits are eliminated: the value added that is created by production is totally distributed to the production factors. Every one of the production factors receives its appropriate returns.

Economic theory assumes that firms earn revenues by selling the products they produce. As the firm sells more products, prices decline, so the contribution of additional sales to revenues will decrease. This additional revenue is called "marginal revenue" in economics. The *costs of the products sold* consist of both the costs of input materials and the factor costs. That is, the costs considered are costs of materials, labor, capital, and all relevant costs pertaining to the production and sale of the products. Again, under the assumptions of economics, the costs of additional production and sale follows first a decreasing, then an increasing trend. The additional cost is called "marginal cost" in economics. Since profit is the difference between revenues and costs, as it is commonly known, profit is maximized when the marginal revenue is equal to the marginal cost. This profit-maximization rule of economics is the best-known rule of economics. But, profit defined in this way is not something approved of in economics. Because, this profit earned is in excess of the earnings from the factor inputs. It is a return without an input; therefore it is not justified. As we have said before, some people justify this profit by considering it to be the return for entrepreneurial skill.

According to capitalist theory, profits arise only in monopolistic markets; or if the companies have monopolistic powers to manipulate the markets. The monopolistic markets in the theory are the markets where there is only one seller who sells a product, which has no substitute, with barriers to entry. Since the theory does not approve of profits defined in the above way, in capitalistic economies, there are rules and regulations to eliminate monopolies and to prevent the development of monopolistic power and to constrain monopolistic behaviors.

According to the capitalist free market economy, profits do not arise in purely competitive markets. In markets that are fully competitive, only a homogeneous product is traded among a great number of buyers and sellers, none of whom is able to influence the market. It is also assumed that in these markets there is no barrier to entry, transportation costs do not exist and there is full information on anything relevant to the markets. Under these assumptions, the competition among sellers will eliminate profits, costs will be minimum, and the price, marginal revenue, average cost and marginal cost will all be the same. In perfectly competitive markets, there would be no profit or income that is not deserved.

As we have explained in previous chapters, in real life, and under recent economic developments, it is not possible to talk about homogeneous products. We have explained that in the current conditions the products are split into two parts: hardware and software. Even if the products' hardware is the same, their software differentiates them. And we know that in the *new economic design* that has emerged after the GATT and the establishment of the WTO, the software of the products is fully protected in order to grant their owners monopoly power. We may say that in the *new economic design*, profit is the return on the products' software.

The accounting definition of profit is quite different. In accounting, profit is the income of the stockholders, the capitalist owners. Profit is defined as the difference between revenues and expenses. Accounting profit is defined very precisely. Expenses are defined as expired costs. And profits are determined by deducting expenses from the revenues that they help to generate.[1] In turn, the expenses are the costs of goods sold, selling and administrative expenses, and the interest expense. Labor is a cost item in production together with the material and overhead costs. As it is seen, accounting considers all factors other than the stockholders' capital to be cost factor. Therefore, accounting methodology is designed to determine the profit of the stockholder, who provides the capital stock of the enterprise. The other part of the capital, which is in the form of the company's debt, is an expense item also, called the "interest expense." From the accounting point of view, the profit is not something unearned. It is the return for the capital stock of the owner and the risk they take. The profit concept of everyday understanding is this accounting concept of profit.

The Definition of Value Added

Economics defines the income generated by production as "value added." The value added is the income generated by the production unit by using the factor inputs. Thus we can say that the value added is the sum of the incomes of the production factors.

The value added is calculated by deducting the payments made for the goods and services purchased from other production units from the revenues obtained from the sale of the goods and services produced. The value added in a production unit is distributed somehow to the factors of production of the

---

1   Technically in profit determination the "matching concept" is used. That is, in profit determination the expenses are matched with the revenues that they help to generate.

production unit. These factors of production are the workers (blue- and white-collar labor), lenders and the stockholders. Government gets its share from the value added through collecting income and corporate taxes. Viewed from this perspective, the value added is the sum of wages and salaries, interest paid, taxes and profit.

The value added is distributed to the factors of production under different schemes. In the capitalist system, wages, salaries and interest expenses are cost factors. The prices paid for these factors are determined either by collective bargaining, as it is the case in wages, or by the markets, as it is the case in interest expenses. When wages, salaries and interest expenses are deducted from the value added of the company, the company's profit is obtained.

What is important in our case is the owner's profit is only a part of the income produced by the factors of production in a firm.

The Conflict between Profit and Value-added Maximization

As stated above, in capitalist free market economies, firms try to maximize their profits. That is, profit maximization is the ultimate objective of the firm. The question we asked earlier was, would this profit maximization of firms lead to value-added maximization? The answer was, not necessarily. Under the economic conditions and trends we are living through, it does not lead to value-added maximization. In fact, companies may decrease the value they add in order to increase their profits.

The reason is quite obvious. In a capitalist economy, firms are owned by stockholders and are run for the interests of the stockholders. All decisions are made under a single goal: the goal of maximizing profit. As explained earlier, in profit maximization, wages and salaries are considered cost factors. The capitalist theory assumes that the revenues are not influenced by costs: costs and revenues are assumed to be independent of each other. In reality, the revenues may increase by increasing costs. There are many examples of companies who are able to charge higher prices for their products by claiming that they are paying *fair prices* to their suppliers, or paying *fair wages* to their labor. Another assumption of economic theory is that wages and the productivity of labor are independent. That means the motivation and efforts of the workers are not influenced by the money spent for better working conditions and the wages paid to the workers. In reality, in the new era where the labor has become transformed into *knowledge workers*, improvements in working conditions and salaries may increase the motivation and efforts of labor. Still another assumption made by the capitalist economic theory is that the situation is a *zero-sum game*. That is, what labor will gain will be the loss of the stockholder, and what labor loses is the gain of the stockholder. In reality, the case may not be a zero-sum game. If labor and capital work for a common purpose, the benefits to both may increase. But the capitalist theory does not allow for establishing any such common purpose. Only if the value added is shared by labor and capital might labor and capital also share a common objective. Considering labor a cost item may be the most significant error of the capitalist economic system.[2]

We should also consider the case where labor is not a cost factor. In such a case, labor would share the value added under a sharing mechanism. In such a case, labor and capital would share the same objective.

With today's technological developments, the capabilities of machines, robots and computers are increasing rapidly. On the other hand, we do not observe similar developments in the portfolio of workers' competencies. Companies are able to save costs by replacing labor with appropriate machines, robots and computers. But labor costs are the incomes of the laborers. When workers are laid off, profits may increase, but wage incomes will decrease; so would be the value added created by the company.

Due to today's technological developments and the profit maximization objectives of companies, the practice of mass labor layoffs are becoming to be an increasingly common phenomenon. These practices of capitalist firms are the main cause of the increasing unemployment and worsening income distribution in a period of increasing profits. We want to explain in summary the trends behind replacing labor in the production processes of firms. The topics we will discuss will be the developments in technology and the increasing capabilities of machines, robots and computers; and re-engineering, privatization and globalization.

Labor's Replacement by Robots

Capitalist theory does not differentiate between the nature of human beings and that of machines in the process of production. It considers labor and capital to be substitutable production factors. This means that labor on one hand and the machines, robots and computers on the other are rivals competing to

---

2   Let us recall that Jaroslav Vanek calls it the "negative sign syndrome".

be hired in the process of production. The competition between production factors applies to all kinds of factors. Over recent decades, machines have become more intelligent, robots more competent and computers much faster and more accurate. For example, just a few computers are able to do quickly and accurately the job of many administrative personnel; automated machines and robots can perform many functions that only people could perform before. In addition to the increase in their performance, the costs of automated machines, robots and computers have been decreasing rapidly. Since the objective of the capitalist owner is to reduce production costs in order to increase profits, all these developments provide opportunities for the firms to replace their workers with non-human counterparts. In fact, this process of replacement is understood to be driving investment in technology, which has become a world-wide trend. For more than a decade, companies have been investing in new technology and discharging their workers in thousands. This process of investing in new technology has in some cases increased the profits and profitability of the relevant companies, but in many cases it has reduced the value added generated by companies. This means their contribution to the national income has decreased in many cases.

A hypothetical example will contribute to the understanding of how the mechanism works. Let us assume a company that uses only the funds of the stockholder and no borrowed funds, creates 100 units of value added. Let us assume that 60 units of this value added are paid to workers as wages and 40 units is the profit. In order to make the example more striking, let us assume the stockholders increase their capital stock by 25 percent, invest in machinery and discharge half of their workers. Let us assume this operation increases the profits of the company by 50 percent. In such a case, profits will increase to 60 units, and the workers' income will be reduced to 30 units. As a result, profits and profitability will increase, but the value added will decrease from 100 to 90 units.

The hypothetical case above is not a fantasy, but a simplified version of hundreds of cases that we have encountered in real life. Recently, in both developed and developing countries, unemployment has been increasing due to this kind of replacement of labor with machines, robots and computers. Other trends have also been contributing to mass layoffs of labor by companies; namely, re-engineering, privatization and globalization, to which we now turn.

Re-engineering

According to its founders James Champy and Michael Hammer, re-engineering is the most important paradigm change since the Industrial Revolution. Re-engineering breaks down an organization down into its component parts and then puts them back together in a way to make the organization more efficient in fulfilling its functions:

> *In a typical re-engineering project ten to twenty young consultants descend on a company, draw up maps of process flow, propose ripping up old accounting procedures and suggest that people from different departments work together in one team (with a good portion of them losing their jobs). Rather than focusing on what comes out of the machine at the end. A re-engineered company's edge comes from its efficiency. Process is more important than product; indeed good products should naturally follow good processes.[3]*

Re-engineering became popular in the 1990s, not only in the US, but also in nearly every country around the world. It can be considered to be the result of the rapid increase in technological developments, especially in computers. Hammer and Champy's book, *Reengineering the Corporation*, has sold millions of copies in many countries. Its Japanese edition sold 250,000 copies in its first three months.[4]

The most important characteristic of re-engineering turned out to be the replacement of human beings in the processes that were reshaped, with machines or computers. Soon the term "re-engineering" came to mean "downsizing"; in the process, millions of workers lost their jobs or had to learn to work in a different way. The stress of re-engineering on the people working in the company was great. But the interesting thing is that, in spite of job losses and income reductions as a result of these operations, the stock markets responded very favorably to the re-engineering announcements.[5] The main purpose of re-engineering was to cut costs, especially labor costs, in order to increase profits: "In 1994 corporate America's profits rose 11 percent, yet it also eliminated 516,069 jobs and announced $10 billion of restructuring charges."[6]

---

3   John Micklethwait and Adrian Wooldridge, *The Witch Doctors*, London: Mandarin, 1997, p. 31.
4   Ibid., p. 29.
5   " … when Mobil announced its plan to shed a tenth of its workforce in early 1995, the oil company's shares jumped to a fifty-two-week high": ibid., p. 34.
6   "When slimming is not enough," *The Economist*, September 3, 1994, as quoted in Micklethwait and Wooldridge, *The Witch Doctors*, p. 34.

The most important problem with the re-engineering concept is considering the employees not only as a cost factor, but also as a cost factor that can be eliminated by redesigning the operations and using more and more computers or machines. The human element in the performance of the organizations is exceedingly important, especially under the new concepts of goods and services. As has been repeated over and over again, the software of products is increasing in importance and the primary factor of production of software is the human element of the companies. The human element is creative, innovative, imaginative and constructive with values and vision. Perhaps, we need to see the developments of computers, robots and machines as the development of tools that will help the employees to increase their creativity, innovativeness and constructiveness, rather than as a means to cut costs.

Another factor to consider is the motivation of the employees. A motivated employee can be very productive. There are many signs that re-engineering has decreased the motivation of employees in their work.

In time, the re-engineering concept itself had to be re-engineered, when the costs to society were considered. In its approach, to its credit, social costs received much more recognition than it had in its earlier implementations. In spite of the changes in its implementation, its objectives did not change. Sadly, the profit maximization goal of the capitalist system, which is spreading all around the world, has become unquestionable. Questioning its validity is a cardinal sin in the new capitalistic faith.

At present, re-engineering is not as popular as it used to be, but the practice of mass labor layoffs is still increasing, making news in the global media. One of these cases that we believe to be very informative is that of Deutsche Telekom. Some information without comment is presented below for the reader to make their own decision about the reasons, the implementation and the expected results of Deutsche Telekom's major employee reduction plans:

> *Due to the massive changes in the industry, Deutsche Telekom faces comprehensive staff restructuring measures. [Basically due to] The worldwide realignment of the industry, the rapid pace of technological development and, in particular, the tough competitive environment in the fixed network and broadband sector in Germany imposed by the regulatory situation ... In the next three years, about 32,000 employees in Germany will leave Deutsche Telekom ... around 6,000 new staff is to be employed. These will comprise, for example, young experts and*

trainees for T-Punkt shops. Thus, the net reduction of jobs over the next three years will be 19,000. The cost of the entire program is about EUR 3.3 billion spread over three years. Job cuts are to be made via voluntary measures, such as old-age, part-time work and severance payments.[7]

The Human Resources and Sustainability report of Deutsche Telekom states that "Deutsche Telekom's employees are its most valuable resource." And the human resource strategy is stated with a slogan of "Motivated staff means happy customers." The human resource strategy is stated as "Structuring work to benefit the company, employees and customers alike," with a strategy goal of lowering costs and increasing efficiency.[8]

Today, we observe significant numbers of mass layoffs in spite of the fact that they may result in reductions in the national income, increases in unemployment and the destruction of motivation.

Privatization Practices

Privatization has been a trend since the 1980s. It has a significant role in the new economic model spreading world-wide, especially in developing countries, due to the efforts of the World Bank and the IMF. Here we will limit our study to indicating privatization's effect on profitability and unemployment.

Privatization of state enterprises is a strategy, designed to reach defined objectives. Early in the 1980s, privatization was introduced as a strategy to increase the efficiency of state-owned enterprises, and became a subject for extensive research and discussions by academicians. In those years, according to the assumptions made, state-owned enterprises were not operating efficiently. This assumption about the efficiency of state-owned enterprises brought about a solution automatically: state-owned enterprises were to be privatized to serve the well-being of the economies of the countries.

In reality, using the same argument, privately owned enterprises had been nationalized just after the Second World War; at that time, private enterprises were assumed to be inefficient. Early in the 1980s, the Thatcher government in the United Kingdom started comprehensive privatization activities, starting

---

7   Deutsche Telekom Press Release, November 2, 2005.
8   "New Ways New Ideas: Making Tomorrow Happen," *The 2004 Human Resources and Sustainability Report* <www.deutschetelekom.com>.

with re-privatizing the state-owned enterprises which were nationalized after the war. Shortly after getting the numerical results of the privatization implementations, academic circles started analyzing the economic implications of privatization. These academic studies reached important conclusions and also served to theorize privatization implementations. Two professors from Oxford University – John Vikers and George Yarrow – wrote perhaps the best book on the subject, *Privatization: An Economic Analysis*. The authors concluded that

> ... *the allocation of property rights does matter because it determines the objectives of the "owners" of the firm (public or private) and the system of monitoring managerial performance. Public and private ownership differ in both respects ... Indeed, it can be argued that the degree of product market competition and the effectiveness of regulatory policy typically have rather larger effects on performance than ownership per se.*[9]

Another conclusion these authors reach is that it is possible to defend, using micro-economic theory, the claim that state enterprises can be more efficient then private companies in many fields.

Many researchers reached similar conclusions in their empirical studies. Research showed that as there are cases where private companies perform better, there are also cases where state-owned enterprises perform better in terms of efficiency. After reaching those results in empirical studies, the evaluation criterion was changed, from efficiency to profitability. When the profitability of state-owned enterprises and privately owned enterprises were compared, the conclusions of the studies were much more robust: the state-owned enterprises were not as profitable as the privately owned companies. Again, the result was as expected. Since, in the capitalist system, the objective of companies must be profit maximization, the state-owned enterprises had to be privatized. In reality, although the state-owned enterprises were not as profitable as the privately owned companies, they were creating more value added and making a larger contribution to the national income.[10]

---

9   John Vikers and George Yarrow, *Privatization: An Economic Analysis*, Cambridge, MA: MIT Press, 1988, p. 3.

10 In Turkey, especially since 2001, the value added created as percentage of the sales of the state-owned enterprises (around 20 percent) is much higher than it is in the private companies (about 11–13 percent). This is mainly due to high labor intensity in the public sector. Ozer Ertuna, *Türkiye'nin 500 Buyuk Sanayi Kurulusunun Yirmi Yili (1983–2004)* [*20 Years of Turkey's 500 Big Industrial Companies (1983–2004)*], Istanbul: ISO [Istanbul Chamber of Commerce], 2005, p. 62.

After defining the objective of a firm to be profit maximization, these privatization activities gained momentum and spread all around the world; and implemented in developing and developed countries.[11] Especially after 1990, East Germany, Poland and Russia widely used mass privatization techniques to convert their socialist economies into free market economies. Soon, rapid privatization's *virtues* became the common creed in many countries. When privatization became a religious conviction, scientific studies lost their importance, and privatization became sacrosanct. Even though studies of privatization reached inconclusive and conflicting results about the consequences of privatization activities, the developing belief structures ignored these results.

As privatization was gaining world-wide acceptance, Turkey was one of the pioneering privatizing countries, as its relations with the IMF gained importance. After the economic crises and the military coup of 1980, Prime Minister Turgut Ozal tried to liberalize the Turkish economy by implementing the IMF's recipes, which included privatization. Ozal described the state-owned enterprises as "bleeding wounds." Large-scale privatization was believed to be a remedy for most of the problems Turkey was facing. As a result, Turkey has sold many state-owned production plants, large refineries, and its telecommunication network.

As we have implied above, state-owned enterprises can be generalized to be less profitable, but are very effective in contributing to national income. And the basic reason for this is their more labor-intensive production or redundant labor utilization. For that reason, most privatization applications result in discharges of labor. When labor cannot be fired due to legal rights, which is usually the case in state economic enterprises, labor is moved to other state-owned enterprises, thus not losing employment but losing their jobs. That is, they continue to receive their salaries but without working. This is an awkward situation. Privatization is implemented to increase the profits of the companies; usually profit increases but the contribution of the enterprise to national income decreases, and still the wages of the redundant labor are paid by the other enterprises. The contribution to national income decreases but the burden on the public sector continues.

---

11 In this spread of privatization, the World Bank and IMF played a vital role. The privatization of state-owned companies was imposed on the developing countries as a pre-condition for loans, under the so-called "Washington Consensus."

The economic costs of privatization practices in socialist economies like Russia were colossal. In the period 1990–2000, Russia's national income was reduced by half, mostly due to mass privatization operations. Of course, privatization was not the only reason for this decline, but must have played a significant role.

Before privatization became a creed – that is, during its early stages – academic studies arrived at some principles to follow in good and effective privatization implementations. One important principle was that the reason for privatization must be to increase efficiency. This implied that the reason should *not* be to raise money for government budgets. Unfortunately, after privatization became a creed, this principle was also forgotten. In many countries, including Turkey, the purpose of privatization became to raise money to support the budgets of governments.

Currently, privatization and re-engineering are used together. Privatized companies, in order to increase their profits, discharge great numbers of employees. For that reason, labor unions and many NGOs (non-governmental organizations) go to the other extreme and take positions against any kind of privatization. As a tool to revive unproductive enterprises in the economy, a privatization strategy can be implemented efficiently and effectively.

Globalization Trends

The present wave of globalization is preparing the ground for the spread of supranational companies. For supranational companies, their contribution to national incomes and income generation has lost its meaning completely. For these companies, the concept of "national income" has no meaning. The sole objective of these companies is the maximization of their profits.

Under the opportunities created by globalization, these supranational companies are able to purchase their raw materials from any country where they cost less, produce their products in any country where the wages are lowest, and sell their products in countries where they can sell under the most lucrative conditions. The only criterion they use in all decisions is the maximization of their profits. These supranational companies have no concern about the welfare of the countries where they carry out their operations. This developing globalized structure makes them only stockholder-oriented and leads them to miss the stakeholder vision. The consequences are seen in various dimensions: as the profits increase, the income generated may decrease; the workers' share in the income generated may decrease, and employment can shift from developed countries to countries where labor is cheap.

Supranational companies can move quickly and have been moving their production facilities from one country to another, whenever they see an opportunity to increase profits by doing so. When wages increase in the country they are operating in due to unionization or other reasons, they move to another country where the wages are still low. This freedom the supranational companies enjoy puts pressure on any improvements in the working conditions and wages in those countries. Many countries, developed or developing, face a bitter choice between low wages or unemployment.

Conclusion

Increasing their national income is still the most important economic objective of both developing and developed countries today. On the other hand, in capitalism as currently practiced, companies seek solely to maximize their profits. They do not consider the impact of their decisions on the national incomes of their home countries. Due to the rapid developments in technology and widespread unemployment, the maximization of companies' profits may not be consistent with the contribution they make to national incomes. Companies' profit maximization objectives may not even be consistent with creating employment and increasing production. Economic theory shows that maximizing the value added generated by companies would result in an increase in output and employment, but it may decrease the profits of these companies.

The technological developments of our times provide companies with opportunities to increase their profit at the expense of generating income. With technological advances, the efficiency of machinery, the competencies of robots and the capacity and speed of computers are increasing with a rapidity never seen before. In a capitalistic system, labor is viewed as just another cost factor like the costs of machinery, robots and computers. Thus labor must compete with other production factors in cost-reduction situations in order to earn its employment. Since the machines, robots and computers are becoming more and more cost-saving, workers are facing the danger of being replaced by them. In fact, mass labor layoffs and discharges have become common practice. These mass labor layoffs have a negative impact on the national income created and the distribution of income, increasing unemployment in both developed and developing countries, and causing serious social problems.

There is a strong need for a change in paradigm. Labor should not be seen as a cost factor. In the twenty-first century, the human element in production is increasing in importance. Investing in human capital has become a must. The technological advances that increase the capacities of machines, robots and computers should be directed towards increasing the capabilities of the human element. Machines, robots and computers should not be seen as competitors of workers, but should enhance the productivity of human beings in production. We need to create such an environment in the workplace that it will motivate people and give people a chance to derive utility from their work.

Since currently the sole objective of companies in the capitalist system is profit maximization, mass discharges of labor have been a common practice for many companies. Popular trends like the re-engineering and privatization of the last three decades and spreading globalization have also contributed to these practices. Re-engineering has come to mean downsizing and employee discharges for the sake of cost reduction; privatization has come to mean elimination of *redundant* labor, and globalization has become an opportunity to seek out and (ab)use cheap labor.

Under the *new economic design* of our times and globalization, unemployment has become one of the major economic problems of both developed and developing countries alike. This, in turn, increases the income gap between rich and poor both in developing and developed countries.

10

Foreign Trade

As for the charge of being anti-trade, many of the movement's leaders are actively involved in the promotion of fair trade – in contrast to the often exploitative free trade they oppose – as a means of improving the economic conditions of poor people and their communities.

(The International Forum on Globalization)[1]

Trade certainly serves the benefits of people. In an environment with no trade, each individual would have to produce all they needed. Trade enables individuals to specialize, produce the products where they have developed comparative advantages and exchange these products with the products produced by others. These are facts even in the most primitive economies. If we consider the complexities of the products of our time, trade increases in importance since we cannot individually produce almost any single one of the products we consume in this modern world. Trade contributes to the nature and the quality of whatever we are consuming. Perhaps the trading systems humanity has developed helped the physical, social and cultural development of humanity more than anything else. Yet the world has not found *the best* trading system. *Free price* versus *fair price* discussions have been very important issues throughout history, and they still are.

Today, people participate in the production of goods and services by selling some of the competencies they have developed; they derive their income from such a production; and they purchase the things they need with their income. In fact, they may not be producing any one of the tradable products or services they are consuming. Through this mechanism, people reach higher levels of income and satisfaction. The case is the same for foreign trade.

---

1   The International Forum on Globalization, *Alternatives to Economic Globalization – A Better World is Possible*, San Francisco, CA: Barrett-Koehler Publishers, Inc., 2002, p. 2.

In a world where there is no foreign trade, each country would have to be self-sufficient. All the needs of each country would have to be fulfilled by its people or its companies. However, they may not possess the resources to produce what they need. Countries differ in their climates, natural resources and the competencies of their people. On the other hand, in the absence of foreign trade, countries may not be able to benefit from the abundant resources they have; they may use only part of these resources in their consumption. Foreign trade enables countries to produce the products where they have comparative advantages, and exchange them for products which are more costly for them to produce. This is what the economics of foreign trade is trying to explain. According to the economics of foreign trade, such trade works to the advantage of all trading countries.

It seems that the benefits of foreign trade are so obvious that there may not be any need to prove their worth. In fact, the benefits are not as clear as it is believed. Let us take an example; let us assume that Country A has comparative advantages in rice production, while Country B's comparative advantages lie in the area of automobile production. At first glance, it seems advantageous for Country A to produce rice and sell it to Country B in return for the automobiles produced there. That will mean Country A will move its production factors from the production of automobiles to rice production. Similarly, Country B will move its relevant production factors from rice to automobile production. This factor mobility may not be possible. The land endowment of Country A may not allow it to move more labor to rice production. It applies to Country B also: Country B may not be able to move its rice farmers into the production of automobiles. Rice and automobile production may require very different talents. Determination of prices in this rice and automobile trade has some questions requiring answers also. The response of demand to the price of rice and automobiles may be different, and may differ in two countries also. This may provide an opportunity to one of the countries to exploit the other. In real-life cases, these kinds of questions need clear and satisfactory answers. The simple example cited above seems very similar to the case presented by the comparative advantages of the United States and Japan. The US has a comparative advantage in rice production and has been trying hard to sell rice to Japan, and Japan has a comparative advantage in automobile production and has been promoting its car sales in the American market. But Japan prefers to protect its rice farmers and does not welcome the imports of American rice. And the US protects its car producers in Detroit. The practice seems to contradict the theory. But does it?

The theory of international trade tries to find answers to these types of questions.

The Foreign Trade Model

The foreign trade theory benefits from a simple model to reach some meaningful conclusions. The model assumes that there are two countries each producing the same two products. The theory studies how trade will take place and what will be its benefits to the countries involved. Constructing the theory on the assumption of a two countries, two products model is not a necessary condition; it is just for simplicity. The conclusions reached are applicable for any number of countries where any number of products are produced. On the other hand, in order to reach its conclusions, the theory makes some assumptions that are necessary for the conclusions to be possible. Or, we should say these additional assumptions made are the necessary conditions for the results reached, and if the assumptions changed, the results would also change. The most important assumption is the full mobility of resources (factors of production) from any one of the products to any other. The theory assumes that resources can be moved to the production areas where the country has, or has developed, comparative advantages.

Another assumption is that demand depends only on price and the prices are determined by costs. Under these assumptions, comparative advantages in the production of a product enable a country to produce that product at a lower cost. Products produced at lower costs can be sold at lower prices. Customers base their purchasing decisions only on the prices of products only. Therefore, specialization of production in countries that have comparative advantages will enable people to purchase goods at lower prices. That means that with the same budget people will be able to purchase and consume more. Therefore people will benefit from foreign trade.

So far everything seems very logical. There seems to be nothing new in our explanations above, but this is not the case. The foreign trade theory proves something very important, which is easily overlooked in our daily observations. The theory proves that a country does not have to have an absolute advantage (producing a product at a lower cost) in order to export it to benefit from foreign trade. It would have to have only a comparative advantage on the production of the product it is exporting. This is so important a conclusion that it is called the "law of comparative advantages."

The Law of Comparative Advantages

As we have stated above, the most important conclusion of the theory of international trade (foreign trade) is that in order to benefit from the opportunities of foreign trade, countries do not have to have an absolute advantage in the production of goods to export; a comparative advantage in their production is sufficient. Let us try to illustrate what is meant by comparative advantages.

To simplify the illustrations, let us use the simplified version of the two countries, two products model used in the theory. Let us also assume that labor is the only production factor. Let us assume the countries are the US and Japan, and the products are rice and cars.

Let us assume for illustrative purposes that the US produces a car for 3,000 units of labor while Japan produces the same car for 3,600 units of labor; it would mean that the US has an absolute advantage in the production of cars. But absolute advantage in the production of a product is not a sufficient and necessary condition to export and to benefit from the advantages of foreign trade. Let us also assume that the US produces a kg of rice for 3 units of labor, while Japan produces a kg of rice for 4 units of labor. As we see, the US also has an absolute advantage in the production of rice. Both cars and rice are cheaper in the US when measured by the amount of labor used in production, and in Japan both products are more expensive as measured by labor spent. Foreign trade theory shows that the countries can still improve their welfare by trading. Country A has an advantage in rice production compared to the production of cars. If the US was to import a car from Japan and to move the labor used in its production to rice production, it could produce 1,000 kg of rice. At current prices of cars and rice in Japan, the US would have to pay only 900 kg of that rice to Japan, keeping 100 kg for its additional consumption. The opposite is true for Japan. Japan has a comparative advantage in the production of cars. When it produces an extra car to sell to the US, it would have to sacrifice only 900 kg of rice production. At market prices in the US, Japan could buy 1,000 kg of rice for the car it exports to the US. In our example, in the trade of one car there is a benefit of 100 kg of rice. We can state the basic conclusion reached by the theory at this point. When the two countries are taken together, the total production of the countries, and also their total income, will increase if the countries specialize in the products in whose production they have a comparative advantage. Our numerical example above verifies this conclusion.

The law of comparative advantages is so impressive that it has become well accepted by many economists, in spite of its too strong assumptions.[2]

Price Impositions in Foreign Trade

In free market economies, the markets are assumed to play a very important role in the operation of the economy. Prices determined in fully competitive markets guide the economy. In fully competitive markets, there are so many buyers and sellers that none of the participants, buyers or sellers, can influence the market. They are all assumed to be price takers in the market. On the other hand, in the case of foreign trade, it is not appropriate to make such an assumption. In foreign trade markets, there are few buyers and sellers; all are specialized in the products in whose production they have comparative advantages. The buyers and sellers in the markets may influence the markets due to the differences in the price elasticity of demand each product faces. In fact, some countries may be able to impose prices on others in the foreign trade markets.

As is the case in all decisions relating to economics, in foreign trade also, each country is assumed to be seeking its own interest. This means each country tries to impose prices on the others. An importer tries to benefit from the low prices in the exporting country; the exporting country, on the other hand, would like to benefit from the high prices in the importing country. When a country imposes prices on another one, it will get all the benefits of foreign trade. In such a case, there will be no incentive for the other country to enter into trade. Perhaps the price in foreign trade will settle somewhere in between the prices in the two countries. And the benefits each country gains from foreign trade will depend on its bargaining power. The foreign trade theory does not spell out solutions for the distribution of the benefits. The economic theory is based on *free* prices. *Fair* price is not a concern of foreign trade theory. The theory proves that increasing foreign trade will increase the cake; countries can share this somehow.

---

2   Paul Krugman, well-known professor of economics at MIT, Cambridge and winner of the Nobel Prize for Economics in 2009 has stated: "If there were an economist's creed, it would surely contain the affirmations 'I believe in the principle of Comparative Advantage' and 'I believe in free trade'": Krugman, "Is Free Trade Passé?", *Journal of Economic Perspectives*, Vol. 1, No. 2 <http://www.jstor.org/pss/1942985>.

Foreign Trade in Real Life

Economic theory supports foreign trade. Under the assumptions made, the theory reaches very important conclusions and makes very strong assertions: in order to benefit from trade, a country does not have to have absolute advantages in production of products; a comparative advantage is sufficient. By definition, each country has comparative advantages, and foreign trade creates benefits, a cake to be shared. But in reality, the case for foreign trade is not as clear as it is stated in theory. For that reason, proponents of foreign trade, even the countries that try hard to promote free trade all around the world, resort to protectionist policies in the cases of some products. In fact, the behavior exhibited by these countries does not contradict the capitalist theory. These countries seek their benefits. As long as foreign trade serves their interests, they support free trade, but if foreign trade were to hurt their interests they deviate to protectionist policies. Free trade among countries does not serve the interests of the trading countries under all circumstances. There are many real-life conditions that do not fit well with the assumptions of the theory. The theory assumes the perfect mobility of factors of production. In real life, resources (factors of production) cannot easily be moved to the production areas where the advantages lie. The theory assumes that demand depends on price. It may not be the case nowadays, since the software of products is gaining importance. These are some of the considerations that are not covered in the theory. In real life, developed countries may be able to impose prices on the developing countries. And, there are products that cannot be traded in foreign markets.

The Lack of Mobility of Production Factors

As we have just mentioned above, the foreign trade theory assumes full mobility of production factors. This means that resources like labor and capital can be moved at no cost from the production of one good or service to others. Whereas, in real-life cases, it may be impossible to move labor or capital from one line of production to another, or the move can only be accomplished at a high cost. Production of different products requires different kinds of labor and capital. Different products or services need different natural conditions, a different climate, different labor competencies and different endowments. People develop competencies applicable for narrow ranges of products. For example, the US has a very strong competitive advantage in the production of motion pictures. On the other hand, we may say that Japan has a comparative advantage in automobile production. The US tries to protect its automobile production sector from Japanese competition. We may ask why the US does not specialize in the motion picture industry and purchase its cars from Japan. Even this question would seem quite funny for most of us. But the answer is even more humorous: in order to accomplish such a specialization, the US would have to be able to convert all its workers in Detroit into movie stars in Hollywood.

Misunderstanding Prices

One of the assumptions of foreign trade theory is that price alone determines the demand for goods and services. In other words, this means if you can produce at a lower cost you can sell your product, because you can charge a lower price. In fact, this is the basic assumption of capitalist market economic theory, because market theory believes in homogeneous products. Whereas, as we have repeated over and over above, the assumption of the capitalist theory about the role of prices does not reflect reality today. The capitalist theory considers the price of a product to be a burden the consumer must bear. In fact, as we have discussed before, since price is only one of the factors that constitute the identity of products, and since the identity of the products is increasing in importance, the price may not be the burden of possessing a product: it may itself be a factor contributing to the amount of utility derived from consumption. We know that consumers, in their pattern of consumption, try to enhance their own identities, or the identities they see fit for themselves. In fact, due to the increasing complexity of products and product technology, price is the only quantitative factor that gives information about the quality and identity of the products. At this point, what is important is the identity of the product: it is more important than price and price is only one of the factors making up the identity. Countries may have comparative advantages in the production of some products and could sell those products at lower prices, but that does not mean that those products will be favored in international markets. Product images are also influenced by the images of the countries. Some countries' products give an impression of better quality and others of a more exclusive design, and still others more state-of-the-art fashion. Some countries are able to set trends in quality, design and fashion, benefiting from the opportunities created by the advances in communication technology and their hold on the communication channels. We can say that as demand and production have done, comparative advantages have split into comparative advantages in production of physical products and the production of the software of these products. Less developed and developing countries may not have the chances the developed countries have in developing the latter comparative advantages.

Imbalance in Bargaining Power

The foreign trade theory shows that liberalized international trade will increase the welfare of the world. It is also shown that this gives countries a chance to improve their income distribution. For that reason, countries are in favor of liberalization of international trade. Again, for the same reason, the GATT was signed and the WTO established. But since the establishment of the WTO, income distribution throughout the world has not improved. In fact, there is some evidence supporting the observation that under the *new economic design* established by the creation of the WTO, foreign trade has *increased* the gap between the rich and the poor, both among nations and within nations. These observations do not contradict the theory. International trade increases the world output, as the theory implies. But the problem is income distribution, or sharing the increase in income. In the distribution of the gain, free market assumptions do not hold. The bargaining powers and the economic conditions of importers and exporters are different and not balanced.

Developed countries usually have the stronger bargaining position in foreign trade. As we have explained earlier, the software of the products – image of quality, design, brand names and prices that make up the identity of the product – are increasing in importance. Currently, the developed, rich countries have developed and own these factors that constitute the software of products. These factors are called "intellectual properties" and are very well protected in the *new economic design*. In many cases, even the production factors of the hardware of the product, such as know-how and industrial design, and industrial secrets, are protected under the TRIPS agreement. Developed countries also mostly own these factors. Under the *new economic design*, the hardware of the products can be produced anywhere in the world, wherever they are produced at a lower cost. Under the new technology, physical quality has been a must. Quality is not a differentiating factor of many products any more. There is a keen competition in the world among countries with abundant and cheap labor in the production of the hardware of products. Under the *new economic design*, as a result of liberalized foreign trade, countries that design these products get the chance to produce them in the countries where labor is cheap, add their brand names and images on the products, and sell them in any country where the market conditions are appropriate. The *new economic design* helps developed countries gain a greater share of the benefits of the foreign trade.

In the *new economic design*, the importers and exporters may not be different economic entities. Supranational companies can establish production facilities in countries where labor is abundant and wages are low. This is another way to increase the share of the developed countries in the benefits of trade. In the *new economic design*, the supranational companies can access raw materials from the most appropriate markets in the world, have their products produced in the labor-abundant countries at local labor costs, and sell their products in rich markets where prices are high. That means in the *new economic design*, there is no case for bargaining on sharing the benefits created by foreign trade. After all, both exporters and importers are the same supranational companies of the *new economic design*.

Existence of Non-tradable Products

Finally, we want to mention that the foreign trade in goods and services would apply to only tradable products. In reality, there are many different types of services that cannot be traded in the international markets. In fact, we can claim that most services are of this type since they are location dependent. For example, hairdressing services are very cheap in labor-abundant countries compared to those of developed countries, but people of developed countries cannot benefit from these low prices. If, in one country, domestic air flights are very cheap, you cannot benefit from them in another country.[3] Because of these differences in prices of non-tradable products in different countries, the per capita national incomes of countries measured in local currency translated into a foreign currency are not comparable. For that reason, for comparative purposes, per capita incomes in purchasing power parities (PPP) are also calculated. For example, the per capita income in Turkey in 2003 was about $3,730 in official exchange rates, but it was $6,710 in purchasing power parity according to the United Nations statistics. But the measurement of per capita income in PPP also requires some assumptions, and when these assumptions change, the calculated per capita incomes change also. The Turkish textile producers syndicate has estimated the Turkish per capita income in PPP to be $11,800. The prices of products that are non-tradable and foreign exchange rates cause the difference between the per capita income and the per capita income in PPP.

---

3   The economic theory assumes the goods and services can be transferred to any place at no cost.

According to economic theory, the prices of tradable products would reach equilibrium in international and national markets under the ongoing exchange rates. But there would be no market forces to make non-tradable product prices to move towards equilibrium. The important issue in our case is that in a national market the prices of non-tradable products also influence the prices of tradable products. Therefore, it is not very difficult for the supranational companies to impose their prices on the local producers and to benefit from their low factor prices.

Conclusion

It has been proven by the economic theory of foreign trade that liberalized international trade serves the interests of the countries trading and the interests of the world at large. Two basic assumptions lie behind this proof. The first of these assumptions is that the factors of production can move without any cost from one type of production to another. The second assumption is that the demand for a product depends only on its price, and the price is determined by the costs of production. The results obtained by the theory under these assumptions are very important. In order to benefit from foreign trade, a country does not have to produce its goods to export at lower costs than anyone else; that is, it does not have to have absolute advantage – comparative advantage is sufficient. That is, it must have an advantage in its production of some of them compared to its production of others. Since a country's production efficiency cannot be the same in all the products it is producing, all countries will have a comparative advantage in the production of some products. The theory shows that if countries specialize in production of products where they have comparative advantages and export them in exchange for other products, they will have a chance to benefit from increasing production and productivity; that is, they will have a chance to share a bigger cake.

But, in real life, there are some problems countries face in benefiting from liberalized foreign trade. The assumption of the theory may not fit the specific cases, and difficulties faced in sharing the cake under the *new economic design* are expanding in the world.

Moving the factors of production from one type of production to another may not be possible or feasible when the costs involved are considered. The free mobility of labor assumption may mean transforming automobile production laborers into Hollywood artists at no cost. On the other hand, in the *new emerging economic design*, products are composed of both hardware and software. The software of the products constitutes the identity of products created by their quality image, design, brand name and price. The factors that produce the product's software are strongly protected by intellectual property rights in the *new economic design* created by the establishment of the WTO. The importance of products' software is increasing day after day. Currently, the developed countries own most of these intellectual properties. Under these conditions, the developed, rich countries have better chance to benefit from the fruits of foreign trade liberalization.

Additionally, in the process of sharing the benefits of foreign trade, the bargaining about the terms by the importers and exporters does not make sense since, under the *new economic design,* supranational companies can have their production plants in countries where labor is abundant and cheap. These supranational companies can have distribution outlets in countries where their products are sold. The *new economic design* has provided opportunities for the supranational companies to gain ever bigger shares of the cake provided by liberalized foreign trade.

For the reasons above, in spite of the fact that foreign trade theory favors liberalized foreign trade, even those countries that support the liberalization movement may, in some cases, resort to protecting some of their industries at the expense of free foreign trade.

11

The *New Economic Design*

I have written this book because while I was at the World Bank, I saw firsthand the devastating effect that globalization can have on developing countries, and especially the poor within those countries.

(Joseph Stiglitz)[1]

Today, with capitalism's conversion into a religion, a new type of capitalist market economic model is under implementation. This new religion is constructing its own institutions and its own creed; in fact, it is conditioning humankind. There are various names given to this new system. Some call it the "neoliberal economy," some call it the "globalized economy"; still others describe it as "free market democracy."[2] Here we will call it the *new economic design*; it is becoming such a belief system that its principles and rules cannot tolerate any discussion or argument. Some of its disciples declare, "You are either with us or against us." Some scholars have even claimed that this is the end of history; the world has found its economic design. The *new economic design* is built on competition and seeking individual interest.

Competitive Conditions

Today, the competitive environment is expanding. Competitive behavior is gaining increased approval and acceptance, and is conquering the domains of cooperation and solidarity. Competition among individuals, firms, economic

---

1   Joseph E. Stiglitz, *Globalization and its Discontents*, New York: W.W. Norton, 2002, p. 27.
2   Economic democracy is not a proper concept to define the *new economic design*. In Jaroslav Vanek's words, "I have had several interests in my life, including the area I call economic democracy. Economic democracy is a transposition of the idea of political democracy. It implies that economic life is governed by people who are involved in that economic life. Capitalism is based on property rights, and democracy on personal rights": *Cooperative Economics: An Interview with Jaroslav Vanek*, interviewed by Albert Perkins <http://www.ru.org/51cooper. html>.

blocs in order to gain advantage over one's rivals is believed to be the driving force of all economic advances and development. Individuals, firms and economic blocs seek to fulfill their own interests rather than what is right and fair. This behavior is admired in the newly transformed society as the new faith expands globally.

For many centuries of human history, those who were strong and powerful were able to gain the lion's share in the distribution of income and other means. The transfer of wealth among countries and continents was secured mostly by power. Even though this is still the case in our time, the current colossal developments in telecommunication technologies make it difficult to exercise power in seeking self-interest. In gaining the lion's share in distribution, convincing people that it is right and fair proves to be much more effective. This in turn creates a need to develop a faith, one which exalts capitalism based on conclusions reached by economic theory under certain theoretical assumptions.

Today, the *new economic design* under construction strives to preserve the affluence of developed countries. It has no concern for narrowing the gap between the incomes of the rich and poor. But this is not something that one can accomplish easily. In a world which is integrating, where location differences are becoming meaningless, and with improvements in communication, any design must take into consideration people's desires and aspirations. But these desires and aspirations are not always in line with the values of the *new economic design*. On the other hand, the free movement of capital among countries accompanied by a free movement of labor force may reduce the differences that exist between the welfare of countries. For that reason, developed countries need to supplement and redefine liberal economic concepts and coverage, and reshape people's values in order to preserve their affluence.

In this framework, a *new economic design*, which is based on competition and self-interest, is under construction. This design is developing under two dimensions that may seem contradictory: globalization and the formation of trade blocs. As the world is integrating into a single market, regional economic blocs become increasingly important as rival markets. Globalization is trying to spread competition to all markets in the world through trade liberalization. Member countries of trade blocs try to cooperate and support each other to improve their competitive position in international markets.

Globalization is taking its shape under the General Agreement on Trade and Tariffs (GATT). Some major trade blocs are already in operation and some are in the process of development. The three most important regional blocs are the European Union (EU), which started as the European Common Market, the North American Free Trade Agreement (NAFTA), and the Shanghai Cooperation Organization (SCO).[3] Among these blocks, the EU has broader objectives than just economic ones: the EU seems to also have an objective of social and political integration.

Below, we will try to review the development of GATT in order to understand the foundations of the *new economic design*.

The General Agreement on Tariffs and Trade (GATT)

The most important step in the direction of foreign trade liberalization can be said to be the signing of the General Agreement on Tariffs and Trade, or GATT. The GATT is trying to establish a global *new economic design*. Under this *new economic design*, all barriers to the free flow and trade of goods and services will be eliminated, and efforts will be made to provide improved conditions for the flow of capital among countries. The *new economic design* is claimed to integrate the world's economies, and therefore called *globalization*. But the *new economic design* does not allow for the free flow of labor; labor mobility has not been an issue in its formulation. The GATT has been deaf on labor mobility and immigration matters. In practice, each country formulates measures to prevent the flow of labor from poor to rich countries. The *new economic design* requires the creation of cheap labor pools in order to produce more cheaply the hardware of products, in order to increase profits. This requires containing workers within their present national boundaries.

The GATT was an agreement reached in 1947 to promote multilateral trade with the minimum of barriers to trade, the reduction of import tariffs and quotas, and the abolition of preferential trade agreements. Members of the agreement pledged to abide by the principle of the "most favored nation" clause. This clause obliged the signatories to extend to each other any favorable trading terms offered in subsequent agreements to third parties.[4] The exception to this rule is the regional trade blocs. Regional trade blocs are regarded as a single country. Therefore the members of regional trade blocs could extend

---

3   The Shanghai Cooperation Organization (SCO) is an intergovernmental mutual-security organization which was founded in 2001 by the leaders of China, Russia, Kazakhstan, Kyrgyzstan, Tajikistan and Uzbekistan.
4   Graham Bannock, R.E. Baxter and Ray Rees, *The Penguin Dictionary of Economics*, Harmondsworth: Penguin Books, 1980.

favorable terms to each other without the burden of extending the same terms to all other signatories of the GATT.

Since 1947, the members of the GATT have had eight rounds of meetings to liberalize international trade. In each of the rounds, some tariff cuts were realized and tariff concessions were made. The last of the rounds, the Uruguay Round, started in 1986 and lasted for seven years. The Uruguay Round was the most ambitious round to date, hoping to expand the functions of the GATT to important new areas such as services, capital, intellectual property, textiles and agriculture. The round ended on December 15, 1993, with an agreement to make the GATT more operational in trade and services and in the establishment of the *new economic design* (later called globalization). Its members signed GATT on April 12–13, 1994 in Marrakesh, Morocco.

The Uruguay Round has had a very significant role in the development of the *new economic design,* and the discussions and disputes of the round can help us to understand the objectives and means of the design.

Discussions on two issues extended the time length of the Uruguay Round. The first was agricultural subsidies. On this issue, the US's interests conflicted with the interests of the EU and Japan. The EU subsidized its agriculture under the Common Agricultural Policy (CAP). A major portion of the EU budget – 44 percent, about €43 billion in 2005 – is allocated to these subsidies. The US, on the other hand, was against providing agricultural subsidies, and wanted them to be eliminated. The US claimed that the subsidies provided by the EU to its member countries provided them competitive advantages, resulting in unfair competition. By moving its subsidies from production areas to income protection and production restrictions, the EU helped to reach a solution. But even today agricultural subsidies in developed countries are a source of great concern for developing countries. Developing countries seem to suffer from the agricultural subsidies still implemented in developed countries.

The second issue was the quotas applied to textile products. The US and Europe wanted to continue protecting their textile sectors and did not want them to be liberalized. They claimed that labor employed in the textile sector had to be protected from the competition originating from developing countries. Developing countries on the other hand wanted the textile trade to be liberalized. Their position was, since the textile sector is labor intensive, textile products were their only hope of exports benefiting from their comparative advantages. Since 1974, the Multi Fiber Arrangement (MFA) has governed the world textile trade, and provides for the imposition of quotas on the amount of textiles developing countries can export to developed countries. The developing countries had argued for the elimination of the MFA.

Perhaps the best way to understand the *new economic design* brought about by the GATT is to listen to the words of those participated in the discussions. Below, we present in summary the testimony of Mickey Kantor, the US trade representative in the Uruguay Rounds. Following is that portion of his prepared testimony summarizing the major components of the agreement:

Industrial Market Access

> *The United States achieved substantially all of its major objectives in the industrial market access negotiations. As a result, increased market access opportunities will be available to U.S. exporters of industrial goods.*

Agriculture

> *U.S. agricultural exports will benefit significantly from the reductions in export subsidies and the market openings provided by the agreement.*[5]

Textiles and Clothing

> *The textile and apparel sector has always been a critical one in this Round. From the very beginning of the negotiations at Punta Del Este, the developing countries have linked their willingness to accept disciplines in services and intellectual property, as well as further market opening, on the achievement of the phase-out of the Multifiber Arrangement (MFA). The MFA has governed trade in textiles and clothing for the past 20 years.*

> *The Administration, however, was equally insistent on five key goals: 1) that the phase-out occur in a gradual manner that would permit our industry to adjust over time to the changes in the trading system; 2) that foreign markets be opened to U.S. textile and clothing exports for the benefit of U.S. workers; 3) that the U.S. retain the control over*

---

5   According to a study conducted by the World Bank, OECD and GATT, the results of the Uruguay Round will increase world income in ten years by \$213–274 billion. Of this amount, \$190 billion will be realized in the agricultural sector and the remaining \$23 billion will come in industry due to the liberalization of trade.

which products would be integrated into the GATT at each stage of the phase-out period; 4) that strong safeguards be included in order to provide protection in the event of damaging surges in imports during the phase-out period; and 5) that in light of the phase-out of the MFA, that tariff cuts in this sector be held to a minimum.

We believe we have done very well in achieving those goals.

Subsidies and Countervailing Measures

The subsidies agreement establishes clearer rules and stronger disciplines in the subsidies area while also making certain subsidies non-actionable, provided they are subject to conditions designed to limit distorting effects.

Services

The General Agreement on Trade in Services (GATS) is the first multilateral, legally enforceable agreement covering trade and investment in the services sectors. The principal elements of the GATS framework agreement include most-favored-nation (MFN) treatment, national treatment, market access, transparency and the free flow of payments and transfers.

Trade Related Intellectual Property Rights

Trade in U.S. goods and services protected by intellectual property rights reflect a consistent trade surplus. For example, U.S. copyright industries – movies, computer software, and sound recordings – are consistently top U.S export earners.

U.S. semiconductors are found in the computers and appliances we all use each day. U.S. pharmaceutical companies are among the most innovative, and our exports of these important products have been growing. Strengthened protection of intellectual property rights and enforcement of those rights as provided in the TRIPS agreement will enhance U.S. competitiveness, encourage creative activity, and expand exports and the number of jobs.

… The Agreement obligates all Members to provide strong protection in the areas of copyrights and related rights, patents, trademarks, trade

secrets, industrial designs, geographic indications and layout designs for integrated circuits.

World Trade Organization

The Agreement establishing the World Trade Organization (WTO) encompasses the current GATT structure and extends it to new disciplines that have not been adequately covered in the past.

The new organization will be more credible and predictable and thus benefit U.S. trade interests.[6]

As it is clearly seen in the testimony of Mickey Kantor, the GATT is bringing a new design to world trade. In fact, it is not just a new design for trade relations, but its objective is much more comprehensive; it aims to set the foundations for the establishment of a *new economic design* all over the world. This new design is characterized by the free flow of goods and services, increased competition in the area of production, no labor mobility, and a full protection of intellectual property rights. The interesting aspect of the design is while all the barriers for the flow of goods and services among countries are eliminated, workers are imprisoned within the boundaries of their countries, and monopoly rights are provided to the designs, brand names and images of the goods and services. Let us try to understand the role of these characteristics of the *new economic design*.

Until very recently, products (goods and services) were items with observable qualities. Those who were able to produce high-quality products at low cost had the advantage in the competitive markets. Recently, products have split into two aspects: their hardware and software. Their hardware is their physical characteristics, which can be seen or touched by everyone. The way they look, the way they operate may be considered their physical nature. The software of the products cannot be seen or held easily, instead they create a perception or image for people: the perceived quality, design, brand name, image, relation to fashion are examples of products' software. With the new technology, the hardware of the products can be produced anywhere in the world. They all would look alike. But today, the software is produced primarily by developed countries with what are called intellectual properties

---

6   Mickey Kantor, "Kantor Outlines Uruguay round Agreement for Congress," *Washington Economic Review*, Special Issue: GATT and NAFTA II, February 1994, pp. 13–22. This testimony was before the US House of Representatives Ways and Means Committee, January 26, 1994.

and with access to communication channels. The *new economic design* puts these intellectual property rights under full protection. That is, only their owners can benefit from them. They cannot be used by anyone else. We should also note that although the products are split into two, the components together make up the identity of the products. And, today, product identities influence demand more than their physical nature.

Under the *new economic design*, developed countries and supranational companies obtained the chance to buy their raw materials from any market in any country in the world, produce the products in any country where labor is cheap, and sell it in any market that has the potential for high profits. Raw materials, parts and products can flow freely among countries and markets in the *new economic design*.

Market structures in hardware and software of the products differ also. In the area of hardware production, there is keen competition. Countries with abundant and cheap labor compete with each other. Competition is mainly on the cost of production. The supranational companies provide them the production know-how needed and the product designs. Under the new era, the quality is not a differentiating factor but a must. Under these conditions, low labor cost is the only competitive advantage of producers, and usually labor wages are reduced to subsistence levels.

On the other hand, in the software side of products, the component parts of the software grant strong monopoly power to their owners. Since these are protected by the TRIPS agreement of the *new economic design*, in these monopolistic markets supranational companies have an opportunity to increase prices to maximize their profits. Developed countries own most of products' intellectual properties. For the time being, developed countries also have greater potential to develop these intellectual properties. These countries also have control over communication channels and the media in order to influence customers' preferences.

It can also be argued that the *new economic design* also serves the interests of the developing countries that have abundant and cheap labor. The supranational companies' eagerness to earn profits guides them to have their goods produced in developing countries, which brings income and employment to countries where the production is done. This, somewhat, reduces poverty in those countries. While this is correct, it may also be seen as an exploitation of workers. When production facilities move from one country to another, the total impact on employment may not change, but labor costs go down. That means the share of labor in the income generated by operations decreases. That is why we observe increases in unemployment and poverty in developing countries and not much of an increase in global welfare. Since the free mobility of labor is not considered in the GATT, there is no tendency for wages to move towards equilibrium. A tendency towards equilibrium may mean an improvement in global income distribution, but an improved income distribution would also require workers to gain a more equitable and fair share from the income generated by operations. Liberalized international trade most probably will increase global total production, but if more equitable and fair income distribution schemes are not developed, only rich countries and the supranational companies based in these countries will benefit from the increase in output as supranational companies will be able to increase their profits.

Rich countries have accumulated their wealth by exploiting their colonies. In order for them to sustain consumption levels compatible with their wealth, they need to take a lion's share from the income generated by production and marketing operations. The *new economic design* is developed to provide them with that opportunity.

Since the construction of the foundations of the *new economic design* in 1994, the ensuing *globalization* has not helped to narrow the gap between the rich and the poor. In fact, income distribution in and among countries has deteriorated: as the rich became richer, overall poverty in the world has increased.

The Missing Pillar of the *New Economic Design*: MAI

The *new economic design* is constructed on providing full mobility to goods and services among countries and restraining the mobility of labor, keeping workers within the boundaries of their countries. In spite of all the efforts of the developed countries, it was not possible to reach an agreement on the free mobility of all types of capital. Extensive discussions were held to pass a Multilateral Agreement on Investment (MAI),[7] but the discussions did not lead to an agreement. This can be considered to be the missing pillar of the *new economic design*.

---

7   The Multilateral Agreement on Investments (MAI) has the following objectives: the opening of most economic sectors and natural resources to foreign ownership; fair and equal treatment of foreign firms; the removal of restrictions against the movement of capital; allowing for individual firms to sue foreign governments before an international mediation panel; and full and proper compensation for expropriation.

It can be claimed that the foundations of the *new economic design* go back to the Washington Consensus of 1978.[8] The Washington Consensus required the free flow of capital among countries in order to establish the sovereignty of capitalism all around the world. That is the reason why the World Bank and the IMF imposed on the developing countries the liberalization of capital markets and favorable treatment for the foreign capital as part of the recipe provided for structural adjustments which were the pre-condition for IMF credits.

Three types of capital flow exist among countries: direct foreign investments, long-term loans and short-term capital movements. Free flow of foreign direct investments among countries is an essential requirement of the *new economic design* in order for it to achieve its objectives. The benefits of foreign direct investment are so much advertised that an undisputable belief is created among people world-wide in the virtues of foreign direct investments. In general, foreign direct investment has great potential to benefit countries receiving these investments. Foreign direct investments come to a country to create income and employment. But there are varieties of these foreign direct investments. Some foreign direct investments come to a country to benefit from the local market and to replace the domestic production. These investments may not have positive contributions to income and employment. If a foreign investment comes to a country to benefit from low wages, it may leave the country when it finds another country where wages are lower. Some foreign direct investments bring technology, know-how and intellectual properties to a country. These investments may make significant contributions to the development of the host country. In short, foreign direct investments may or may not serve a country; they should be considered as tools to reach objectives and not as the end themselves.

Foreign direct investments have objectives when they come to a country. The host country must also have some objectives. The host country must be able to reconcile the objectives of the foreign direct investments and their own objectives. These types of investments are called "strategic alliances." Many countries do exercise caution in selecting the foreign direct investments that will serve their national interests.

Long-term foreign loans are also a form of capital flow among countries. Good examples of these loans are the development loans provided by the World Bank to developing countries. Countries may benefit greatly from these

---

8   The consensus among the World Bank, the IMF and the US Treasury in 1978 was called the "Washington Consensus" in 1989 by John Williamson. This title is accepted by many.

loans. But if the loans come with strings attached, these loans may not serve the purposes of the receiving country. As it is seen in the Washington Consensus, these loans may be used in order to impose policies on developing countries, which may not be always in the interest of the recipient country. Long-term foreign loans may or may not serve the interests of developing countries.[9]

Short-term capital movements among countries require utmost care, especially by the recipient country. There is a huge amount of capital in the world trying to earn money by making short-term investments in emerging markets and government securities in those markets. These are mostly pension funds and mutual funds trying to earn high returns for their investment portfolios. These funds invest most of their funds in secure investments at low returns, but allocate part of their funds to investments in emerging markets at very high returns; such returns may go as high as 30–40 percent. These are risky investments. In most cases, the risks themselves are created by the behavior of these capital flows. When these funds move into a country with an expectation of return, usually returns increase and more funds are attracted. But if these funds decide to leave a country, especially if they try to escape a probable hazard, they may cause a market crash. Since 1980, the numbers of market crashes have increased world-wide. For that reason, some governments try to regulate the flow of short-term capital movements in and out of their countries. This short-term capital is called "hot money" in daily use.

As we have mentioned above, after signing the GATT, developed countries, especially those who are exporting foreign capital, worked hard to reach an agreement to eliminate all barriers to the free flow of capital among countries. The WTO has been instrumental in supporting campaigns for reaching an agreement. A draft was prepared and discussed behind closed doors by the leadership of the Organization for Economic Cooperation and Development (OECD). In 1997, the first draft of the MAI drew widespread criticism from non-governmental organizations (NGOs) and developing countries. Developing countries feared that the agreement would make it difficult for them to regulate foreign investors and thus it was not possible to reach an agreement on the MAI. However, developed and capital-exporting countries continue to push for similar investment provisions, since the free flow of capital is an integral part of the *new economic design*.

---

9   In his book John Perkins explains how long-term loans can be used and have been used as a means to reach political objectives, see John Perkins, *Confessions of an Economic Hit Man*, San Francisco, CA: Barrett-Koehler Publishers Inc., 2004.

Globalization and Trade Blocs

While some people believe globalization and trade blocs to be contradictory, other believe that the trade benefits of regional blocs make globalization more attractive. The signing of the GATT and the establishment of the WTO did not slow the formation of new economic blocs; in fact, it increased it. In 1998, there were more than 90 trade blocs operating in the world. Three-quarters of these trade blocs were established after 1994; that is, after the GATT came into effect. One-third of these agreements relate to the European Union.

The former Director-General of the WTO, Renato Ruggiero, believes that regional trade blocs may become useless:

> *Their contribution to the promotion of liberalization cannot be called into question. And yet the logic of regionalism makes less economic sense in an era of globalization. As production and distribution become increasingly global and as economies become more integrated and more driven by borderless technologies, it is in no one's economic interest to have a fragmented system with fragmented rules and even a fragmented dispute settlement system.*[10]

The WTO is trying to establish a unified, rule-based world with free trade and improved dispute settlement system. In spite of this, trade blocs in Europe, in North America and in the Asia-Pacific region are increasing in importance.

Trade blocs are expanding their functions beyond the economic interests of their members. Although the EU was formed to serve the economic interests of its members, it is converting itself to a political and cultural unity. The Black Sea Economic Cooperation group is promoting the economic development of its members. Trade blocs are also trying to establish relations amongst themselves. Discussions to establish relations are carried under the auspices of the WTO. The objective of all these regional developments is claimed to be the establishment of economic and political freedom, respect for human rights and social solidarity.

It seems that the free trade environment created by the WTO will be reinforced by the democratic values secured by the activities of the trade blocs

---

10 The speech delivered by the former Director-General of WTO, Renato Ruggiero in 1998 at the
    Brookings Institute <http://www.wto.org/english/news_e/sprr_e/wash_e.htm>.

in the development of the *new economic design*. In this context, the issue of how we define *democratic values* gains importance.

The Objectives of the *New Economic Design*

Globalization is a name for the *new economic design*. In spite of my calling the design a new one, in reality it is not new at all. The design is an income distribution design created to sustain the income levels of rich countries so that they will be in accord with the wealth they possess. The design is built to use the opportunities of the century, avoiding conflicts with the new trends in people's perceptions. Similar income distribution schemes, using the opportunities of their day, were developed and used throughout the centuries.

Until very recently, European countries accumulated their wealth by exploiting their colonies. They were able to consume more than they produced since they could acquire goods and services from their colonies at very low cost. Although the American case was somewhat different, the results were the same. The US was able to use slaves in its production at very low costs, to reach a high level of affluence.

After the First World War, oppressed countries and the colonies began to gain their independence, putting an end to their exploitation by wealthier countries. This in turn posed a threat to the developed rich countries in sustaining their consumption behavior. Since those days, rich countries have been in search of new designs to preserve – and perhaps increase – their level of consumption compatible with their level of wealth. The *new economic design* has the potential to meet the desires of rich countries to preserve their level of affluence. The architect of the new design is the US, and the design reflects American aspirations. As we have seen above, with the establishment of the new design, the interests of the US and Europe, and the interests of the US and Japan were in conflict. Europe and Japan tried to preserve their interests during the discussions of the GATT, and they were successful to a certain extent. On the other hand, poor and developing countries also tried to seek their interests, but they had to settle for the promises and the alleged benefits of the *new economic design*.

The *new economic design* was established under the name of *globalization* in the framework of the capitalist market economy in two phases. In the first phase, through an efficient propaganda machine, both developed and developing counties were persuaded about the *virtues* of capitalist market economies. In this stage, the capitalist market economy was converted into a creed. In the second phase, the capitalist market economy was reshaped to serve the interests of the developed rich countries.

The First Phase of the *New Economic Design*

To reach the objectives of the first phase, the IMF, The World Bank and the US Treasury reached a consensus that was later called the Washington Consensus.[11] This consensus brought a radically different approach to economic development stabilization. The World Bank, which was established to provide support to countries that could not develop without institutional support and the IMF, which was established to solve the problems countries faced in financing their current account deficits, started to impose the principles of the Washington Consensus as a single recipe to solve all kinds of problems. After the Washington Consensus, the phrase "free market economy" became a mantra,[12] and the concept was imposed on all developing countries as a precondition for any IMF loans. This imposition was in line with the objectives of the *new economic design*. It included the liberalization of foreign trade and capital markets, privatization, and the expansion of the principles of free markets. Shortly after implementing these policies, these countries faced severe foreign trade, and current account deficits. The emerging market economies of Asia and Latin America attracted huge inflows of foreign money in the forms of loans and speculative investments. Increases in their foreign trade deficits, and the subsequent financing of these deficits with loans and speculative investments ended up in crises in 1994 in Mexico, and in 1997 and 1998 in Asia, Russia and Brazil.[13]

As short-term foreign capital flows into a country, it creates a euphoric mood and speculative setting. The influx of short-term foreign capital increases short-term gains, inviting new inflows of capital. Soon, a speculative bubble

---

11 Initially, this consensus appeared as a reform package prepared for the Latin American countries; later, this package became a standard recipe, which was imposed on all developing countries; about ten years later, John Williamson named the package the "Washington Consensus." This name received wide acceptance. This "reform package" (a recipe) included the following policies: financial discipline, setting priorities for public spending, tax reform, market determination of interest rates, competitive exchange rates, liberalization of trade, liberalization of foreign direct investments, privatization, deregulation and respect for property rights.

12 A *mantra* is the sacred word repeated during prayers or meditations in Hinduism. Joseph Stiglitz used this term in his book on globalization: Stiglitz, *Globalization and its Discontents*, p. 16.

13 A report of the International Forum on Globalization, *Alternatives to Economic Globalization – A Better World is Possible*, San Francisco, CA: Barrett-Koehler Publishers, 2002, p. 39.

is developed in the capital markets. But as the current account deficit grows – which is the natural result of the inflows – the expectation of a devaluation of domestic currency increases the investors' nervousness and anxiety. At one point, any unfortunate event may trigger a rush to the foreign exchange market to save the value of the invested capital. The mass behavior of crowds leads to a market crash and financial crises. The boom and bust resulting from the inflows of short-term foreign capital has been experienced in most of the crises that have occurred since the 1980s. The economic crises since 1980 have inflicted great economic and social costs to the countries experiencing them.

Joseph Stiglitz explains the way the Washington Consensus was imposed on the developing countries:

> *When crises hit, the IMF prescribed outmoded, inappropriate, if "standard" solutions, without considering the effects they would have on the people in the countries told to follow these policies. Rarely did I see forecasts about what the policies would do to poverty. Rarely did I see thoughtful discussions and analyses of the consequences of alternative policies. There was a single prescription. Alternative opinions were not sought. Open, frank discussion was discouraged – there was no room for it. Ideology guided policy prescription and countries were expected to follow the IMF guidelines without debate.*[14]

After all the crises, the IMF comes to the country to protect the rights of the lenders, forces the government take over the responsibility for debts of the private sector and grants new credits to the country. These new loans provide an opportunity for the IMF to impose new policies.

The breakdown of the USSR in 1990 is interpreted as the defeat of the socialist system, and was celebrated as victory for the capitalist system. This event created a great opportunity for the World Bank and the IMF to enforce their liberal recipes. The World Bank and the IMF rushed to the formerly socialist countries in order to help them to transform their economies to a market-based capitalist form. The recipe used was the same recipe used for developing countries: the Washington Consensus. Foreign trade and capital markets were to be liberalized, the state-owned enterprises were to be privatized, and the principles of the liberal market economy were to be spread to all parts of economy. Reforms in the formerly socialist countries were implemented at high speed. The Russian economy lost about 40 percent of its level of income in the process.

---

14 Stiglitz, *Globalization and its Discontents*, pp. 17–18.

The East Asian crises in 1997 had destructive effects on one-time Asian "Tigers." The IMF's policies were also behind these crises. Walter LaFeber claims that Asian peoples accused the West, and primarily American capitalists, for the crises and their aftermath. In their opinion, the Western countries had created the speculative bubble in these Asian countries, made huge profits in a short time and then departed, leaving behind devastation. According to LaFeber, the result was widespread poverty, and social and political chaos in many countries. LaFeber also believes that the IMF made important mistakes in all the issues in which it was involved (such as development and crises management) and in transforming the communist countries to capitalist economies. In countries where limited growth was observed, the benefits of the rich (top 10 percent) increased while the incomes of poor remained the same, or decreased.[15]

At this point, we should also say a few words about the privatization policies of the World Bank and the IMF. The privatization strategy of the World Bank and the IMF is essential for the establishment of the *new economic design*. In developing countries, State Economic Enterprises (SEEs) operate in strategic sectors. These strategic sectors, which provide the infrastructure of almost all the developing countries, are the transportation, telecommunication and the energy sectors. Since these infrastructure sectors require huge amounts of investment, they cannot be undertaken by the private sectors of developing countries. The targets of the privatization strategy of the World Bank and the IMF are these sectors.

In the capitalist economic system, enterprises operate to serve the interests of the owners of capital or the shareholders. The ownership structure, therefore, is very important. If the firms are private firms, they will seek profits for their owners. On the other hand, if the enterprises are owned by the state, they have a public mission to accomplish and they will strive to reach national objectives under a national identity. The private companies are transforming themselves into supranational companies. We may call them "globalized companies":

> *The economic clout of global firms is equally staggering. As Sarah Anderson and John Cavanagh of the Institute for Policy Studies report, the combined sales of the top two hundred firms grew faster than overall global economic activity between 1983 and 1999, reaching the equivalent of close to 30 percent of world GDP.*[16]

---

15   Walter LaFeber, *Michael Jordan ve Yeni Kuresel Kapitalizm* [*Michael Jordan and the new Global Capitalism*] (trans. Aysel Morin), Istanbul: Cep Kitaplari, 156/21 (Yüzyıl Dizisi), 2001, pp. 15, 39–40.
16   As cited in International Forum on Globalization, *Alternatives to Economic Globalization*, p. 31. It is interesting to note also that these firms employ only 0.75 percent of the global workforce.

These companies have no nation (at least so they claim). These companies also seek to serve their stockholders. In the *new economic design*, these companies have a very significant role. As it is often asserted, the world is becoming a unified one, without boundaries or barriers to hinder the free flow of goods and services. In the *new economic design*, economic operations must serve the interests of these supranational companies.

Let us return to the issue of privatization. Privatization of the SEEs is essential for these supranational companies to acquire ownership of the infrastructures – such as the transportation, telecommunication and energy sectors – of developing countries. Since the 1980s, privatization propaganda has benefited from justifiable arguments against state ownerships of enterprises. At that time, it was argued that state enterprises were "nests of corruption", a burden on government budgets, and the "bleeding wound" had to be healed. It was also asserted that the objective of privatization needed to be efficiency increases, and the purpose of privatization should never be to create funds for government spending. It took some time to convince the public about the virtues of privatization. But as soon as the public was convinced, privatization returned to its main objectives. Today, privatization activities are concentrated on energy power plants, refineries and telecommunication networks. Privatization in these areas require such huge amounts of funds that the local private sector cannot raise them. Supranational companies, together with their local partners, compete among each other to buy these SEEs.

To summarize, the first phase of globalization was convincing the public about the *virtues* of the capitalist market economy through pervasive and efficient propaganda. In this endeavor, the World Bank, the IMF and the US Treasury assumed significant roles and they were successful. Today, the principles of the Washington Consensus have become indisputable truths, the basic principles of a new creed, a new faith.

The Second Phase of the *New Economic Design*

We have already defined the second phase of globalization as a reshaping of the capitalist market economy to serve the interests of the developed rich countries, with the help of the new faith. These two phases do not follow one another in time. They are synchronistic, supporting each other and creating synergy in the establishment of the *new economic design*. However, in spite of this, we need to state that the first phase is the prerequisite of the second phase.

We believe that it may help to clarify a related issue before we explain the concepts, institutions and the operating modalities of the second phase. The statement that the *new economic design* will serve the interests of the rich countries brings a question along with it: will the *new economic design* serve the interests of countries or the supranational companies? As the *new economic design* eliminates national boundaries, is it meaningful to talk about nations? Or will it serve the affluence of those who are already rich?[17] One thing that is clear is that while the supranational companies have significant roles in the establishment of the *new economic design*, the agreements are discussed and shaped by nation states. It is not clear whether the supranational companies are using the countries as means to reach their ends, or whether the countries are using the supranational companies for their own interests. But we believe that this ambiguity will not affect our understanding of the concepts, the institutions and the operating modalities of the *new economic design*.

We need to clarify at this point a very important choice we have made about the concepts we have been using. In our explanations above, we were timid in defining the *new economic design* as *globalization*, and we were hesitant in calling supranational companies *global companies*. There was an important reason behind this caution. Globalization is a very broad term, which encompasses many different trends that will finally shape the world's design, hopefully a design that will serve humanity. What has been developing recently is only one such attempt, hopefully a futile attempt to shape the world. We call the current attempt a *new economic design*. For the same reasons, we hesitate to call supranational companies *global companies*.

Let us return to the second phase of the *new economic design*. Today, the concept known as "the product" has undergone an important transformation. Economic theory assumed a product to be something that granted utility when consumed. The hardware of the products was important. Theory also assumed that the products that satisfy a need are homogeneous, not differentiated and not perceived differently. Today, the same can be said only for the hardware of the products, in fact this is even more so. With current technology, the hardware of the products can be produced anywhere in the world, by any producer. But also, today, the software of the products has become important. The software of a product is the image of the product developed by its brand name, design, quality image and its price. The product's software is produced by the creativity

---

17 The results obtained so far give an impression that it will serve the rich and help them to be richer. The income gap within and among the countries is widening. As small number of rich are getting richer, great masses of people are getting poorer.

and imagination, aspirations and visions of the human element of production. Laws under the name of intellectual property rights protect the things that make up the software of the products. Intellectual properties are factors like patents, copyrights, brand names, designs, printed circuits, trade secrets and geographical indicators. The new economic order provides strong protection to these rights. Together, hardware and software form the products' identity. When consumers purchase products, they consider the identity of the product. They try to match somewhat the identity they develop for themselves with the identity of the products they buy.

An important aspect of the *new economic design* is the separation of the production of the hardware and software of the products.[18] Under the *new economic design*, the hardware and software are produced separately by different production factors in different places.

Today, there has been another change in people's perception that has contributed to the image of the product. This relates to the perception of the price of the products. Economic theory assumes the price to be the burden one must bear in order to buy the product. With the developments in the complexity of the products, price became an integral part of the product's image. Price as a part of the product's image must be consistent with the other elements comprising the image. In fact, each component of the image must contribute to the others and create synergies to enhance the image. In addition, the product's price is the only concrete element of the image that conveys important quantitative information about the product's identity. Under these considerations, prices may be a source of satisfaction, rather than being a burden.

These conceptual changes have provided some actors great opportunities to gain a bigger share from the cake produced by economic operations. Those who possess the software of the products, such as brand names, designs, patents, copyrights, can get the hardware of the products produced in any country in the world where labor is abundant and the wages are low, at very low cost, and then ship them to the markets where opportunities exist to charge more for the product. In these operations, the intellectual properties that produce the image of the products are under full protection.

---

18 The split here in the separation in production is of utmost importance. In previous centuries too people used to talk about the hardware and software of the products. For example the products of some artisans used to be perceived differently. Differences in perception can be understood to be differences in the software. But in those centuries there was no separation in the production. The artisans were the people who produced both the hardware and the software.

The operating modalities of acquiring a bigger share of the results of economic operations are the GATT and the institution of the WTO, which implements the rules of the GATT. The GATT is an agreement of countries to liberalize the world trade. Under the GATT's rules, there will be no barriers to the free flow of goods and services among countries.

Again, under the GATT, the cheap labor pools of the labor-abundant countries are preserved. This is so because the GATT is silent on the issue of labor mobility among countries. Since the labor mobility issue is not addressed, labor markets are fractured and the differences in wages do not tend towards equalization. Since the countries where labor is abundant and there is competition with each other to get the production orders of the rich countries, wages in those countries remain at subsistence levels.

In spite of the free flow of goods and services in product markets and keen competition for production in labor abundant countries, intellectual properties are fully protected by GATT. Today, developed rich countries own most of the intellectual properties. These developed and rich countries have better chances to develop these properties further, as they are the countries that have the means to invest in research and development, and in human capital. In the *new economic design*, countries become rich because they own intellectual properties, they can then produce new intellectual properties because they are rich, and the new intellectual properties can make them even richer. This is why in the *new economic design*, the rich get richer while poverty increases in an ever-expanding spiral.

Another institutional requirement of the *new economic design* is the operation of supranational companies.

Capitalist market economics assume a perfect market with great numbers of buyers and sellers. It is assumed that no participant of the markets can influence the price. This assumption does not hold in case of international trade. Economic theory claims that international trade increases the size of the cake to be shared, but how much an importer or exporter will get depends on their bargaining power. Exporters and importers will try to impose prices in foreign trade transactions. Theoretically, in the case of hardware production, the producers in labor-abundant countries and the companies that give the production orders could bargain on prices. In reality, this kind of bargaining cannot take place since the producers are large in number. But in the case of supranational companies, there is no room for bargaining since these companies own the production plants outright, or perhaps the supranational companies have their products produced by their partners in those countries. In these cases, the supranational companies use the labor force of the labor-abundant countries just by hiring them at the prevailing wages of those countries. When wages increase in one country, the supranational companies move their plants to other countries where the wages are lower. Under the *new economic design*, the developing countries are convinced they should welcome foreign direct investment.

Another requirement of the operating modality of the *new economic design* is the power to control communication channels in order to enhance the country's and the product's images. The *new economic design* can also help poor countries to benefit from the rules and principles of the design. Developing countries can also create their own fashions, brand names and designs, which means they can enhance the image of their products. This would make life more difficult for rich countries that have created strong images in markets all around the world. That would mean keen competition in software also. For the *new economic design* to serve the rich countries and the supranational companies, they need to have control over the communication channels and media of the countries where they want to operate. This is provided by the privatization implementations. Privatization has always been an important issue in the agenda of the World Bank and the IMF; it was one of the principles of the Washington Consensus. The US has great potential in image development, for example, Hollywood motion pictures have always been an important export item for the US. These films have promoted not only products by enhancing their images, but they also promoted the concepts, institutions and the operational modalities of the *new economic design*.

We want to complete this chapter by citing Jaroslav Vanek on the sustainability of the existing trends. Vanek adds a new dimension to our analysis above:

> *The inflated standard of living enjoyed by the rich of the world can never, for many reasons, become the way of life of the 80 percent who are poor. The sane levels at which all humanity can survive indefinitely is somewhere near the order of ten times less than today's rich, and ten times more than today's poorest ... This I would call the economics of hope. By contrast, the potentially cataclysmic road of our present, self-centered mainstream economics and "atom defense" of our ill-gotten riches is what I call the economics of damnation.*[19]

---

19 *Cooperative Economics: An Interview with Jaroslav Vanek*, interviewed by Albert Perkins <http://www.ru.org/51cooper.html#author#author>.

Conclusion

The *new economic design* currently under construction has the objective of preserving the affluence of the developed, rich countries. This is not an easy job to accomplish. The advances in communication technologies are making the world smaller and smaller. The free flow of goods and services and capital among countries, if accompanied by the free mobility of labor, may help to narrow the gap between the rich and the poor. In order to take a bigger share from the world output, the developed, rich countries must design a new economic rules and institutions. The *new economic design* needs to look right and fair to people in the world.

For that reason, the new design was launched, claiming that it will serve the interests of all. In the first phase of launching the design, with appropriate propaganda, people were convinced about the virtues of the principles, rules, institutions and the operating modalities of the *new economic design*. The World Bank and the IMF played an important role in this early phase. The design was promoted under an appealing name: globalization. The implementation gained its momentum through the GATT and the establishment of the WTO in 1994.

So far the implementation of the *new economic design* seems to have been successful in gaining acceptance and in reaching its objectives. But since its launch, the gap between the rich and the poor did not narrow. Rich people continued to get richer while poverty levels seem to have remained the same or even increased, while the world's resources are becoming more and more depleted. This situation has created opposition to the *new economic design*. In the next chapter, we will try to analyze the results of, and the opposition to, the *new economic design*.

12

An Interrogation of Capitalism

If the gospels do not apply to the economy what would they apply to?
(Pastor Don Jose Maria, founder of the Mondragon system)[1]

The twentieth century was an era when two economic systems were first experimented with, and then applied with great devotion by their advocates. One was the capitalist free market economy; the other was the socialist centrally planned economy. Although these two systems looked as if they were opposed to each other, they were both the products of Western thought and had great similarities. Capitalism envisaged private property while socialism envisaged the state ownership of property. The basic difference between the two systems emanated from their assumption about humankind. The capitalist system perceived people as basically greedy, self-interested, competitive; the socialist system assumed people wished to seek the service of the state, were collectivist, and inclined to cooperation. The main argument of the capitalist economy was the conviction that it was the source of economic growth and prosperity. The main argument of the socialist economy was the assertion that capitalism exploited the working class. But both the systems were promising heaven on earth. According to the capitalist system, when every individual's efforts are focused on his own interest, this finally will serve the society as a whole; markets will reach their equilibrium with freely determined prices, reflecting the free will of all, and unemployment, one of the major problems of the century, will be eliminated. On the other hand, the socialist system promised a classless society without any exploitation, to be established by an uprising of the working class.

The twentieth century experienced two world wars in 1914–1918 and 1939–1945, and with a similarly devastating effect, an economic depression in the 1930s. In this turbulent environment, both capitalist and socialist economic systems tried to establish superiority against one another and made great efforts to expand their respective domains.

---

1   <http://www.global-co-operation.coop/LinkstoCo-opExcellence.htm>.

In the twentieth century, thanks to enormous breakthroughs in technology, humankind has gained important means to solve its economic problems. But, in spite of these powerful means being in their hands, neither of these systems really brought solutions to the problems people were facing. As technological developments increased their pace in a way unseen in previous centuries, so did the longings of humankind increase parallel to these developments.

On December 10, 1948, the United Nations approved the Declaration of Human Rights. This important document set out the aspirations and longings of humankind. As mentioned in previous chapters, this was a declaration of people's civil, political, economic and social rights. Any new systems developed had the duty to turn to these aspirations into realities. After the Second World War, with the realization that post-war markets might not be able to function properly, institutions like the World Bank and the International Monetary Fund (IMF) were established in the capitalist world to create solutions to the economic problems faced by developing and developed countries. Their apparent purpose was to meet the aspirations of humanity, especially in developing countries.

After the Second World War and until the 1980s, governments played very important roles in the field of economics. However, in spite of the efforts made at both national and international levels, the economic systems failed to meet the aspirations of mankind. As we approached the 1980s, the divide between rich and poor countries increased. As wealthy countries, which represent only a small segment of the world's population, got wealthier, poor countries were not able to increase their welfare standards, and in fact became poorer.

Capitalism Turning into a Religion

Many things changed in the year 1980. Capitalist countries, especially the United States, asserted that the capitalist market economy was not the cause of the unresolved problems of inequality; on the contrary, the real cause was the lack of proper implementation of the rules of the free market economy. The single remedy for the world's problems was the capitalist free market economy, with free trade, privatization and the free flow of capital. These principles became a single recipe to be recommended, in fact imposed, on the developing and underdeveloped countries. At this stage, the capitalist market economy's principles became indisputable, a clear sign that capitalism was becoming a religion.

As the result of the rapid liberalization of foreign trade and capital markets, financial crises became a common event in developing economies. Often, these financial crises turned into economic crises, which inflicted great damage on the economy, and social and political structures of these countries. In spite of the failures of the single recipe used in these countries, not the recipe but its implementation was blamed.

The Joy of Victory

Another turning-point occurred in the year 1990. The socialist system, which had been established in 1917, had glorified the state, but fell short of meeting the aspirations of humanity as we approached the twenty-first century. The year 1990 saw the collapse of the Berlin Wall, and the unification of the two German states. By the end of 1991, the Union of Soviet Socialist Republics, which had been centrally administered by bureaucratic prefectures, disintegrated. The world, previously perceived as divided into two systems, gave the impression that it was transforming into a single-system world. Capitalism's victory was declared. Without any delay, it was claimed that "liberal democracy" was the final stage of ideological evolution of mankind, and for that reason "the end of history" had come.[2] This final claim created a sense of euphoria and generated trust in the capitalist system. However, this trust had no sound foundation, while the religious characteristics of capitalism gained strength. Perfect markets, privatization and liberalization, even increasing unemployment, became unquestionable, undisputable elements of the free market. Unfortunately, some economists were also to follow the popular trend. Stiglitz states that:

> *The standard models that economists had used for generations argued either that markets worked perfectly – some even denied the existence of genuine unemployment – or that the only reason that unemployment existed was that wages were too high, suggesting the obvious remedy: lower wages.*[3]

Over-confidence continued in the years following 1990, causing the proponents of capitalism to commit a very significant error. A consensus was reached to impose a global order based on capitalism; a system which did not respond to all humankind's aspirations, which made the rich richer and poor poorer, which caused masses of unemployment in order to increase the profits of companies,

---

2   Francis Fukuyama, *The End of History and the Last Man*, London: Penguin, 1992.
3   Joseph Stiglitz, *Globalization and its Discontents*, New York: W.W. Norton, p. 12.

and most importantly, which destroyed the world's ecological balance. In the year 1994, with signing and inauguration of the General Agreement on Trade and Tariffs (GATT), the *new economic design*, which had been long in planning, acquired its form. The name used for this *new economic design* was *globalization*.

The *new economic design* was imposed on the world with a promise to improve the welfare of the poor. But its hidden purpose was to serve the interests of the capitalist countries (or supranational companies, according to some).

The Point Now Reached

As we approached 2005, it could be observed that the *new economic design* became much more successful than expected in a period as short as just a decade. The natural economic consequences of the system became apparent soon. In *Globalization and its Discontents*, Nobel Prize winner Joseph Stiglitz explains his reason for writing the book: " … while I was at the World Bank [as an economic advisor], I saw firsthand the devastating effect that globalization can have on developing countries, and especially the poor within those countries." He continues:

> *A growing divide between the haves and the have-nots has left increasing numbers in the Third World in dire poverty, living on less than a dollar a day. Despite repeated promises of poverty reduction made over the last decade of the twentieth century, the actual number of people living in poverty has actually increased by almost 100 million. This occurred at the same time that total world income actually increased by an average of 2 percent annually.*[4]

Yes, under the label of globalization, capitalism has adapted itself to the new technology and world conditions. But it was still serving the same audience, that is, rich countries or supranational companies:

> *In a world in which a few enjoy unimaginable wealth, two hundred million children under age five are underweight because of a lack of food. Some fourteen million children die each year from hunger-related disease. The human tragedy is not confined to poor countries. Even in*

---

4   Ibid., p. .27.

a country as wealthy as the United States, 6.1 million adults and 3.3 million children experience outright hunger.[5]

Naturally, the *new economic design* also served developing countries. Since wages were low in developing countries, the production facilities of rich countries moved to developing countries in order to produce goods at lower costs.[6] This, of course, created employment and income in those countries. In the countries where the production took place, workers were employed at very low wages and were subject to very bad conditions. When wages increased in one country, the production facilities were moved to another country where the wages were still low. Due to the mobility of production facilities, it became more difficult to raise wages, which were often at mere subsistence levels, in low-wage countries. This mobility also caused unemployment to increase in countries with higher wages and is why income distribution worsened both among countries and within countries. In any case, labor's share in the income generated by productive operations decreased.

Resistance to Globalization

Resistance to globalization was also global in its dimensions. Millions of people from all around the world came together to express their aspirations for a better and fairer world to live in. Protestors were not against foreign trade; they were opposing the rules of free trade implemented under the *new economic design*: they were demanding *fair* trade, which would serve the needy as well as wealthy.

After 1999, the protestors' targets were the World Bank, the IMF and the World Trade Organization (WTO). Protestors blocked the Ministerial Conference of WTO in Seattle, whose agenda was to open new discussions on further liberalization. The meeting was disrupted and postponed to 2001. In 2001, the meeting took place in the city of Doha in Qatar, a small Arabian kingdom from which protestors were barred. Since the year 2000, Davos in Switzerland has come to symbolize the power of globalization and liberalization when, in January of each year, CEOs of global companies, political leaders and others from many countries attend the World Economic Forum in order to expand the

---

5   The International Forum on Globalization, *Alternatives to Economic Globalization: A Better World is Possible*, San Francisco, CA: Barrett-Koehler Publishers, 2002, p. 7.

6   "Made in USA Foundation asserts that in the 1980s, when Nike and other shoe companies moved their production facilities to Asian countries, 65,000 American workers lost their jobs": ibid., p. 103.

boundaries of globalization. In 2001, the opponents of globalization scheduled an alternative conference, the World Social Forum, in Porto Allegre, Brazil; the theme of the conference was "A Better World is Possible." This alternative meeting was repeated in the following years in January as an alternative to the World Economic Forum.[7]

The Doha ministerial conference of the World Trade Organization was another turning-point. Some regarded the meeting as a triumph of globalization, but others considered it a sign of submission to the trends opposing globalization. The *Washington Post* asserted that the result of the WTO's meeting came in the form of two successes: First, the Doha meeting did not meet the fate of the disbanded Seattle conference, and showed that even in times of global protest, global integration can make progress. Second, the summit initiated a second trade round that would focus on the needs of the poor countries.

In reality, there were no developments in favor of the developing countries in the Doha meeting. Europe would not accept any steps to open up its agricultural products markets, and the US its textile markets, to poor countries. The proposal to establish a relief fund for the benefit of countries in need did not receive any support. It was accepted that, in case of an emergency, patent rights on pharmaceutical products could be suspended, but no amendment was made in the TRIPS agreement that provides full protection to these rights, in this direction. The countries involved also did not make changes to their laws and regulations.

One of the most important features of the *new economic design* is the full protection of intellectual property rights. Pharmaceutical companies benefit extensively from this protection. Pharmaceutical companies have been claiming that they are spending millions of dollars for drug development, which is reflected in the prices of their products; if not, it would be impossible for them to develop new products that would serve people's health. On the other hand, in the academic world, contradictory arguments have become topics for discussion: it is asserted in the academic world that a significant portion of pharmaceutical research in the US is based on the studies carried by the National Institute of Health (NIH); that since President Reagan's administration in the 1980s drug companies have benefited from very strong monopoly protections; that patent protection terms are extended to products which are reformulations of old ones; that contrary to the claims of the pharmaceutical companies, they

---

7   In the struggle against globalization the International Forum on Globalization (IFG) has been very instrumental <http://www.ifg.org>.

did not spend much for research and development (they spent even less than their profit); that through their advertisements they created illnesses tailored to their drugs, instead of creating drugs for current illnesses, that they made very high profits of around 17–18 percent of their sales, that a few supranational companies dominated the market, and that in this fast-developing, $400 billion industry, the supranational companies have gained the strength to steer national policies in the direction of their own interests.[8]

Poor countries afflicted by the HIV/AIDS epidemic tabled a proposal to the Doha meeting of the WTO. They were unable to wage the fight against HIV/AIDS due to the high price of the drugs which were protected by patent rights. But the spread of HIV/AIDS was a threat to rich countries also. The poor countries requested a reduction in the price of HIV/AIDS drug therapies. While their proposal did not receive much concern during the meeting, a separate Declaration was later adopted, which noted the importance of research and development without recommending any concrete measures. However, "In the case of AIDS, the international outrage was so great that drug companies had to back down, eventually agreeing to lower their prices, to sell the drugs at cost in late 2001."[9]

In fact, the Doha meeting illustrated that capitalism was engaged in a great struggle to establish global domination. But the counter-resistance to capitalism was also gaining strength. The search for various solutions was beginning in many places: in academic circles, in different blocs of developing countries, in the Internet environment. In reality, what was under interrogation was not only globalization, but capitalism itself.

Opposition Against the Global Companies

Supranational companies are an integral part of globalization. The companies that we define as supranational are not accountable to and do not have any responsibility to serve nations; they only seek to maximize their own profits.

---

8   In this respect the studies of Marcia Angell, a professor at Harvard Medical School. represent a good example. See: New York Review of Books, *The Truth About the Drug Companies*, Volume 51, Number 12, and July 15, 2004 <http://www.nybooks.com/articles/17244> and *Frontline: The Other Drug War: Interviews, Marcia Angell* <http://www.pbs.org/wgbh/pages/frontline/shows/other/interviews/angell.html>.

9   Stiglitz, *Globalization and its Discontents*, p. 8.

In the *new economic design*, these supranational companies, after designing their products with the intellectual properties they own, can purchase their raw materials from anywhere in the world where they can get them cheapest, have their products produced in countries at minimum cost where labor is cheap and abundant (mostly in Asian countries), and market them in whatever country they see fit. Since the *new economic design* does not permit labor mobility, vast pools of cheap labor can be found in developing countries. Many supranational companies, through direct investment or by joint ventures established by domestic producers, move their production facilities to the countries where wages and production costs are very low. As soon as wages increase in these countries, the same companies move their production facilities yet again. Wage increases in developing countries usually occur due to the unionization of workers, that is, when workers start exercising their democratic rights. Thus, in the process of unionization, workers face the risk of unemployment. Perhaps this is one of the major causes of labor exploitation in these labor-abundant countries. Supranational companies' exploitation of labor in labor-abundant countries meets with the condemnation of non-governmental organizations and trade unions in rich countries (especially in the US). NGOs and unions protest against the sweatshops operated by supranational companies in labor-abundant countries. Of course, the real concern of the unions is the increasing unemployment in their home countries. US labor unions claim that increasing job opportunities in Asia through the reallocation of production are really jobs stolen from Americans. On the other hand, the NGOs' reaction to supranational companies is due to the inhumane nature of the working conditions and exploitation of the workers in these Asian countries.

The NGOs' protests soon received media support. The NGOs started campaigns urging consumers not to purchase the products produced under such conditions, highlighting how child and female workers were forced to work under severe conditions, extending to torture, with forced overtime, for $1.60 a day. When students organized themselves, universities joined the NGOs' protests. What was actually being opposed was the exploitation of the people of Asian countries under the profit motive by the supranational companies.

The case of the Nike Shoe Company[10] is a good example of a supranational company's exploitation of labor in underdeveloped countries, and the

---

10 Nike's operations in East Asia are used as a case study in academic courses. See Rebecca J. Moris and Anne T. Lawrence, *Nike's Dispute with the University of Oregon*. Thompson and Strickland, Strategic Management, Concepts and Cases, New York: McGraw Hill, 2003. pp. c759–c775. A good book on the issue is Walter LaFeber, *Michael Jordan and the New Global Capitalism*, New York: W.W. Norton, 2001.

opposition and resistance this exploitation faced in developed countries. We will examine this case briefly.[11]

Phil Knight and his partner, with $1,000 in capital, officially founded Nike Inc. in 1963. By the year 2000, Nike had become a company which provided employment to 20,000 employees directly and indirectly to half a million people through 565 factories in 46 countries where production is subcontracted. The company had a share of 45 percent of the sports shoes market and $9 billion of sales turnover. In the factories in Asia where Nike's products are produced, woman (who made up 90 percent of the workforce) toiled in awful conditions for 14 cents an hour.

The labor cost of a pair of Nike shoes was $2.75; while selling and administrative costs were $5 and advertisement expenditures $4. After deducting material and supplies costs, Nike's profit share was $6.25. The wholesale price of a pair of Nike shoes was $35 and the retail price about $70.

In the early 1990s, serious criticism of Nike's global labor practices and exploitation of laborers in Asian factories started to appear widely in the media. According to the claims, in the factories where Nike's shoes were produced, laborers were forced by the managers to work six hours of overtime, and were subjected to sexual harassment and physical torture. Human rights associations and Christian organizations immediately responded to the news in the media. Shareholder activists, organized by the Interfaith Center for Corporate Responsibility, submitted a shareholders' proposal at Nike's annual meeting, calling on the company to review labor practices by its subcontractors. The proposal received only 3 percent support from the shareholders. In 1996, Nike established a new Labor Practices Department. Again in the same year, President Clinton established the White House Apparel Industry Partnership on Workplace Standards (AIP). The initial group comprised 18 organizations. Participants included several leading manufacturers, such as Nike, Reebok and Liz Claiborne. The goal of the AIP was to develop a set of standards and

---

11 The issue that labor employed in the Nike shoe company's factories in Asia worked in inhumane conditions is a well-discussed matter. "Since the beginning of 1990s, media (in Asia) was reporting regularly that some of the laborers were working in very inhumane conditions. It was clear that working conditions showed very little improvement till the end of the 1990s. In the factories where 70 million pair of shoes were produced, labor received an average 2.23 dollars a day ... Indonesian workers were being forced to work 6 hours of overtime and they were subject to sexual harassment and aerating." "Working conditions in Vietnam were also awful." Ninety percent of the 30,000 employees were female. These female workers were receiving only 2 dollars pay for 12 hours of work. See: LaFeber, *Michael Jordan and the New Global Capitalism*, pp. 121–2.

to monitor them to ensure that apparel and footwear were not made under sweatshop conditions. The AIP established a new organization, the Fair Labor Association (FLA), to oversee compliance with its workplace code of conduct.[12] In October 1999, these developments were followed by the establishment of the Workers' Rights Consortium (WRC) by the leadership of students from more than a hundred colleges. This consortium asked the companies to pay wages sufficient to sustain life, to supply the addresses of the factories where their products were produced, and asked the universities not to purchase goods from companies which do not meet these conditions.

On April 12, 2000, the University of Oregon joined the WRC. Shortly after the university's decision, Phil Knight, the founder of Nike and its major shareholder, withdrew his philanthropic contributions to University of Oregon.

This example deserves analysis from various points of view, and is a case used in the education of master's degree policy course students. The example indicates the importance people assign to ethical values and the corporate responsibilities assumed by the companies. This case questions the behavior of global companies within the rules of globalization.

An Interrogation of Capitalism

The *new economic design* called globalization is the latest attempt of capitalism to establish its sovereignty. Implementation of capitalism on a broader scale has also helped us to understand the consequences created by the capitalist system. Income distribution among and within countries worsened, and poverty became more widespread. Worse than that, in spite of the fact that only a small number of people benefit from the blessings of the system, it became clear that the ecological balances of the world are not able to carry the burden of the material hunger of capitalism and the waste produced by this hunger. The greenhouse effect caused by carbon emissions due to excessive consumption of petroleum, has resulted in melting of the polar icecaps, changes in the course of the Gulf Stream and change in climate.[13] As the ozone layer thins, the world is deprived of its protective shield.

12　Moris and Lawrence, *Nike's Dispute with the University of Oregon*, p. c771.
13　The United States is the major country that consumes and promotes consumption, and the country that blocks the reforms on energy consumption. For that reason, the US has declined to sign the Kyoto Protocol signed by many countries, which attempt to take moderate steps in environmental protection. The US which produces 4 percent of the world's petroleum consumes about 25 percent of the world's petroleum.

These developments engendered two political movements: the first being the wars to establish control over the world's natural resources, and the second being terrorism. As rich capitalist countries kept on their race to establish control over the world's natural resources, poor countries came to the conclusion that resorting to terrorist measures was the only way they could preserve their existence. Joseph Stiglitz evaluates the point reached by applying globalization for ten years in the following words:

> The barbaric attacks of September 11, 2001, have brought home with great force that we all share a single planet. We are a global community, and like all communities have to follow some rules so that we can live together. These rules must be fair and just, must pay due attention to the poor as well as the powerful, must reflect a basic sense of decency and social justice.[14]

At first, it seemed that the interrogation of capitalism was focused on globalization and the interrogators were against globalization. In reality, what is being questioned is capitalism itself, and comes from very different groups of people from various professions, and from an expanded geography. This interrogation is organized in various forms, benefiting from advanced technology, and aims at creating an alternative to capitalism with a broad participation using democratic means.

An interesting aspect of this is that the teaching of economics is also being questioned. The reason for this is that in the past the economic teaching promoted and defended capitalism without discussing any alternatives. Here, we want to briefly mention two institutions as examples of academic interrogation: the Post Autistic Economics movement, which is known as *PAE*, and the Santa Fe Institute.

The Post Autistic Economics Movement[15]

This movement was started in France in June 2000, when a group of students, under the banner *"autism-economie,"* published a petition on the Internet, protesting against:

---

14 Stiglitz, *Globalization and its Discontents*, p. 15.
15 <htpp://www.btinternet.com~pae_news/history.htm>.

- economics' *uncontrolled use* and the treatment of mathematics as *an end in itself*, and the resulting *autistic science*,

- the repressive domination of neoclassical theory and derivative approaches in the curriculum, and

- the dogmatic teaching style, which leaves no place for critical and reflective thought.

In this petition, the students demanded:

- engagement with empirical and concrete economic realities,

- prioritizing science over scientism,

- a pluralism of approaches adapted to the complexity of economic objects and the uncertainty surrounding most of the big economic questions, and

- that their professors initiate reforms to rescue economics from its autistic and socially irresponsible state.

Initially, this petition was backed by some of the professors; after getting their support the topic was opened to discussion in *Le Monde*, on June 21, 2000. The topic caught the attention of French Minister of Education and the Ministry formed a commission to discuss and report its findings in a year. Eventually, the discussions became a forum where the current concepts of economics and the capitalist economy are debated. The *Post Autistic Economics Newsletter*, which was disseminated in the early days, is now a quarterly e-mail journal.[16]

According to the supporters of the Post Autistic Economics movement, by creating a comprehensive forum of discussions "such an open environment would preclude the standard practice of keeping the ideological content of neoclassicism hidden from students."[17] Again, according to the same belief, economic science has never been under such pressure since the 1930s. The complaint then was economic science's inability to explain and develop

---

16 <http://www.paecon.net>.
17 Edward Fullbrook, *The Post-Autistic Economics Movement: A Brief History*, November 21, 2001, p. 20 <http://www.altruists.org/static/files/The%20Post-Autistic%20Economics%20Movement%20%28Edward%20Fullbrook%29.pdf>.

a solution to the 1930 Great Depression. This led to the development of macroeconomics. Today, the accusation is more general and more serious: the way economics is taught in universities is unable to explain today's realities or to present a framework for in-depth discussion of the problems in democratic communities.

The journal of the Post Autistics Economics movement questions the way economics is understood today – its assumptions, methods and the conclusions it reaches – and tries to produce alternatives; in short, it is questioning capitalism as a whole.

The Santa Fe Institute[18]

The Santa Fe Institute was established in 1984 as a non-profit institution, devoted to creating a new kind of scientific research community, which would emphasize multi-disciplinary collaboration in pursuit of understanding the common themes that arise in natural, artificial, and social systems. The institute has a great number of renowned scientists from economics and other disciplines; some are Nobel Prize winners. It promotes multidisciplinary collaborations in the physical, biological, computational and social sciences. The institute attempts to uncover the mechanisms that underlie the deep simplicity present in our complex world. The institute believes that the understanding of complex adaptive systems is critical to addressing key environmental, technological, biological, economic and political challenges.

From the point of view of economic science, the Santa Fe Institute diverges from the neoclassical stand completely. Neoclassical economics, diminishing returns, static equilibrium rely on absolute rationality.[19] On the contrary, the Santa Fe Institute emphasizes the increasing return, constrained rationality, and evolution and dynamics of learning: "Instead of viewing the society as some kind of Newtonian machine, they would see it as something organic, adoptive, and alive."[20]

Some of the studies conducted by the institute show how wrong a path the capitalist free market system is following. Since the Santa Fe Institute

---

18 <http://www.santafe.edu>.
19 Rationality is a well defined concept in economics. This concept assumes individuals to be consistent in behavior and that they know what is good for them.
20 M. Mitchell Waldrop, *Complexity: The emerging Science at the Edge of Order and Chaos*, New York: Simon and Schuster, 1993, p. 252.

defined itself using a broader mission, it is not conducting studies to develop alternatives to capitalism.

Capitalist Companies' Search for Solutions

Resistance to globalization and the interrogation of capitalism has redirected capitalist companies to search for new relations. Capitalist companies redirect themselves to "sustainable profits," a new concept they have defined to replace short-term profits. "Respect for ethical values" and "sensitivity to social responsibility" as concepts lay at the base of the sustainable profits concept. In time, companies understand that their behavior, which will not be accepted by human conscience, will impair their achievements. The concepts of "working ethics," "corporate social responsibility" and "environmental protection" are gradually gaining advocates and are spreading. Still, companies regard these concepts as a means to increase their profits. Companies realize that they must respect the customer's ethical values in order to make a profit. In reality, here lies a contradiction: consumers seem to be ready to make sacrifices, though small, paying a higher but fair price to purchase products that are environmentally friendly and that help to preserve ecological balances. Companies that benefit from these concerns of the consumers do not seem to show the same sensitivity their customers are showing, but instead, use their customers' concerns to increase their profits.

In fact, the capitalist company's awareness of the ethical values is a very important step forward. This development can also be considered a revolution in economic science. Economic science claims that it is not a *normative*, but a *positive* science. That is, economic science states that it does not account for value judgments. Whereas it is being understood that individuals make their choices not as *homo economicus*, which is likened to a machine by economics, but as individuals who assign high importance to their value judgments. This is another example that shows how much the economic sciences are removed from the realities of real life. Similarly, economic institutions and companies, recognizing these facts, reshape their policies accordingly.

A good example for companies redirecting themselves to sustainable profitability objectives and assuming a kind of behavior that pays respect to people and to the environment is available in an article published in *Made in*

Holland, a publication of the Netherlands Foreign Trade Agency (NFTA), part of the Ministry of Economic Affairs.[21] Let us briefly summarize this article:

> *Corporate social responsibility is in fact nothing other than a business that behaves properly in relation to people and the environment. The international marketing term is accordingly "People Planet Profit". But that is easier said than done: A business earns its place in the world by making profit. Environmental measures and a good social plan, by contrast, eat into profits.*
>
> *Nevertheless, ever more Dutch businesses are actively exploring ways of taking the environment more closely into account in their business management. They prove that this is not just possible but also commercially interesting. Shell is working hard and developing hydrogen as a source of energy and a fuel and on windmills and other forms of sustainable energy. C&A is no longer doing business with suppliers who make use of child labor; and DSM is developing more environmentally friendly production processes.*
>
> *With its Max Havelaar coffee brand, the coffee-roasting house and tea dealer Simon Levelt was one of the first Dutch companies to base a consumer product on corporate social responsibility while at the same time managing to turn the brand into a commercial success. Since 1988 many Dutch people have been happy to buy the more expensive coffee in the knowledge that the Simon Levelt coffee farmers in South America are paid a proper price for their coffee beans. In the mean time, not just "fair" coffee but also cocoa, tea, honey, bananas and orange juice are being sold under the Max Havelaar brand – and not only in Holland but in 17 other countries.*
>
> *After looking for profits alone for years, large Dutch companies and multinationals have now recognized this to be a short-term strategy and acknowledge that sustainable entrepreneurship is a long-term investment … Corporate social responsibility is not a matter of charity or a subsidy but an investment in the continuity of the company.*

---

21 Tina Reinders, "Doing business in the Netherlands on the People Planet Profit principle," *Made in Holland*, 2003–04, pp. 16–19. Also see <www.maxhavelaar.nl>; <www.natureandmore.com>; <www.eosta.com>; <www.w-concern.com>.

As can be seen from this example, companies have started to recognize the need to place importance on the aspirations of individuals. But for the time being, this recognition is directed to the profit objective. Another interesting point about this example is that this article was published in a magazine trying to promote Holland.

The Insistence on Capitalism for Survival

In the previous paragraphs above, we have explained the increase in resistance to globalization, the interrogation of capitalism, and how humanity is searching for solutions. Today, facing these challenges of resistance and interrogation, the proponents of capitalism (the fortresses of capitalism), instead of reshaping capitalism in the direction of the aspirations of humankind, are making an effort to spread their ideology with greater devotion and greed, and to implement capitalism to serve their interest.

After the fall of the USSR, we see that the advocates of capitalism, and more than that, the defenders of the US's interests, have initiated efforts to develop a new world vision.[22] In 1992, Francis Fukuyama, in his book *The End of History and the Last Man,* declared that the arrival of the end of history. According to Fukuyama, with the Cold War over, the world is no longer a bipolar world but a single order; liberal democracy has become the future of the world. There is no room in the world for distinct ideologies, and liberal democracy may be the final stage of the ideological evolution of humanity.[23] In this context, liberal democracy is liberalism as a political, economic and social system. Accordingly, as Fukuyama visualizes, capitalism is the future world order. In fact, what is being accomplished is the idealization of a non-ideology, that is, idealization of a lack of ideology. What is being accomplished is very important: people will be convinced that they should not be in search of systems and ideologies to meet their aspirations (longings). This does not seem to be a scientific approach. It is an act of faith.

How will capitalism spread over the world in a medium where no ideology exists? The answer to this question had to be incorporated into the new world vision. This did not constitute any problem at all. In 1993, Zbigniew Brzezinski published his book, *Out of Control,* which had great influence on world politics. Brzezinski claimed that twentieth-century politics can be defined as

---

22 We may call this a new paradigm.
23 Francis Fukuyama, *The End of History and the Last Man,* London: Penguin, 1992.

one of "organized insanity," and that an innumerable amount of people were destroyed in ideological clashes.[24] Now a global look would be required to advance humanity, and the United States stand as the only truly global power; if the United States failed to establish global authority, the world would enter a stage of intensified global instability.[25] According to the assertion, if the US fails in this mission, the world will drift into a terrorist environment.

Though there is no need for *ideologies* to clash in the twenty-first century, there must be a clash somewhere, in order to help capitalism dominate the world. In 1996, Samuel P. Huntington produced an answer in his often-cited book, *The Clash of Civilizations*. According to Huntington, down the centuries, clans, kings, nations and ideologies have clashed. Since these all have become history, it is now time for the clash of civilizations. The twentieth century had become a scene for the competition of superpowers. Now this competition will take place among civilizations. In the world of the 1990s, the major civilizations that have a significant role in the identity of individuals can be named as the Western, Latin American, African, Islamic, Chinese, Indian, Orthodox, Buddhist and Japanese civilizations. Among these existing cultures, the Christian Western culture is most susceptible to economic and democratic development, while Islamic culture is seen as an important barrier to the development of democracy. In our times, the Western culture is strong. But, it is losing its strength over time. The West will be involved in an effort to preserve its values. Non-Western cultures are confronted with two options: to join the Western cultural caravan, or to take sides with the Confucian and Islamic cultures, which try to achieve a balance with Western civilization by increasing their military and economic power. The post-Cold War order will be a scene of a cultural race between the Western and non-Western cultures. And major clashes will take place on the fault-lines between civilizations.[26]

Since the end of the Cold War, the US has been in search of an operating theory of the world and a military strategy to support it. The clearest explanation of this model came from Thomas P.M. Barnett, who is a professor of warfare analysis and an advisor to the Office of the Secretary of Defense since September 11, 2001. Barnett gave this explanation in an article in *Esquire* in 2003, and in his book *The Pentagon's New Map*, published in 2004. According to Barnett, the twenty-first century's clashes will take place between the countries that are

---

24 The communist system whose failure has been proven now, had a cost of the lives of 60 million people.

25 Zbigniew Brzezinski, *Out of Control: Global Turmoil on the Eve of the Twenty First Century*, New York: Scribner's, 1993.

26 Samuel P. Huntington, *The Clash of Civilizations*, New York: Free Press, 1996, p. 28.

successful in adopting themselves to globalization and those that are not. The "Core" countries, which are successful in globalization, are the countries which have stable government and improving standards of life. The "Gap" countries, on the other hand, are those countries with oppressive governments, where misery is widespread, and most important of all, where terrorism is nurtured. The objectives of the wars in the twenty-first century must be to expand the Core country areas and shrinking the Gap. Between these Core and Gap countries lie the "Seam" countries.[27] Seam countries must take their positions, either siding with the Core or Gap countries – there is no room for detachment in this world. The position of the Seam states is important. In spite of their efforts and intentions, the Seam states face severe difficulties under globalization.[28] Cooperation with these states is essential to protect the US from the threats of the Gap countries, and terrorism, and as such, the US must use its power on these countries.[29]

The United States – acknowledged as the fortress of capitalism, and architect of the *new economic design*, that is, globalization – is trying to expand its global hegemony, under different labels, such as the "war on terrorism" (WOT), protecting human rights and democracy, expanding liberal economics. According to the US's view, the world is divided into two camps: those who side with the US and those who oppose it. During the Iraq War, the US's official stance was: "You are either with us, or against us."

Although the world is unable to carry the burden of the present level of petroleum consumption; although for this reason, the climate is changing, the glaciers are melting, and the world's ecological balances is shifting, and although the rich countries account for most petroleum consumption, rich countries do not reduce their consumption, nor do they make any effort to find alternative sources of energy, but instead compete or fight to expropriate the world's remaining oil reserves.

These efforts are the insistence of capitalism for survival.

---

27 Seam states that lie along the Gap's bloody boundaries are strategically very important.
28 Here we would like to mention that, Turkey lies on the "seam line" on Barnett's classification.
29 Thomas P.M. Barnett, "The Pentagon's New Map," *Esquire*, March 2003.

Inconsistent Principles and the Conflicting System

Today, the capitalist system is in conflicting with the aspirations of the people. These aspirations are bound to create a new economic system. We can briefly define the conflicting principles as follows:

- The focal point of the capitalist system are individuals, who are rational, and try to maximize their affluence. Their environment (which can be other individuals, and the social, economic and ecological environment) is not considered in their decision mechanisms. *However*, in people's aspirations, individuals are an inseparable part of the society, part of nature, and a part of a whole. When the individuals make their decisions, they would seek a harmony between their own and society's well-being.[30]

- In the capitalist system, individuals (person, companies, countries and blocs) promote their own interest. Standards are not important when that interest is at stake. A country that is a strong advocate of free trade can resort to protective measures if its interest dictates. This is also the case for individuals. The capitalist economy lets individuals enter into fierce competition with their colleagues at work.[31] *However*, in the aspirations of people it is not self-interest, but being right and fair (*hak*)[32] that is important. In these aspirations, it is not military power, force, economic power or propaganda, but being right that matters. Being defeated in a right cause is accepted as being more valuable than being victorious for a wrong cause. The concept of *hak* is a broad one that influences the philosophy of life. *Hak* is a very old and deep-rooted concept, known as a*sha* in the Zoroastrian religion, *rita* in the Vedas, and *dharma* in Buddhism.

- Capitalism is built on the competition principle. Competition among individuals, among companies, among countries and among blocs is assumed to be the main source of development and improvement. Competition as defined by capitalism means overcoming, or even destroying rivals. Defined as such, a very thin line differentiates competition and clashes. It is for this reason

---

30 The breakdown of the Soviet Socialist Republic has also shown that emphasizing the society by neglecting the individual is also wrong.

31 This practice has been implemented with success especially in corporate downsizing operations, which are in fashion.

32 The Turkish word is *hak*, is more comprehensive than right; it also means being fair and just.

that the capitalist mentality is even able to talk about the "clash of civilizations." *However*, aspirations are in favor of cooperation and solidarity. Today, competitive and cooperative behaviors and their interaction are not well understood. It is possible to discern a closer relation between competition and *collaboration*.[33] In order to compete, parties may have to collaborate. But the goal of cooperation may not be competition. For that reason in the aspirations of people, competing to serve humanity (*hizmet yolunda yarışma*)[34] holds a very special place.

- Capitalism is built on *dissatisfaction*. People are assumed to be greedy. Increased consumption grants diminishing satisfaction (utility), but always increases satisfaction. There is no saturation point, no upper limit for satisfaction. Currently, the per capita income of the rich countries is about $30,000. How much can this per capita income increase? Capitalism has a clear answer to this question: as much as it can be increased. Capitalism's goal is to increase consumption at the expense of everything: the "others," the environment and nature. In capitalism, it is not satisfaction, but dissatisfaction is the rule.[35] However, people's aspirations lead them to yearn to be satisfied with less, a sufficient level of consumption, which is in harmony with our world, our environment, and our society. Our aspirations are not focused on consumption but focused on moral satisfaction and happiness. In reaching moral satisfaction and happiness, our relations with our environment, our loved ones, and nature is of utmost importance. Our aspirations are humanistic: it is the peace, happiness and welfare of all people.

---

33 In the book *Complexity*, M.M. Waldrop quotes John H. Holland: "...despite all the work in economics and biology, we still haven't extracted what's central in competition. There is a richness there that we've only just begun to fathom. Consider the marginal fact that competition can produce a very strong incentive for cooperation, as certain players spontaneously forge alliances and symbiotic relationships with each other for mutual support. It happens at every level and in every kind of complex, adaptive system, from biology to economics and politics. Competition and cooperation may seem antithetical, but at some very deep level, they are two sides of the same coin": M.M. Waldrop, *Complexity*, New York: Simon and Schuster, p. 185.

34 *Yarışma* is a concept different than competition. In *yarışma*, there does not have to be an opponent.

35 In *Complexity*, Waldrop quotes Gell Mann: We need cross-cultural ferment, "of particular importance may be discoveries about how (our own culture can) restrain the appetite for material goods and substitute more spiritual appetites": Waldrop, *Complexity*, p. 352.

- In capitalism, companies consider the consumer as king in order to make a profit. But here also, people are not the end but only a means to reach the end. People are not kings because they are human beings, they are kings when they have money to spend to increase profits. In order to reach the profit objective if it is possible to exploit (by forming monopolies) the king, this chance should not be missed. Capitalism has regulations to prevent the formation of monopolies, but recently these regulations are being loosened by new definitions. As the supranational companies become widespread, question marks arise about who is defined as the king. The *new economic design* is being shaped in order to serve the interests of these supranational companies. *However*, in our aspirations, people are precious precisely because they are *people*. The objective is the people. All other things are means. Systems ought to be shaped to serve people: *"Serving people means serving God."*[36]

- In the areas of production, capitalism looks upon human beings as a factor of production that is in competition with the other factors, and as a mean that must be cheaper in order to be employed. Capitalism considers man as a cost factor. In a competitive environment, in order to maximize profits, companies must reduce their costs. For that reason, labor can be replaced by machinery if machinery is cheaper. This would be considered acceptable by capitalist standards. Today, machines are becoming more intelligent, robots more skilled and computers faster and more accurate. Humans must compete with all this machinery. For that reason, unemployment has been an unsolved problem in capitalism. During the economic crises created by capitalism, massive numbers of laborers lose their jobs, which also reinforces the crises. *However*, in our aspirations, humans are the primary source of production. They create the technology, design, and brand names and fashion; in fact they created capital. Man is productive. In the area of production, participation, unity in destiny, and sharing are the rule.

---

36 In Denizli, on the gate of Babadağ bazaar there is an inscription (tablet) which says: "Show affection to every one ha! Do not withhold your greetings./Do not differentiate people ha! Give them all their rights with justice/Your purpose must be good ha! Tell the truth about everything./Do not part with whatever is beneficial ha! Be in accord with everyone./Disperse friendship around you ha! Your work remains but you go./Learn by heart, do not forget ha! First count your service, then yourself."

- In capitalism, humans seek leisure. Capitalism considers work as a burden and the wage received as bliss. *However*, in our aspirations, work itself, having good work to do, being constructive and creative are blessings in their own right. The wage received is only one of the blessings received from work. Working gives a chance to people to prove themselves and to excel in what they do. Working provides status and identity to human beings.[37]

- When we take into consideration the two points mentioned above, capitalism considers man as a means of production, which is not different from machines (we can say as a slave under certain conditions), but considers him as a king as a customer. This is an important conflict in capitalism. When we consider the dynamics of this, when capitalism reduces wages or causes unemployment, labor loses its income; this means the "king" is deprived of his purchasing power. We face these events repeatedly in economic crisis. On the other hand, let us assume that machines or robots will carry in the future all production. Where will workers get their income to spend? Perhaps in such an order, each person will have to own a robot! *However*, our aspirations view humans not only a means of production or as a "king," but considers them as complete persons with a culture, beliefs, motivation to work, in fact, an integral part of their nature.

- In capitalism, the comparative advantages of people make them advantageous in the economic race (competition) and provide them with success. Those who are successful are admired, receive good wages, and make profits or gains. Those who are not successful are pushed outside the system and must depend on social security systems or charity organizations. There are two sources for superiority: either God-given, or developed by the individual's own efforts, benefiting from the means and opportunities provided by society. In capitalism, whatever the source, the reward is personalized, and the benefit is the right of the one who possesses the advantage. In the *new economic design*, rights like patents, copyrights, printed circuits, brand names, trade secrets

---

37 It is claimed that, the military type of hierarchy consciously structured in Japanese companies helps them to pay as much as American companies are paying to their chief executives. American companies pay about 10 times, sometimes 100 times more to their chief executives than the Japanese companies. This is another source for competitive advantage of the Japanese companies.

and geographic indicators are fully protected under intellectual property rights so that only those who possess them can receive the benefits. *However*, in our aspirations, those endowments that are the blessings of God are given to the fortunate as a test, to share them with others. This holds true for intellectual, for moral superiorities as well as monetary riches. The superiorities developed by the individual are developed benefiting from the means of the society. These superiorities assign them responsibilities as well as rights. Our conscience cannot accept losing the war against HIV/AIDS because medicines are prohibitively expensive on account of intellectual property right protection. Killing innocent people in wars launched to gain control of petroleum reserves encouraged by military power also cannot be accepted.

Social systems are the products of people's faith, beliefs and values. As in the systems, in value structures there are opposing forces. In the Zoroastrian religion, the clash is believed to be between light (enlightenment) and darkness, between Ahura Mazda and Ahriman. People are advised to take sides with Ahura Mazda of their own free will. In the Vedas, this clash is the clash between good and evil. In the Islamic religion, it is between *hak* (right, justice, truth) and *batıl* (false, null and void). In most belief systems, humanity has the capacity to follow the right path. What leads a person to stray is his or her *nefs* (physical body, self and ego as opposed to spirit). For that reason, people should control their *nefs*. In some beliefs, the cause of all suffering is "the thirsts of the physical body and in the illusions of worldly passion," which cause dissatisfaction and misery. People must free themselves from these wants and ambitions.[38] Throughout history, humanity has accomplished great steps forward and come to the point of accepting principles such as those described in the Universal Declaration of Human Rights, which represents the aspirations of humankind in *our* time.

Technological developments of our day have given us a chance to make great progress in meeting our aspirations. Unfortunately the capitalist system is carrying on its resistance, setting strong barriers on the realization of our aspirations.

---

38 "If desire, which lies at the root of all human passion, can be removed, then passion will die out and all human sufferings will be ended." The *Teaching of Buddha*, Tokyo: Foundation for the Promotion of Buddhism, 1980, pp. 74–6.

Epilogue

After 1980, capitalism seized the chance to spread its principles globally by benefiting from the needs of the developing countries. The United States and the international organizations of the day were successful in presenting the principles of capitalism as the only solution to their problems. The 1990s presented a new turning-point for the world. In those years, the Eastern bloc that had applied centrally administered state socialism collapsed. Advances in communications technology were one of the driving forces of this collapse. The collapse and the developments in communication technology presented golden opportunities for capitalism, under the leadership of the United States, to declare victory. The US acquired the chance and the courage to impose the principles of capitalism on the countries that were trying to transform their economies from socialist economies to market economies, and on the developing countries that were in search of models to benefit from the advances of the technology. The years after the 1990s are the years when the *new economic design* was rapidly established. Very significant steps were taken on liberalization and privatization issues in these years. When the GATT was signed in 1994, all avenues were opened for the development of a brand new world under capitalist principles.

But the implementation of the *new economic design,* which was called *globalization,* produced its results in a very short period: the income allocation among countries and within countries entered a worsening trend, as a minority rich grew even richer; while a greater majority of people entered the stage of poverty. Initially, this situation gave birth to a resistance against globalization, but later this resistance transformed itself to a questioning of the capitalist system in academic circles. At present, the search for alternatives to globalization is continuing, and accelerating globally, in various media and channels. Capitalism, which was trying to reinforce itself all over the world with great confidence, had to turn to defend itself in a short time period. This defense is implemented under an active resistance strategy. Capitalism is trying to capture the *final fortresses* with increased rage. On the one hand, capitalism is converting itself to a faith (a belief system); on the other hand, it is trying to reinforce its dominance in the economic and political fields by establishing dominance over the non-renewable resources of the world through supranational companies. This is the insistence of capitalism for survival.

The principles that capitalism has reinforced all over the world and converted to a belief system are contrary to the aspirations humans have developed over thousand of years. The scene that has emerged under capitalism is not at all comforting to the human conscience. The ecological balances of the world are facing severe threat; the gap between the rich and poor is widening. The ecological environment, destroyed by the material hunger of capitalism, is unable to carry the burden of expanding welfare to more people, let alone expanding it to all humankind. The political consequences of all of these developments create an unacceptable lack of principles and widespread terror.

The world will have to create an alternative or alternatives to capitalism. Today, as yet, there is no ready recipe we can use. The solution will emerge through the wide and increased participation of people enabled by the advances in technology. Creating solutions in line with the aspirations of humankind requires increased awareness. This is what we have tried to accomplish in this book.

Index

References with *f* and a number refer to the footnotes at the bottom of that page.

acquisitions, making 13–15
advertising 12–13, 184
aesthetics 4
agency theory 24
agricultural subsidies 70, 180, 181
Anatolian culture 7, 61–3
aspirations 4, 7, 10, 200
    vs. capitalism 3, 122–3, 125, 178, 217–21
Avesta 94*f7*

Barnett, Thomas P.M. 215–16
behavior types 55, 59
    competitive 21, 56–8, 177–8, 217–18
    cooperative 59–61, 61–3, 218
    cultural differences 25, 52, 58, 61–3
    directed by belief systems 64–6
belief systems
    behavioral guidance 6, 49, 52, 64–6, 124, 133, 221
    and economics 36
    human beings, view of 52, 66
    intellectual properties, views on 93–4, 124
    role 4
    vs. science 40*f7*
benefits *see* utility

benefits not reflected in markets 17–18, 84–5, 114*f2*, 123–5
Brandenburger, Adam J. 59*f4*
Brzezinski, Zbigniew 214–15
Buddha 127, 221*f38*

capital 138
    in capitalism vs. in socialism 26–7, 119–20
    defined 20, 138
    in foreign trade 185–8
    human 45, 90, 123–4, 137, 142–3, 163
    and labor 23, 65, 119–21, 144–6, 154–5
    mobility of 185–8
    as production factor 119, 140
    see also capital markets
Capital Assets Pricing Model (CAPM) 105, 105*f6*
capital flows, international 74, 77–8, 99–100, 104, 107
capital gains 102
capital markets
    'hot money' effects 100
    interest rates determination 78–9, 104–5
    international capital flows 74, 77–8, 99–100, 104, 107
    liberalization of 190, 201
    power balance 94–5

risk 77, 79, 98, 100, 101, 105–7
see also foreign exchange markets
capitalism 3, 4–5, 20–26, 217–21
   assumptions
      capital and labor 23
      consumption 43, 47–8, 128,
         130–131
      efficient markets 94
      equilibrium prices 71–2, 76, 78,
         80, 88
      foreign trade 167, 171, 196
      goods and services 147
      human beings 38, 199
      labor 44, 140, 153
      national vs. private enterprises
         158
      vs. reality 37, 95
   consequences of 5, 208, 209, 222–3
   and consumption 46–9, 50, 132–3
   ethical values, move towards
      212–14
   first concession of 86
   vs. human aspirations 217–20, 222
   human beings, view of 6, 38–42,
      52–3, 66, 199, 220
   imposition of 73–4, 186–97, 202–3,
      222
      resistance to 203–8
   interrogation of 208–9
   objectives of 4–5, 149, 219
   poor, indifference to 51, 56
   promises vs. reality 37, 53, 75, 85,
      217–21
   as religion 1, 29, 36–7, 52, 177,
      200–202, 214
   rise of in 1980's and 1990's 1–2, 73,
      222
   rules, indifference to moral/ethical
      41, 41*f8*, 53
   vs. socialism 29–31, 199
   unsustainability of 3, 48, 113

see also competition; free market
   economies; globalization;
   labor; *new economic design*;
   specific markets
Champy, James 156
civilizations, clash of 215–16
Çizakça, Murat 121
Clash of Civilizations, The
   (Huntington) 215
collective bargaining system 23,
   88–92, 96, 122
Columbus, Christopher 9
communication, control of 171, 183–4,
   197
comparative advantages 20, 165–7,
   171, 220
   law of 168–9
competencies 45, 137, 154, 170
competition 17, 21, 31–2, 56–8, 92,
   147, 217–18
   in classical economic system 71–2
   vs. cooperation/solidarity 38–9,
      59–61, 217–18
   expanding environment of 177–9
   'monopolistic' 18*f15*
   in non-western cultures 21*f20*, 58,
      61–6
   'perfect' 21–2, 70–72, 92, 127–8,
      127*f1*, 151
Competitive Strategy (Porter) 57*f1*
Confessions of an Economic Hit Man
   (Perkins) 14*f6*, 187*f9*
consumers 46–7, 51, 53, 56, 61, 132–3
consumption 12–13, 43, 48, 49–50,
   115–16, 128–9
   unsustainable 18, 32, 49, 53, 125,
      216
   utility from 41, 47–9, 128, 130,
      132–3
cooperation 6, 58, 63, 65–6
   vs. competition 38–9, 59–61, 217–18

co-opetition 38–9, 39*f3*, 59*f4*

Co-opetition (Branderburger and Nelebuff) 39*f3*, 59*f4*

costs not reflected in markets 17–18, 46, 84–5, 114–23, 114*f1*

Cowan, George 2

crises in developing countries 74, 190, 201

customers 46–7, 51, 53, 56, 61, 132–3

Declaration of Human Rights, 1948 27, 87, 123, 200

demand and supply rule 76, 114
 capital markets 78–9, 101–2, 104, 106
 foreign exchange markets 76–8, 99
 goods and services markets 76
 labor markets 80–81, 87

demand theory 128–31

Deutsche Telekom, re-engineering of 157–8

developing countries
 capitalist models, choice of 25–6
 exploitation of 14*f6*, 15, 184–5
 'hot money', effects on 74, 77–8, 99–104
 imposition of free market on 24, 73, 186, 190–1
 privatization of state enterprises 158–60, 160*f11*, 192, 193
 supranationals' effects on 143, 184–5, 200, 203, 206
 unfairness towards 180–181, 204

direct foreign investment 74

Don Jose Maria, Pastor 199

East Asian crises of 1997 25, 192

economic crises 25, 99–104, 107, 191–2

economic systems 3, 10–11, 13–16, 36–7, 50
 human focus 38, 51
 see also capitalism; socialism

economic theory 42, 53, 97
 assumptions
  capital markets 78–9, 101
  competition 21–2, 92, 127
  consumption 48, 128–9
  demand 131, 171
  foreign exchange markets 76–7, 98
  foreign trade 167, 170, 174
  goods and services 19, 76, 132, 147
  human beings 39–40
  labor markets 80–81, 121, 153–4
  production 140
  revenues 151, 153
  work 44–5
  zero-sum game 154
 demand theory 128–31
 human beings, view of 44
 monopolies 18
 production theory 135–9
 profits 151

economics 11–13, 40–41
 teaching of 2*f4*, 39, 209–11
 and value judgements 39, 41, 41*f8*, 212

economy, defined 11

employment, full 19, 19*f16*
 see also unemployment

End of History and the Last Man, The (Fukuyama) 214

entrepreneurship 20, 21, 138

environmental damage 18, 48, 53, 115, 117, 125, 223

equilibrium prices 71, 85, 87
 capital markets 78, 79, 104, 104–7
 foreign exchange markets 76–7, 98, 99–104
 goods and services markets 76
 labor markets 80, 87, 122

equitable sharing 15

ethics 37*f1*, 41
European Union (EU) 31, 179, 188
exchange rate anchor 104
exploitation 14–15, 32, 59, 138
  of customers 21, 61, 92–3
  of developing countries 14*f6*, 15,
    103–4, 184–5
  of labor 23, 88, 143, 179, 184, 196,
    206–8

fair trade vs. free trade 53, 165, 169,
  203
faith systems *see* belief systems
Fisher, Irving 78
foreign exchange markets
  exchange rates determination
    76–8, 98–104, 107
  high interest–low exchange rate cycle
    84, 99–104, 107
  price parities 83–4
  see also 'hot money'
foreign investment 74, 185–6
foreign loans, long-term 186–7
foreign trade
  benefits of 166
  foreign exchange rates, relation to
    77–8, 98–101
  foreign trade model 167
  free trade vs. fair trade 169, 203
  law of comparative advantages
    168–9
  liberalization of 179, 201
  price impositions 169, 196
  realities of 170–175, 184–5
  restrictions on 82
foundations 16*f12*
free enterprise 21, 21*f18*
free market economies 19–20, 69–70,
  112
  and consumers 46–9, 50–51
  imposition of 73, 190, 191, 200

monopolies 18, 18*f15*
price determination 17–18
social benefits/costs 114–16, 123–5
see also capitalism; competition;
  new economic design
free trade vs. fair trade 53, 165, 169,
  203
Freud, Sigmund 52*f21*
Fukuyama, Francis 214

Galbraith, John Kenneth 69, 72, 81–2,
  97, 110, 111
GATT (General Agreement on Trade
  and Tariffs) 31–2, 73–4, 143,
  179–85, 196, 202
Germany, unification of 28, 73, 201
global warming 115, 117, 119, 125
globalization 2, 2*f3*, 24, 30–31, 161–2,
  178, 188–9, 194
  imposition of 201, 202
  markets 81–2
  problems 75
  resistance to 203–5
  search for alternatives to 222
  see also exploitation; liberalization
    of markets; *new economic
    design*
goods and services markets 76, 109
  foreign trade 173
  liberalization 73
  needs, meeting 132–4
  price determination 76
  see also consumption; hardware
    and software
Gorbachev, Mikhail 29
governments
  national objectives 83
  price fixing 70, 84–5, 85
  roles in market economies 22, 58,
    72–3, 116–17
Gülistan (Sadi) 5, 5*f11*

Hammer, Michael 156
hardware and software 134, 142–3, 147, 175
    separation of production 143, 148, 183–4, 195, 195*f18*
Hayyam, Ömer 40*f6*
Heilbroner, Robert L. 39
high interest–low exchange rate cycle 84, 99–104, 107
Holland, John H. 218*f33*
Holy Bible 9
'hot money' 74, 77, 99–104, 187, 190–191
human beings 6, 27
    aspirations of 35, 200, 217–21
    as consumers 46–9
    as cost factor 119–23, 219
    needs of 12–13, 35–6
    as production factors 44–6, 53, 136–7, 219
    see also customers; labor
human capital 45, 90, 123–4, 137, 142–3, 163
Human Development Index 123*f17*
hunger 5, 202–3
Huntington, Samuel P. 215

identity, personal 48, 133, 146, 147, 220
identity, product 133–4, 141–2, 147, 171, 175, 184, 194–5
IMF (International Monetary Fund) 24, 73, 104, 186, 190–192
    privatization policies 158, 160, 160*f11*, 192
    protests against 203
    see also Washington Consensus
income, generation of 109, 110
income sharing 135–6, 144–6
intellectual properties 93–4, 124, 142–3, 148, 195, 220–221

haves and have-nots 32, 144, 196
    protection of 93, 124*f19*, 183–4, 195, 204
interest 78–9, 104
International Forum on Globalization 165
International Monetary Fund (IMF) *see* IMF (International Monetary Fund)
investment, foreign 74, 185–6
invisible hand 16, 17, 69–70
Islam 64–6, 94*f7*, 121, 136, 146, 215

Japan 23, 26, 58, 146–7, 220*f37*

Kantor, Mickey 181–3
keiretsu organizations 21*f20*, 26, 26*f28*, 58, 58*f2*
kibbutzim 15, 15*f8*
Koran
    economic behavior in 64–6
    quotes from 13*f4*, 35, 48*f15*, 65, 66, 113, 115*f5*
Krugman, Paul 169*f2*

labor
    assumptions about 19, 140, 153, 154
    collective bargaining system 23, 88–92, 96, 122
    competencies 45, 137, 165, 170
    competition vs. team spirit 59–61
    as cost item 22–3, 42–4, 90, 119–23, 145, 153–4, 157
    as customers 51, 53, 119
    under different systems 23, 65
    exploitation of 23, 32, 88, 143, 179, 196, 206–8
    human capital 45, 90, 123–4, 137, 142–3, 163
    immobility of 31, 32, 74, 179, 185, 196

income sharing 135–6, 144–6
mass layoffs 61, 154, 155, 157, 162
  and privatization 160
  vs. technology 42, 43, 57, 123,
    140–141, 154–5
    through re-engineering 156–8
  unions 23, 89, 89*f3*, 90, 206
  see also unemployment
labor markets 80–81, 95, 196
  wages determination 80, 87, 88–92
labor-managed market economy
  19–20, 120, 136, 146
LaFeber, Walter 192
learning organizations 59–60, 59*f5*
liberalization of markets 17, 31, 73–4,
    172, 180, 185, 201
  see also GATT (General
    Agreement on Trade and
    Tariffs); privatization, of state
    enterprises
Lincoln, Abraham 9*f2*
Locke, Robert 26
lockouts 23, 89
long-term foreign loans 186–7

macroeconomic theory 149
Made in Holland journal 212–13
managers 24, 60, 138
market crashes 107, 187
market economies 16–20
  evolution of 16*f13*
  market types 73–4
  prices, effects of 75–81
  see also capitalism; free market
    economies
market exchanges 108–11
markets 16, 22, 69, 81–2
  see also specific markets
Marshall, Alfred 38
Marx, Karl 27
Marxism 28–9

mercantilist period 81–2
mergers and acquisitions 93
Miller, Merton 97
Mondragón Cooperative Corporation
  15, 15*f9*, 20
monopolies 18, 18*f15*, 92, 93, 151
  vs. competition 71
moral rules 37*f1*, 41
mudaraba system 65, 121, 136
Multi Fiber Arrangement (MFA)
  180–181
Multilateral Agreement on
  Investment (MAI) 185, 185*f7*

national income 121, 135, 149, 150
  and current account deficit
    100–101, 107
  privatization, effects of 160–161,
    161
  vs. profit maximization 150, 162
  through state-owned enterprises
    159, 160
needs, human 12–13, 35–6, 132–4
negative sign syndrome 23*f21*, 42–3,
    119*f8*, 136*f9*
Nelebuff, Barry J. 59*f4*
Netherlands 212–13
new economic design 2–3, 2*f3*, 28, 73,
    177, 181–3, 198
  capital, mobility of 185
  communication, control of 197
  competition 31–2
  consequences of 74–5, 163, 202,
    203, 208, 222, 223
  imposition of 190, 201–2
  intellectual properties,
    protection of 93, 142–3, 148,
    152, 184, 204–5
  labor, immobility of 74, 179, 203
  liberalization of some markets
    31, 179

objectives of 179, 183, 189–90, 198,
    202
Phase One 190–193
Phase Two 193–7
privatization, importance of 192
serving supranational companies
    172–3, 175, 184, 192–3, 196–7,
    206
serving the wealthy 178, 185, 194,
    196, 202–3
see also capitalism; free market
    economies; globalization
NGOs (Non-governmental
    organizations) 187, 206
Nike shoe company 134f8, 203f6,
    206–8
North American Free Trade
    Agreement (NAFTA) 31, 179,
    188

objectivity 4–5
Out of Control (Brzezinski) 214–15

parities, price 83–4
Pentagon's New Map, The (Barnett)
    215–16
people see human beings
Perkins, John 14f6, 187f9
personal identity 48, 133, 146, 147, 220
persuasion 12–13, 184
pharmaceutical companies 204–5
poor 15–16, 17, 47f12, 51
Porter, Michael E. 57f1
Post Autistic Economics movement 2,
    2f4, 209–11
poverty 5, 129
    increasing levels of 74, 143, 185,
        196, 202
prices
    determination of 16, 17–18, 71,
        84–5

fair vs. free 14f7, 165
fixing of 70, 84–5, 169
guiding economy 69, 75, 82–3, 97
markets, effects on 75–81
not reflected in markets 114
parities 83–4
and product identity 133–4, 147,
    171, 195
and utility 130–131
see also equilibrium prices
privatization
    of social services 124, 124f18
    of state enterprises 63, 93, 158–62,
        160f11, 192–3
product differentiation 92, 132–3
product identity 133–4, 141–2, 147,
    171, 175, 184, 194–5
production 18, 42, 170–171
    factors of 10, 42, 119, 135–9
        see also labor
    human beings, defined in 38,
        42–6, 53
production function 139–41, 143
production theory 135–9
profit motive 10, 21, 56, 138
    vs. labor's goals 23, 42–3, 51, 53,
        88, 119, 154–8
    vs. national concerns 117, 158–61
profit-maximization rule 151
profits 119, 145, 150–152
    vs. income generation 149–50
    as main objective 1, 3, 42, 51, 138,
        149, 161
    sharing 146
    sustainable 212–13
    vs. value-added maximization
        153–4

rationality 211f19
re-engineering 156–8, 163
religion see belief systems

'right' and 'wrong' 37*f1*
risk 77, 79, 100, 101, 104–7, 187
rivalry *see* competition
Robinson, Joan 18*f15*
Ruggiero, Renato 188

Sadi 5, 5*f11*
Samuelson, Paul A. 71*f2*
Santa Fe Institute 2, 2*f5*, 211–12
satisfaction *see* utility
Schumpeter, Joseph Alois 18*f15*, 28–9
science 3–4, 5, 39–41, 40*f7*
scientific methodology 3–4, 11, 40–41
self-interest 55, 217
Senge, Peter M. 59*f5*
service and goods markets *see* goods
        and services markets
Shanghai Cooperation Organization
        (SCO) 31, 179, 179*f3*
short-term capital flows,
        international 74, 77, 99–104,
        187, 190–191
Smith, Adam 71
socialism 26–8
    vs. capitalism 29–31, 199
    price fixing 70
software and hardware *see* hardware
        and software
speculation 110–111
stakeholder concept 89–90, 91–2,
        91*f4*
Stiglitz, Joseph 25–6, 177, 191, 201, 209
stockholders 22
strikes 23, 89
subsidies 70, 180, 181, 182
supply and demand rule *see* demand
        and supply rule
supranational companies 192–3, 196–7
    countries, relationship with 194
    exploitation of labor 206

free mobility of 162, 173, 184–5
    opposition to 205–8
systems 9–11
    see also economic systems

team spirit 59, 60
technology 139, 143–4
    vs. labor 42, 43, 51, 123, 140–141,
        154–5
    through re-engineering 156–8
terrorism 209, 215, 216
textile quotas 180–181
trade blocs 31, 178–9, 179–80, 188–9
trade unions *see* unions
TRIPS (trade-regulated intellectual
        property rights) 31, 93–4
Turkey 58, 63, 70, 103, 106, 159*f10*, 160
    see also Anatolian culture

unemployment 19, 43–4, 45–6, 51,
        121–3, 219
    causes 140–141, 143, 154, 155, 162,
        185, 203, 206
unions 23, 89, 89*f3*, 90, 206
    collective bargaining system 23,
        88–92, 96, 122
United States
    advantages 166
    globalization 215, 216, 222
    Kyoto Protocol 118, 208*f13*
    poverty 202–3
    Treasury 1, 190, 193
    Uruguay Round, points won at
        181–3
Universal Declaration of Human
        Rights 87, 89*f3*, 123
Uruguay Round 180–181
USSR (Union of Soviet Socialist
        Republics) 1–2, 28, 29–31, 84,
        191, 201

utility 41, 218
   from consumption 41, 47–9, 128,
      130–132, 171
   defined 17
   from foreign exchange 98
   and needs 132–4
   non-market sources 129

value added 109–110, 121, 135–6,
    152–4, 162
values, ethical/moral 39, 41, 41*f8*, 212,
    221
Vanek, Jaroslav 23*f21*, 26–7, 42–3,
    119*f8*, 136*f9*, 177*f2*, 197
Vedas 1*f1*, 94*f8*
   economic behavior in 64
   quotes from iv, 1, 55, 64, 149
Vikers, John 159

wages determination 80, 87

wars 14, 209
Washington Consensus 1, 186, 186*f8*,
    190, 190*f11*, 191
Wilber, Charles K. 41*f8*
work
   non-pecuniary benefits of 146–7
   perceptions of 44–5, 80, 146, 220
World Bank 24, 73, 158, 160*f11*, 191
   privatization policies 192
   protests against 203
   see also Washington Consensus
World Resources Institute mission
    statement 113
WTO (World Trade Organization) 24,
    31, 73, 172, 183, 187–8, 196
   Doha ministerial conference 204
   protests against 203

Yarrow, George 159
Yesevi, Ahmet 49*f16*